Working Childhoods

Working Childhoods draws upon research in the Indian Himalayas to provide a theoretically informed account of children's lives in a remote part of the world. The book shows that children in their pre-teens and teens are lynchpins of the rural economy, spending hours each day herding cattle, collecting leaves and juggling household tasks with schoolwork. Through documenting in painstaking detail children's stories, songs, friendships, fears and tribulations, the book offers a powerful account of youth agency and young people's rich relationship with the natural world. The 'environment' emerges not only as a crucial economic resource but also as a basis for developing gendered ideas of self. This book is essential reading for anyone interested in better understanding childhood, youth, the environment, and development within and beyond India – including anthropologists, sociologists, geographers, development studies scholars and south Asianists.

DR JANE DYSON is a Research Associate at the University of Oxford.

Working Childhoods

Youth, Agency and the Environment in India

Jane Dyson

CAMBRIDGE
UNIVERSITY PRESS

CAMBRIDGE
UNIVERSITY PRESS

University Printing House, Cambridge CB2 8BS, United Kingdom

Published in the United States of America by Cambridge University Press, New York

Cambridge University Press is part of the University of Cambridge.

It furthers the University's mission by disseminating knowledge in the pursuit of education, learning and research at the highest international levels of excellence.

www.cambridge.org
Information on this title: www.cambridge.org/9781107058385

First published 2014

Printed in the United Kingdom by Clays, St Ives plc.

A catalogue record for this publication is available from the British Library

Library of Congress Cataloguing in Publication data
Dyson, Jane
Working childhoods : youth, agency and the environment in India / Jane Dyson.
pages cm
Includes bibliographical references and index.
ISBN 978-1-107-05838-5 (hardback)
1. Rural youth – India – Social conditions. 2. Rural youth – Employment – India.
3. Human ecology – India. I. Title.
HQ799.I5D97 2014
305.235′0917340954 – dc23 2013048912

ISBN 978-1-107-05838-5 Hardback

For Craig,
Florence and Finn

Contents

Figures

Map

Tables

Abbreviations

BPS	Bemni Primary School
FD	Forest Department
GC	general caste
GP	gram panchayat
JFM	joint forest management
KI	key informant
OBC	other backward class
SC	scheduled caste
SPS	Sunti Private School
SSBS	Sunti Senior Basic School
UP	Uttar Pradesh
VFJM	village forest joint management
VP	van panchayat

Preface

As I write, the central Himalayas area is struggling with the worst floods for nearly a century, a natural disaster that some have termed the 'Himalayan tsunami'. The village featured in this book is located right in the heart of the monsoon devastation, in the Indian state of Uttarakhand. Thankfully, it sits on a mountain ridge high above the swollen rivers, and remains relatively safe. While some villagers have had property damaged and lost the livestock on which they depend, the basic infrastructure remains intact, and no human lives have been taken. Other villages have, tragically, fared much worse. The flooding is a reminder of the difficult and sometimes catastrophic events that characterise life in Uttarakhand. People in the 'high Himalayas' (above about 2,500 feet), and those living away from the main road network, face particularly intense struggles to maintain their farms, raise families and adapt to environmental change.

This book explores the lives of some of these people. I focus particularly on a group who have been routinely ignored in research in India: children, especially those aged between about ten and eighteen. I argue that children and youth are central to the rural economy in the high Himalayas, drawing on fifteen months of research conducted in 2003 and 2004 in a village that I call Bemni. (All names of places and people in this book are pseudonyms, with the exception of place names of larger settlements.) I examine the everyday lives of these children, which differ so hugely from those of young people in most parts of Europe or North America. Children as young as ten in Bemni spend many hours each day washing dishes, fetching water, herding cattle or collecting wood, often in forests far from home. These children are now increasingly going to school, but have to juggle their education with a range of household work. I lived and worked alongside these children, trudging up and down the mountains, lugging backloads of leaf litter or winter hay or getting blistered hands weeding fields of potatoes. We also had lots of fun. We made impromptu picnics from freshly fallen snow, foraged for wild strawberries, played games in the meadows and fooled around in the forest.

This is a fine-grained ethnography that tells a set of stories about what children in a remote part of the world were doing at a particular point in time.

Through these stories, though, the book asks a number of questions that have much broader implications for understanding the lives of young people. What do children think about their work? And what does their work tell us about children's social practices, and the ways in which life is rendered meaningful? And what do these social practices reveal about their place in, and relationship to, their environment? I pay particular attention to children of different ages and caste, and explore the social differences between boys and girls. In addressing these compelling and previously unasked questions, I offer new perspectives on young people's agency, the social meaning of work and the role of the environment in people's everyday lives.

The book will, I hope, interest those working with children and youth in any part of the world, as well as general scholars of south Asia. It speaks, too, to scholars exploring the relationship between people and their environment. It is a book that is hopeful about young people's resourcefulness but that also chronicles stories of poverty and hardship. Risks and fears, such as those elicited by the recent floods, are part of daily life.

As is often the case in academic writing, this book has been ten years in the making, and over that time I have accumulated enormous debts. The people of Bemni village have been immeasurably kind, and I am hugely grateful. On my first day in Bemni, when I explained that I was visiting several villages in my search for an appropriate field site, Saka simply laughed and said, 'Well, go and look at the other villages, but of course *this* is the best village for you.' She was right, and, just as I was that day, I am repeatedly astonished and humbled by the willingness of friends in Bemni to open their lives to me. They have so generously shared their time and knowledge, their houses and food, their hopes, sorrows and love. It is difficult to express how keenly I appreciate this privilege. In recent trips, people have rightly asked what has come out of that first period of fieldwork. I hope this book goes some way to reassuring them that there is some point to my endless wondering and questioning.

In particular, I am indebted to *tai-ji* and *tao-ji*, to Vinod, Hema, Mukesh and his wife Purnima, and to Saka, for welcoming me into their lives and their home, and for sharing the delights and cruelties of life in Bemni. I am honoured to consider them my extended family. I give heartfelt thanks to the children and young people with whom I worked for their patience, for guiding me gently into their worlds, for watching over me, for making me laugh and for only rarely complaining about my relentless pestering. Huge thanks especially go to my key informants: Ashish, Basanti, Bina, Devendre, Diraj, Janki, (the late) Papita, Parwati, Prema, Manoj, Mehendre, Rakesh, Saka, Sanjay, Sarita and their parents. I remember with fondness and gratitude the late *sarpanch-ji* for his help and support, and for being both an inspiring leader and father. I am grateful to the last three pradhans, and to the current sarpanch, for their kind permission for me to work in Bemni.

There are many others I could name – friends and neighbours, young and old – whom it has been such joy to know and who have given so much. I thank them all. I continue to work in Bemni and have been back several times since my arrival in early 2003. Now, villagers joke that it is my *mainka*, my natal home, and that there is little wonder that I still weep every time I say goodbye, just as a newlywed daughter does. I hope I will have cause to weep for several years to come.

My research assistant in 2003/4, Anita, became a dear friend; my time in Bemni and this book would have been very different without her. I am extremely grateful. I appreciate, too, the kindness and trust of Anita's family.

In Ghat, I thank Bhatt-*ji* and his family, Sukvir *Bhai* and Hoshiyar *Bhai*. I am grateful to a number of people in Gopeshwar: the district magistrate and the superintendent of police for granting me permission to work in Chamoli district, Tomar-*ji* (and his family) for being the most caring neighbour, friend and guide, and Shri P. B. Kandauri and his wife. Everyone at the Himalayan Society for Alternative Development was exceptionally kind, unremittingly picking up the pieces during my trips to Gopeshwar. Special thanks go to Dr Pundir, Omar Shankar Bhist, Hemla, Geet, Gita, Rekha, Sudha and Surendra. For their expert advice, I am grateful to Ramesh Pahari, Chandi Prasad Bhatt, Bhopal Singh and Bharat Singh, and, in particular, to Sudarshan Kathait and Om Prakash Bhatt for pointing me towards Bemni. I thank the district judge and his family for their hospitality. A number of shopkeepers regularly went out of their way to help and welcome me. Finally, I remember and pay my respects to Kamla.

In Mussoorie, I am grateful to Anuradha and Pawan Gupta (and others at Sidh), for their inspiration, wisdom and cosy home, and to Darab Nagarwala and Yusuf. In Dehra Dun, I appreciate the advice of Hem Gairola, and to Adarsh Kaushal and all at the Rural Litigation and Entitlement Kendra for taking care of me and encouraging me along the way. Shomie and the late Pheroza Das provided a real haven, of which I have such fond memories. In New Delhi, I am grateful to those at the Institute of Economic Growth (IEG) for my affiliation, particularly Professor Kanchan Chopra and Dr Sushil Sen, and to Anna Lake for making me so welcome in her home in Delhi.

The fieldwork in 2003/4 was conducted while I was a doctoral student at the University of Cambridge. I am very grateful to my supervisor, Bhaskar Vira, for all his advice and support, and to my examiners, Elizabeth Watson and Jens Lerche, for their insightful comments. The book has developed in many ways since that thesis, morphing as I moved from Cambridge, to the University of Washington, and then to the University of Oxford. It has benefited from a decade of comments by and discussions with a number of friends and colleagues. Many thanks go to Bina Agarwal, Ann Anagnost, Andrea Arai, Amita Baviskar, Tim Bayliss-Smith, Heather Plumridge Bedi, Jo Boyden, David Butz,

Ashwini Chattre, Moushimi Chaudhury, David Citrin, Isobel Clark-Deces, Purnamita Dasgupta, Ritwick Dutta, Anthony Dyson, Rowan Ellis, Peggy Froerer, Liz Gagen, David Gellner, Ann Gold, Ramachandra Guha, Danny Hoffman, Dhana Hughes, Tim Ingold, Alex Jeffrey, Craig Jeffrey, Patricia Jeffery, Roger Jeffery, Krishna Kumar, Heather Lovell, Francesca Marchetti, Emma Mawdsley, Linda McDowell, David Mills, Brian Milne, Ginny Morrow, Shekhar Pathak, Chris Philo, Sam Punch, Priti Ramamurty, Haripriya Rangan, Esther Rootham, Sahar Romani, Mitch Rose, Vasant Sabarwal, Sushil Saigal, 'Shivi' Shivaramakrishnan, Jonathan Spencer, Wynet Smith, Janet Sturgeon, Nandini Sundar, Kathryn Tanner, Rajesh Thandani, Sudha Vasan, Henrik Vigh, Susan Wadley, Philippa Williams, Anand Yang and Steven Young. I thank the many students in several different classes at the Universities of Washington and Oxford who have helped form my ideas. Thanks are due to Phil Bartie and Phillip Stickler for their lending their expertise to my GIS mapping, and to Aisla Allen for her assistance with the photographs.

Different parts of the manuscript have benefited from participants' comments at conferences held by the Association of American Geographers in Denver (2005), Chicago (2006) and Seattle (2011), the Association for Asian Studies in San Francisco (2006), the International Association for the Study of Common Property in Oaxaca, Mexico (2004), and the Center for South Asia at the University of Wisconsin–Madison (2005), and at seminars held by the IEG in New Delhi (2004), the Department of Geography at the University of Cambridge (2004), the London School of Economics and Political Science (2004), the Department of Anthropology at Brunel University (2005), the Center for South Asia Studies at the University of California–Berkeley (2006), the Department of Geography at the University of Washington (2006), the University of Oxford (2009), the Department of Anthropology at Princeton University (2011) and the Economic and Social Research Council (ESRC) in its 'Childhood' series at the University of Edinburgh (2011). An earlier version of Chapter 5 appeared in my article in *Annals of the Association of American Geographers* 98 (1), 160–79. Parts of Chapter 6 are revised versions of my article in *American Ethnologist* 37 (3), 482–98. Sections from Chapters 4, 5 and 6 have also appeared, in other guises, in my chapters 'Saka', in *Telling Young Lives: Portraits of Global Youth* (Jeffrey and Dyson 2008), and 'Respite and rupees', in *Childhoods in South Asia* (Behera 2007).

I was privileged to hold a studentship from the ESRC and the Natural Environment Research Council from 2001 to 2005, and am grateful to the following for funding aspects of the research and writing: the John Fell Fund, the Smuts Memorial Fund, St John's College Cambridge, the Suzy Paine Prize, the Phillip Lake Trust, the William Vaughan Lewis Fund and the Isaac Newton Trust. I thank the government of India, for granting me permission to conduct the research, and the IEG, for my affiliation between September 2003 and April 2004.

At Cambridge University Press, I am very grateful to Andrew Winnard for believing in this project and for making it happen, and to Helena Dowson, Emma Walker and Mike Richardson for their efficient help and support.

Finally, I am very appreciative of my family. My parents have, as always, been unfailingly supportive throughout the several research trips and writing. I am so grateful to Florence and Finn for both their alacrity and their patience during their early introduction to ethnographic fieldwork. And, most of all, my thanks go to Craig, without whom none of this would have happened, and who, with kindness and love, has been there every step of the way.

1 Working with young people in the Himalayas

On a frosty morning in November 2004 I was huddled against a tree in a forest high above a village called Bemni in Uttarakhand, India. Far below I could see the river Nandakini; above stood the 7,000 metre crimson peak of Trishul. I was with two girls, Bina and Basanti, who were collecting leaf litter to be used as bedding in livestock stalls. Bina and Basanti were only twelve years old. Their thin hair was plastered to the side of their faces with sweat and mist as they stuffed their baskets with leaves, wove twigs across the top to keep them in place and fastened their back-breaking loads with thick rope over their shoulders. Basanti was taller and more athletic, but Bina seemed the more adept at constructing a leaf basket. Before they set off back down the hill they checked that their loads were big enough. They asked me to compare the two piles of leaves. When they were absolutely sure that they had what their parents would regard as 'good baskets' (*atchchhe kandhe*) they tore down the steep hill singing songs, their nimble feet picking expertly over the rough, stony ground.

This book examines the working lives of young people in a remote part of north India. During fifteen months of ethnographic research in Bemni I charted young people's involvement in rural household labour. I followed girls such as Bina and Basanti through fields, up mountains and into forests, and spent hours chatting in the village with children and adults. At one level, *Working Childhoods* is a study in the social geography of children's everyday labour in a high Himalayan village. It chronicles what work children did in Bemni in the early 2000s, when they did it, with whom, and with what consequences for their own developing identities and for broader household livelihood strategies. The book stands as a record of a set of work regimes. It describes the resilience of young people, who worked in difficult and sometimes dangerous conditions to fulfil household obligations, even as their lives were being transformed by the extension of the nearby road network, the expansion of schooling and changes in local marriage practices.

The book also examines how young people's agency might be theorised, agency being defined as 'the ability to act effectively and exercise a measure of power' (Durham 2008: 175). I argue that young people developed a sense of agency not primarily through opposing older villagers but by acquiescing to their demands. The concern that Bina and Basanti showed to stuff their baskets with leaves and meet village expectations of what constitutes 'good work' was indicative of a general desire among children to conform to prevailing norms. I also argue that young people's agency was not primarily about asserting autonomy but focused on building relationships of mutual dependence with each other and their parents. In addition, I highlight the crucial importance of the forest in young people's work and in developing a sense of themselves as competent, 'good' people. Young people cultivated a sense of their own capacity for work and identity through their tactile use of the environment and its materials: trees, leaves, branches and streams, for example. This focus on young people's complicated and rich relationship to the natural world provides a counterpoint to the focus in most of the literature on children and youth in urban areas. It also underlines the importance of thinking about the 'environment' as a setting for cultural practices as well as an economic resource.

Throughout the book I use the word 'children' to refer roughly to young people aged five to thirteen and 'youth' to indicate young people aged fourteen to seventeen. This distinction is broadly in line with how parents and young people in Bemni understood the terms 'child' and 'youth'. I use the term 'young people' as an umbrella term for children and youth. I am nevertheless aware that the terms 'children', 'youth' and 'young people' are slippery, and they are deployed in different ways in different circumstances (see Durham 2008; Solberg 1997).

Young people's agency

There is now a great deal of scholarly research on the burdens being placed on younger sections of the population in the contemporary global South. In the context of the rise of new media and heightened expectations around education, parents and wider society are often looking to young people as sources of hope. At the same time, market-based economic policies have often increased social uncertainties and undermined state welfare mechanisms, such as government-funded schools, health care programmes and development schemes. The extension of new forms of governmental and non-governmental power has frequently had the effect of marginalising young people or pathologising their behaviour (see, for example, Gibson 2011), and environmental degradation and the restructuring of families often complicate young people's lives still further (Comaroff and Comaroff 2005; Jeffrey and Dyson 2008).

My research points to the capacity of young people to respond actively and creatively to some of these pressures. The agency of young people is, of course, a well-established theme in studies of childhood and youth (Boyden and Ennew 1997; Bucholtz 2002). In childhood studies, the shift to stress agency came in the 1960s and 1970s and marked a move away from sole emphasis on the socialisation of children (James, Jenks and Prout 1998). In youth studies, the move to emphasise agency came earlier and was bound up in an interest in 'rebellion' (Hall 1904; Keniston 1971; Willis 1977). Since the 1990s the children's agency literature and the youth agency literature have both expanded enormously, with a welcome increase in studies of girls and young women (see McRobbie 2004), young people in the global South (for example Ansell 2004; Honwana and de Boeck 2005) and children and youth as political actors (such as Philo and Smith 2003; Hirschkind 2011). Among notable studies is Jennifer Cole's (2004) account of how poor and lower middle-class young people in Madagascar reacted to economic scarcity in the 1990s. Cole shows that young women in her research area were able to make money through sex work and actually came to support young men financially. In the process, they questioned and partially contested established gender norms. Kate Swanson's (2009) work on young beggars in urban Ecuador is similarly compelling, demonstrating how young people survived in the early 2000s through migrating to cities, where they managed to use the money they earned from begging to finance their studies in urban schools. The picture emerging from such studies is of young people's extraordinary resourcefulness, even in unpromising circumstances.

Another theme that stands out in these recent studies is the significance of work as a site for young people's social and cultural agency, and, especially, the capacity of young people to instil meaning in their work. For example, Pamela Reynolds' (1991) assessment of children's labour in rural Zimbabwe documents the creative way in which children may imbue their work with a sense of purpose and achievement. Reynolds shows that children imagined their work simultaneously expressing their love for family members, fulfilling moral duties to their parents and contributing to the costs of attending school. In a markedly different case, Paul Willis (1977) comes to somewhat similar conclusions. In his classic study of young working-class men in a town in the English Midlands, he shows how a set of working-class 'lads' – through their everyday practices of fighting, sex, smoking and other means of 'having a laff' – came to view manual labour as an 'authentic' basis for masculinity and successful adulthood. As Willis's research shows, children and youth, in imbuing their work with meaning, often develop distinctive gendered subjectivities, for example as masculine wage earners or diligent workers (see also Jackson 2000; McDowell 2003; Ramamurthy 2010).

Young people also try to negotiate their work within the constraints imposed on them by employers, parents or broader social structures in order to develop their own work 'regimes' (Gidwani 2001). For example, children may alter the content and nature of their labour, change the spaces and timing of their work practices or reshape the social context of their work. Samantha Punch's (2000) research in Bolivia provides a good case. Drawing on participant observation in rural Bolivia, Punch shows how children accommodate their own needs and desires within work settings through a range of micro-strategies aimed at moderating the burdensome nature of their labour. Similarly, Reynolds (1991) identifies how children in rural Zimbabwe altered how they conducted herding, agricultural work and fuel wood collection in order to bolster their social links with kin and neighbours and improve their future security. Cindi Katz (2004) focuses more resolutely on the ways in which children mix 'work' and 'playful' activity and how these combinations may shift over time. Building on close observation of children's herding, water and fuel wood collection, and agricultural work, Katz documents how a state-sponsored agricultural project initiated in their village in the 1980s disrupted children's capacity to combine work and play by expanding irrigated agriculture for the market, encouraging deforestation and reducing cattle herds. In undermining the subsistence-oriented economy of the village, this development project also reduced the capacity of children to 'manage' their everyday work in meaningful ways.

My study is centrally taken up with examining how young people instil meaning in their work and negotiate their labour in a context of social transformation – especially in light of their growing commitment to acquiring an education. In drawing attention to the importance of how children negotiate labour, I point to the difficulties associated with 'reading off' the burdensomeness of work with reference to the physical arduousness of their activity (Jackson and Palmer-Jones 1999). Rather than assuming children's work to be exploitative, or seeking an easy measure of burden and effort, I highlight the value of fine-grained accounts of young people's everyday experience of labour.

Generation is also a prominent topic in this recent work on young people's agency and working lives in the global South, and it is an issue that surfaced quite often in discussions with parents and young people in Bemni in 2003 and 2004. In the 1970s and 1980s in Bemni, young people usually married in their teens, frequently in their early teens in the case of girls. This meant that they became 'adults', in local terms, at a fairly early stage. But rising education and an increase in young people's age at marriage has altered this pattern and precipitated the emergence of a new generation of 'youth' (*jawaan*) aged between their early teens and early twenties. In his classic essay on generations, Karl Mannheim (1956 [1923]) argues that particular generations experience the same events at the same period in their lives and that these shared experiences could become the basis for a type of generational identity. He builds on this observation to suggest that generations could become social and political actors in particular situations, emphasising the young generation, in particular, as an agent of change. Young people are often closer to pressing socio-economic problems and they are more likely to engage in novel cultural, social and political practices. In Mannheim's terms, young people have a 'fresh contact' with their surroundings (Cole and Durham 2006; Shahine 2011).

Mannheim's research is helpful for my purposes because it both emphasises questions of generational change and highlights the importance of young people's relationship to surrounding landscapes, objects and materials. 'Fresh contact' implies an interest in how children and youth use materials at hand, such as leaves, baskets and branches. But Mannheim is only partially useful as a guide to young people's agency in Bemni. By emphasising situations in which people exert agency through opposing established structures, Mannheim downplays the possibility that children and youth might exercise agency through conforming to prior practices and norms. Saba Mahmood (2005) advances a somewhat similar version of this argument about conformity and agency in her ethnography of the Da'wa religious movement in Egypt. Contrary to what many US feminists might have expected, many Egyptian women active in religious organisations are not seeking to challenge patriarchal norms or established gendered hierarchies. Rather, they are trying to find niches within dominant hierarchies that can provide a measure of respect and security while also allowing them to bring their behaviour into line with their religious beliefs. Mahmood builds on these observations to argue that 'agentival capacity is entailed not only in those acts that resist norms but also in the multiple ways in which one inhabits norms' (15). Deborah Durham (2008) makes a related point in research with young people in Botswana. Young people exert their own power in this setting not by trying to escape established social institutions but by reinforcing them. I will develop this argument through discussing how young people in Bemni abide by the wishes of their parents and older villagers while also advancing their own goals.

Another difficulty with Mannheim's work from the point of view of my interest in young people's lives in the Himalayas is that he suggests that youth characteristically become 'agents' through asserting independence, and in particular by breaking from their families. 'Fresh contacts play an important part of the life of the individual when he is forced by events to leave his own social group and enter a new one – when, for example, an adolescent leaves home' (Mannheim 1956 [1923]; quoted by Durham 2008: 168). This argument reflects the intellectual climate of the 1920s and 1930s, when Mannheim was writing. The rise of romanticism in the nineteenth century led to a new emphasis on childhood as a period of dependence on the family. It followed that 'youth' was the stage of life in which people freed themselves of kinship ties. This vision of youth also influenced mainstream youth studies in the twentieth and twenty-first centuries. Much of the early writing on young people referred to youth as a 'stage' in which people gradually learnt to sever links with senior kin and build their own independent lives (see, for example, Hall 1904; Mead 1928; Piaget and Inhelder 1958; Keniston 1971). Likewise, many scholars of young people's agency in the 1980s and 1990s frequently looked for instances in which young people broke from their kin (see Durham 2008).

There are several problems with the notion that young people express agency by emphasising their independence. First of all, those espousing this view risk presenting as a sociological 'fact' what should be analysed as a product of power. As Nikolas Rose (1998) and Graham Burchell (1996) have shown, powerful institutions in the last quarter of the twentieth century and early twenty-first century have often tried to instil in people the notion that they are 'individuals' who must tackle historical disadvantages through assuming responsibility for their own lives (see World Bank 2007).

The notion that youth become more independent as they mature and break from their kin also distracts attention from the extent to which young people build social relationships – with each other and with older kin or non-kin – in order to acquire a sense of agency. This is a theme of numerous recent studies of young people, especially but not exclusively children and youth in Africa, Asia and Latin America. For example, Durham (2008) has argued in research in Botswana that young people's maturity and agency are measured in terms of their ability to invest in traditional social networks. A mature, responsible person in the place where Durham worked is one who is able to maintain multiple relationships of interdependence rather than express his or her own independence (see also Hoffman 2008). The manner in which young people exercise agency through building social relationships emerges even more clearly in research on young people's work. For example, Reynolds (1991) argues that young people in Zimbabwe in the 1980s developed a sense of their own maturity and pursued their goals by conducting household work for elder kin. The transition from child to youth in this context was marked by young people's ability to show through their everyday labour their love and respect for elders. Olga Nieuwenhuys (1994) makes similar points in her assessment of children's work routines in Kerala, south India. In this case children used paid work outside the home and unpaid domestic labour as a means of fulfilling moral obligations to their parents and other senior kin. Paid work outside the home was gendered: boys were mainly involved in scavenging for fish as a means of developing an identity as successful providers, while girls sought respect through producing coir yarn in the home. But boys and girls were united in their desire to strengthen relations of interdependence within the household, and thereby raise their status within it. My study builds on the work of scholars such as Durham, Reynolds and Nieuwenhuys. The agro-pastoral system characteristic of Bemni requires parents and children to coordinate their various activities closely, and to do so in different ways at different times of the year. Children and youth also cultivate numerous connections among themselves, often on the basis of friendship and in their everyday spaces of work.

In the context of Bemni, it is also important to stress the limits to young people's social agency. There is much research highlighting how caste, class, gender and other inequalities shape young people's actions while working (such as Aitken 2001; Da Costa 2010). In addition, young people often reproduce caste, class and gender identities and other pernicious norms. Willis (1977) similarly shows that the lads at the centre of his study often challenged notions of class improvement through education, and thus resisted broader social structures in certain ways. At the same time, however, working-class boys reproduced misogynistic views, and to some extent also racist attitudes. Willis therefore argues that young people often make 'partial penetrations' of wider structures. They apprehend some aspects of dominance but reproduce other dominant norms. Such 'partial penetrations' repeatedly surfaced in the everyday work practices of young people in Bemni.

Young people and the environment

Young people's relationship to the rural environment is the other major theme of this book. I use the word 'environment' to refer broadly to people's natural surroundings. The term is somewhat problematic, though, because of its tendency to suggest a world in which humans are positioned centrally: they are 'surrounded' by an 'environment' (see Gold and Gujar 2002). In addition, 'environment' tends to connote those aspects of people's surrounding landscape that have utilitarian value (Ingold 1992). I nevertheless prefer the term to the alternative terms 'landscape' and 'nature'. 'Landscape' has a rather distant resonance – it suggests 'scenery' and the 'bird's-eye view' – and it tends to connote representations of the land. 'Nature' refers either to a realm untouched by human activity or the entire living world, including humans; neither of these definitions is especially helpful for my analytical purposes (Whatmore 2009). 'Environment' therefore appears the most felicitous term.

Young people's relationship to the 'environment' in Bemni was indeed partly utilitarian: the field and forest were places in which they obtained the basic foodstuffs, fuel and other materials that would sustain them through the year. Indeed, children and young people were crucial to the reproduction of the household economy through the work that they did in the forest and fields. Other studies have noted the significant role that children and youth can play in agrarian societies, including work in Europe (Morrow 1994), Africa (Katz 2004) and Latin America (Wyers 1986; Punch 2001). In Bemni, children and youth were largely responsible for herding cattle in the village, and they provided vital additional labour at peak periods in the agricultural cycle.

Children were also highly knowledgeable about the fields and forest, and, especially, the qualities and availability of natural resources. Local knowledge in rural communities in the global South is a well-established and prominent topic in development studies and anthropology (for example Chambers 1983; Gupta 1998). Many recent studies of nature and society relations draw out the importance of how information about natural processes is acquired, communicated and stored within communities (for example Gidwani 2008; Pandian 2009). But, with notable exceptions (such as Katz 2004), the particular knowledge of children and youth has not been studied in depth. I examine in detail the nature of young people's knowledge and skills. Children in Bemni quickly acquired information about the availability of natural resources and how these resources could be harvested.

Much recent scholarship in geography, anthropology and related disciplines has challenged the common assumption that the 'environment' is interesting only from the point of its economic utility. This literature has examined subjective and affective dimensions of nature–society relations, highlighting the social construction of nature (for example Descola and Palsson 1996; Agrawal and Sivaramakrishnan 2000), the complex manner in which bodies interrelate with environments (for example Ingold 2007; McCormack 2008) and questions around affect and emotion (for example Lorimer 2012). The environment is not a static container or backdrop for human action but intimately bound up with human activity. Scholars have also argued that humans are not in any privileged position within environmental systems and that natural phenomena all have 'effects', contributing to outcomes on the ground (for example Latour 2005; Whatmore 2009).

Commentators on urban youth have in some ways anticipated this interest in how environments intermesh with people's social and cultural lives (Hart 1979; Gagen 2000). Literature on street children, for example, is full of references to young people's complex engagement with the materiality of the city, including their knowledge of the properties of 'the street' and their capacity to rework urban locations to reflect their own goals. This is evident for example in Swanson's (2009) work on young beggars in Ecuador, Andrew Burridge's (2010) work on youth protest in New York, and the anthropological research of Brad Weiss (2009) on urban youth practices in Tanzania. Young people are very much a product of their place in the urban realm, just as they shape the urban world through their practices. This literature on urban youth has also examined how young people imagine the urban neighbourhoods, towns and cities in which they live, and it has probed in rich detail the consumption practices of urban youth and their complicated relationship to new technologies such as the mobile phone (for example Pfaff 2009; Doron and Jeffrey 2012).

My work builds on this research, but through reference to young people's relationship to fields and forests rather than street corners and mobile phones. Young people's relationship to their rural surroundings is a theme of Katz's (2004) social research with children and young people in Sudan, and also Tatek Adebe's (2007) writing on youth in Ethiopia (see also Sugden and Punch 2013). My work extends these studies through focusing in more detail on precisely how young people utilise and imagine their everyday work in the field and forest. More than existing studies, I also discuss how young people express their intimate relationship to natural resources.

I am interested in how the field and forest, and the materials and processes that children encounter in these places, are significant symbolically and socially. The agricultural fields and forest surrounding Bemni constitute the stage upon which young people develop a sense of their own gendered identities and an understanding of themselves as capable, moral subjects. Anand Pandian (2009) has advanced a parallel argument in an analysis of members of the Kallar caste in Tamil Nadu. Pandian is especially interested in the process by which Kallars – labelled a 'criminal caste' by the British – developed a notion of themselves as moral beings over the course of the twentieth century. He argues that their project of self-making occurred in large part through the manner in which they interacted with their agrarian landscape. The physical act of cultivation was centrally bound up with the wider cultivation of a virtuous self. My analysis provides similar evidence for the close connection between people's idea of themselves as virtuous and their tactile engagement with the landscape. I place particular emphasis on how young people develop a sense of self in the environment through practices of what Tim Ingold (2007) terms 'wayfaring': spontaneous movement through the landscape that entails meaning-filled, close and tactile engagement with the materials encountered there.

In addition to being important economically and for the cultivation of the self, the fields and forest are a crucially significant setting for social interaction for children and youth. The forests – like 'the street' in some urban studies – provide a venue for young people to develop intimate relationships. The forest is also a space of fun. There has been some interesting work in recent years on young people, humour and enjoyment. Oskar Verkaaik (2004) has argued that 'fun' (*mazaa*) is a key feature of the social and political lives of young people in urban settings in Pakistan. This is also a theme of Willis's research on factory labour in 1970s Britain, where 'having a laff' was important to the maintenance of friendship networks. Scholars of rural life have made similar points: James Scott (1985) frequently refers to the significance of humour in people's everyday resistance in a Malaysian village, and Katz (2004) argues that young people often blend work with different forms of play. I build on these studies by showing how the forest provides the setting and 'props' for young people to engage in games, mischief and joking. The wider point is that the forest and fields serve both as utilitarian 'resources' and as a primary site of youth sociality. It is both a 'safe space', in which to explore identities and relationships, and at other moments a place of risk.

Improvisation was also a theme that emerged in young people's discussion of everyday work. In many situations, young people in Bemni manage the demands of agricultural work or harvesting resources in the forest through a type of judicious opportunism called *jugaad*. *Jugaad* was often used in a general way to suggest any type of improvisation that made best use of the resources that happened to be at hand. It also referred more specifically to instances in which people combined different materials in an opportunistic, and sometimes unconventional, way; *jugaad* in this sense is similar to the US term 'jimmy-rigging'. The fields and forests are sites of improvisation and provide the raw materials for acts of high-spirited *jugaad*.

The analysis of symbolic dimensions of the environment also entails considering how children and youth talk about and represent the forest and fields. The young people often sang about the beauty of the Nandakini Valley and their village, which they imagined as their 'home' (*ghar*). At a finer scale, young people associated specific sites with particular dangers and opportunities; for example, particular places were regarded as haunted or as especially treacherous sites to collect leaves. The temporal dimensions of these spatial imaginaries are sometimes complex, because young people were constantly reflecting on how their immediate surroundings were changing – seasonally and through time – and because their relationship to the fields and forest was shifting as they grew up. In addition, young people superimposed on their visions of the environment their own ideas about whether a particular place was 'safe', in the sense of being outside the supervisory gaze of their parents and older villagers, or 'risky' – a place in which they could be watched over by their elders, and therefore where it is necessary to accord with wider norms around work and gender.

South Asian approaches

My reflections on young people's agency and environmental engagements in the Himalayas have partly been inspired by a new generation of research on children and youth in south Asia. Work in the past twenty years has examined how young people are responding to processes of rapid social change, including research on higher education (for example Lukose 2005; Rogers 2008; Jeffrey 2010), youth involvement in new forms of the urban economy (Fuller and Narasimhan 2007; Nisbett 2007; Gooptu 2009) and children's experiences in rural and school settings (Gold and Gujar 2002; Sarangapani 2003; Bénéï 2008). These studies have contributed to wider understanding of structures of gender difference in south Asia (for example Chopra, Osella and Osella's 2004 work on masculinities); helped us to appreciate the mismatch between young people's aspirations and economic outcomes (for example Nisbett 2007); and shown how young people's lives – and 'youth' itself – can become politicised (for example Bénéï 2008).

My book complements the existing work on children and youth in contemporary south Asia by concentrating on a set of young people who have not been drawn into globalisation in the manner, say, of the young people studied by Caroline and Filippo Osella (2006) in Kerala. I focus instead on young people in a relatively isolated setting. At the same time, I build upon themes in the existing literature: how young people's lives are changing in the context of the rise of formal education, the gendered nature of childhood and youth, and the vibrant cultural practices and social imaginations of young people in Bemni.

It is important to state what this book is not, however. I have not followed the type of psycho-social 'socialisation' approach that has been prominent in south Asian scholarly circles. This vein of research, which can be traced at least as far back as Morris Carstairs (1958) and Sudhir Kakar (1978), examines the psychological impact of mother–infant bonds on the subsequent emotional development of Indian men. Kakar, in particular, did much to uncover how male children absorb cultural knowledge and experience youth. But he makes rather broad assertions about 'the Indian child' based on the close observation of just a few higher-caste urban individuals (Trawick 1990). Socialisation approaches also frequently dwell on children as in a state of 'becoming', and thereby tend to read all children's actions as part of their preparation for adulthood (Alanen 2007). In addition, these socialisation approaches have tended to downplay children's agency by suggesting that young people passively absorb social and cultural ideas produced by adult society. The story I tell is of children's and young people's active creation of cultural practices.

My study is also somewhat distinct from the burgeoning literature, within academic and policy circles, on child labour in south Asia (Weiner 1991; Burra 2003). The Campaign against Child Labour recently estimated that there are between 40 million and 100 million children working in India (Mishra 2000; Nambissan 2003; Sugden and Punch 2013). Although the vast majority of these children work in rural areas, and are often engaged in household labour, many studies have focused on paid work in manufacturing settings. These include, for example, Lakshmidhar Mishra's (2000) account of the carpet industry in north India, Thérèse Blanchet's (1996) analysis of cigarette production in Bangladesh and Smitu Kothari's (1983) and Mann Kulkarni's (1983) discussions of match manufacturing in Tamil Nadu. Much of this work has drawn attention to the oppressive conditions under which children labour, and to issues such as bonded labour and child trafficking (Burra 2003). It has also usefully highlighted how age and gender intersect to subordinate children (Folbre 1986; Nieuwenhuys 1994; Oldman 1994).

Some of the work on child labour in south Asia has, nonetheless, tended to reproduce, often unwittingly, the Western, twentieth-century notion of a singular, unchanging 'normal' childhood against which children are defined. Commentators typically imagine this 'ideal childhood' as being a condition of dependence and innocence, wholly removed from paid or unpaid work. In addition, many studies of child labour, through focusing on children as victims of wider forces, risk downplaying children's agency (compare Swanson 2009). The stories from Bemni reveal a different picture. They certainly highlight the hardships of children's – mostly unpaid – work. But they also demonstrate young people's capacity to instil meaning in their labour, to acquire skills and to balance their domestic work with formal education. I hope to show not only that children are active agents, but that this agency is necessarily tied up with notions of interdependence that are crucial to children's own sense of themselves as competent young people.

Uttarakhand

My study of young people's working lives emerges out of research I conducted in the village of Bemni, Uttarakhand, in 2003 and 2004, and it is crucially important to situate my study with reference to the wider context. The state of Uttarakhand was established on 8 November 2000, carved out of Uttar Pradesh. As much as 88 per cent of the state is mountainous and it is fairly poorly linked in terms of transport and communications infrastructure to the rest of India. Some 77 per cent of the population lived in rural areas in 2000, and roughly two-thirds of the population was dependent on agriculture (Ministry of Home Affairs 2001). Forest resources have been especially important in the lives of Uttarakhandi villagers. Forests provide fuelwood (the dominant source of energy), building materials, livestock fodder and bedding, medicinal plants and various wild foods, which are increasingly being harvested and sold commercially (Pande and Pande 2001; Sharma 2001).

Uttarakhand has played a significant role in India's history, especially in the post-colonial era. In the early 1970s Uttarakhand witnessed the emergence of the 'Chipko movement', which began when local people, organised initially by a small village cooperative society, began to protest at the unsustainable exploitation of the forests, which provided little in the way of jobs or income for local Uttarakhandis. The Chipko movement came to incorporate a wide range of demands, including calls for more raw material allocation to local people, the abolition of large-scale extraction by non-local forest contractors, the hiring of locally organised labour cooperatives for timber felling and the regulation of external competition to privilege local entrepreneurs. In some cases, Chipko protests were organised by women and environmentalists, and were aimed at protecting the resource base for subsistence farming (Rangan 1997; Mawdsley 1998; Jayal 2001). These demands reflected the broad range of social actors who became involved in the movement, including village agriculturalists, and also students, Gandhians, academics, small businesspeople and politicians. Controversially, the environmental demands articulated by one element of the Chipko movement were met when the state banned green commercial felling at altitudes above 1,000 metres, and the Chipko legend became important within and beyond India (Shiva 1989). The social and economic aspects of the movement were less well recognised, however, causing ongoing resentment in the marginalised hill communities (Rangan 2001).

In the 1990s Uttarakhand was the site of another social movement, this time agitating for a separate state. This protest was triggered in part by the decision of the UP government to reserve 27 per cent of government posts throughout the state for so-called 'other backward classes'. This category refers to castes (*jatis*) that are located relatively low down within the varna caste hierarchy. The quota of 27 per cent was roughly equivalent to the percentage of OBCs in UP's population as a whole. But Uttarakhand's caste make-up was rather different. Upper castes were much more numerous in Uttarakhand than in most other areas of India. Of the 7.5 million people living in the state, 69 per cent were upper caste (Brahmins and Kshatriyas). A further 17 per cent belonged to castes formerly classed as 'untouchable' in the village. The remainder of the state's population was comprised of 8 per cent Muslims, Sikhs and Christians, 3.5 per cent 'scheduled tribes' (including the Bhotiyas, Jaunsaries and Van Gujjars) and just 2.5 per cent OBCs. Thus, what seemed logical for the state as a whole was patently unfair from the perspective of those living in the mountains. OBCs in plains UP began to migrate to Uttarakhand to compete for jobs in the reserved quota. Uttarakhandis' fear of an influx of people from the plains into the mountainous region catalysed longer-standing concerns about being governed by politicians in Lucknow, the state capital. The geographer Emma Mawdsley (1997) heard people in Uttarakhand begin to chant in the streets that 'Peking is closer than Lucknow' – a politically charged (if geographically inaccurate) means of signalling mountain-dwellers dissatisfaction with being part of Uttar Pradesh. Such concerns coalesced into a widespread, largely non-violent popular movement in Uttarakhand in the mid-1990s that, like the Chipko movement before it, involved large sections of the population. This culminated in the establishment of the state of Uttarakhand (formerly called 'Uttaranchal') in 2000 (see Mawdsley 1997, 1999).

Chipko and the movement for a separate state reflected people's long-standing concern about their location, peripheral to major national and international flows of goods, ideas and services. At the same time, the 'remoteness' of Uttarakhand should not be exaggerated. Participants in the movement for a separate state of Uttarakhand were keen to emphasise the region's importance in India's past and present economic, social and cultural life. Throughout much of the twentieth century the state played a key administrative and military role, not least during the Indo-China war of 1962. The role of natural resources, especially forests, has also been significant. Through their historic struggles over forest resources, rural people in Uttarakhand demonstrated not only their dependence on forests but also the extent to which they were capable of sustainable forest management (see Guha and Gadgil 1992; Pathak 1997;

Gururani 2001). Recent shifts in state- and national-level forest management strategies have reflected this by facilitating a move away from state-driven management to models in which authority is returned to local people (Das 2000). This transition occurred in part in Uttarakhand during the 1930s, through the introduction of the Van Panchayat Act, and provided a framework on which the nationwide Joint Forest Management programme was more recently modelled (see Poffenberger and McGean 1996; Sundar, Jeffery and Thin 2001; Kumar 2004).

Uttarakhand also became better integrated into the Indian economy between the early 1980s and early 2000s. The growth of educational institutions and hospitals was important in providing some new employment opportunities to people in the state. In the early 2000s the foundation of the new state led to an expansion of government bureaucracies and educational institutions in Uttarakhand (Moller 2003). Improvements in infrastructure have encouraged the cultivation of new cash crops, such as potatoes, kidney beans, amaranth and soybean, and there has been an associated decline in millet, wheat and barley, grown for subsistence. Some well-connected areas of Uttarakhand also became centres for horticulture in the 1990s and early 2000s (Pandey and Rawat 2000). In addition, improved infrastructure facilitated tourism. The high Himalayan region of Uttarakhand is home to four of the most sacred Hindu temples, at Badrinath, Kedarnath, Gangotri and Yamunotri, and draws large numbers of pilgrims each year (Pande and Pandey 2001). Moreover, in recent years Bollywood directors have increasingly looked to the state as a cheap, homespun equivalent to expensive film shoots in Switzerland, and Uttarakhand even has a nascent indigenous film industry based in Dehra Dun.

The state nevertheless remained somewhat marginal to the Indian economy in the 1990s and early 2000s. In 2000 28 per cent of villages in Uttarakhand remained more than 5 kilometres from a road and 21 per cent lacked electricity, according to the United Nations Development Programme, and, reflecting the mountainous terrain, only 24 per cent of the land in Uttarakhand was cultivated. Moreover, 75 per cent of landholdings were less than 1 hectare in 2000 (Ministry of Home Affairs 2001), inhibiting the emergence of successful commercial farms. The small size of landholdings is closely linked to the prevailing system of partible inheritance, whereby sons formally inherit equal portions of land when their father dies.

Uttarakhand did not share in the expansion of information technology and ancillary services that occurred in the Delhi metropolitan region in the 1990s and early 2000s. The school infrastructure in Uttarakhand is also poor relative to neighbouring Himachal Pradesh (Ministry of Home Affairs 2001; Klenk 2010), and the adult literacy rate in Uttarakhand was 60 per cent in 2000, 73 per cent for men and 42 per cent for women (Ministry of Home Affairs 2001).

The generally depressed state of agriculture during much of the post-colonial period and the paucity of local employment opportunities has meant that many men in rural Uttarakhand have migrated in search of work (Mamgain 2003). In one study conducted in the early 1990s, 60 per cent of households in a sample of villages in two eastern districts of the state were reported to have male members who had migrated away from the village, often to urban centres (Bora 1996). Positions in the army were especially popular in the 1990s and early 2000s.

There is therefore a strong sense in which Uttarakhand is relatively marginal to the processes of economic, political and cultural change occurring in India as a whole (Tewari and Mujoo 2001). At the same time, processes of migration and the establishment of Uttarakhand as a separate state have resulted in new flows of people, ideas and resources into the region, especially since the early 1990s. Moreover, many Uttarakhandis have a powerful sense of belonging to the Indian nation, and display pride at the centrality of the state in India's sacred geography.

There are substantial variations in the degree to which specific locations in the state are integrated into the wider economy. A first set of villages around Dehra Dun, Haridwar and Rishikesh are part of a region of economic development stretching from Delhi, up through the relatively prosperous Ghaziabad, Meerut and Muzaffarnagar districts, to Dehra Dun itself. In the thriving towns of Dehra Dun, Haridwar and Rishikesh it is common to find a wide array of commercial and service activity, including private schools, horticulture businesses and shops. Dehra Dun has a substantial army base, too. These areas include both the fertile 'terai' areas of Uttarakhand and also portions of what is termed the 'outer Himalayas', in which a relatively wide variety of agricultural production is possible, and where farming resembles to a great extent that of the adjacent plains. A second set of settlements is comprised of those located in the 'middle Himalayas' that are close to major roads. Almost all these villages had a regular supply of electricity in the early 2000s, and they were often sites of small business ventures, shops and non-governmental organisation (NGO) activity. A third set of villages is located in the 'high Himalayas' (or 'inner Himalayas'), areas above 1,800 metres and close to the highest peaks. They are typically distant from major roads, or not connected to the road transport network at all. Many of these villages lack electricity or well-developed commercial activity. It was in the 'high Himalayas' that I worked.

Chamoli district

The administrative district in which Bemni village is located – Chamoli district – lies in the far north of Uttarakhand state, bordering Tibet. The population density of Chamoli district is relatively low for the state, just fifty people per square kilometre, and only 9 per cent lived in urban areas in 2001 (Ministry of Home Affairs 2001). Chamoli district contains a broad spectrum of ecosystem types. Climatic conditions vary with altitude, although winter generally occurs between November and March, and most of the precipitation falls between June and September. The river Alaknanda passes through the centre of the district, until its confluence with the Bhagirathi at Devprayag.

Forests comprise 58 per cent of the total area of Chamoli district. The abundant natural resources are the draw for increasing numbers of tourists to Chamoli. Nanda Devi Biosphere Reserve was officially reopened in 2003 for restricted community based ecotourism, after a twenty-one-year closure, and a number of trekking routes thread through the district. It is also an important spiritual location; a large number of pilgrims pass through the district during the summer season.

Livelihood strategies in Chamoli were predominantly rural in the early 2000s, and the population remained dependent on natural resources. Villagers in the high Himalayas once practised pastoralism and agro-pastoralism, which involved varying degrees of transhumance. The vertical linkages in such regimes have most commonly been examined with respect to the large-scale transhumance still practised by tribal pastoralist groups such as the Bhotiyas (Hoon 1996; Nautiyal *et al.* 2003) and Van Gujjars (Gooch 1998), and among the Gaddis of Himachal Pradesh (Saberwal 1999). These groups spend the summer months in the alpine pastures and the winter months at lower altitudes.

There has been less research on the smaller-scale transhumance practices of the agro-pastoralist Hindu caste groups. These regimes involve a mix of cultivated land use and pastoralism and depend on a series of seasonal shifts to varying altitudes to ensure the most efficient and sustainable use of available land. Such small-scale transhumance was once common throughout Uttarakhand and Chamoli district, and several colonial reports refer to such practices (Pauw 1896; Walton 1910, quoted by Somanathan 1991). But small-scale transhumance had largely disappeared from the outer and middle Himalayas by the mid-1990s (Sarkar 1998). In such areas, the loss of agricultural labour through high levels of emigration and the subdivision of land have made the practice unviable. At the same time, the lack of grazing areas and labour has led to the decline of livestock numbers, on which the system depends for draught power and fertiliser. As transhumance practices are gradually abandoned, agricultural systems in the inner Himalayan zone of Chamoli have become increasingly sedentary (Chauhan and Bhatt 2000; Palni, Maikhuri and Rao 2001).

As elsewhere in Uttarakhand, off-farm employment opportunities in Chamoli continue to be concentrated at transport hubs at lower altitudes. A lack of private salaried work and business opportunities has encouraged male migration from the area. In 1991 the female population was 52 per cent higher than the male population in Chamoli district (Bora 1996). A shortage of private-sector work has also promoted intense competition for government employment in the region.

The widespread desire for government employment, for which a class ten (high school) pass is a minimum qualification, partly explains the prominent role played by education in Chamoli district in the last forty years. Between 1961 and 1971 there was a 52 per cent increase in literacy, and by 2001 literacy levels had reached 75 per cent (Ministry of Home Affairs 2001). Although most children lived close to a junior basic school, the hostility of the terrain and poor road infrastructure restricted access to senior secondary schools to a small proportion of the population.

Locating the village

I wanted to explore children's and young people's agency through the lens of their everyday work practices. I therefore looked to work in an area where villagers were still largely dependent on agriculture, and where children juggled their contribution to household and agricultural work with their schooling. Uttarakhand, and Chamoli district in particular, seemed an obvious choice. There was increasing awareness in the region of women's work practices, knowledge and agency in places such as Bemni, as highlighted through the Chipko movement (which itself originated in Chamoli district). But commentators had paid little attention to the important role played by children in rural labour.

As I embarked on finding a place to work, I had in mind critiques of 'the village' as a basis of enquiry. Scholars have questioned the notion that the village in India is a natural sociological unit. The coherence of the village in north India is largely a male construction, since most women migrate to other settlements at the point of marriage. Moreover, villages, even in 'remote' locations, form part of wider networks of social relations and flows of goods and people; analysing 'the village' can convey a false sense of its isolation. In addition, the term 'village' (*ganv*) is itself somewhat misleading in some parts of the high Himalayas, referring not to a single settlement but to a string of two or three settlements, stretched out across the mountainside, to which villagers migrate on a seasonal basis. But, for all these caveats, the village remains an important context for understanding young people's agency in India, especially in Uttarakhand: people depend on the village as a source of food and services; they are proud of their own village; and they are apt to speculate on the different characteristics and reputation of other villages round about. For practical reasons, too, it made sense to be based in one village. Working in a single place would mean that I would be working with a single set of local institutions, and that I would develop closer bonds and a deeper understanding of everyday practices. I would be able to acquire a keen sense of the village as an anthropological entity, and this would provide a comparative framework for understanding the relative position of different households in the settlement.

I relied heavily on friends from a number of small local NGOs, both in Dehra Dun and Gopeshwar, to advise me on suitable areas within Chamoli district. It was finally a combination of two well-known local men – a journalist and a politician – that led me towards the Nandakini Valley, where, at the beginning of 2003, I spent four weeks visiting different villages. These villages lie a few hours by road from the district town of Gopeshwar and close to the small market town of Ghat. But they are relatively removed from flows of commerce and activity trickling up the main valleys of Uttarakhand from the plains. I wanted to work in a village where agriculture was the mainstay of the economy, where there were both higher castes and scheduled castes and in which children were educated locally, rather than travelling to a local town for school. Most villages in the Nandakini Valley satisfied these criteria. I settled on Bemni because it was a relatively large village administered under a single gram panchayat (the lowest level of government administration). Some other gram panchayats in this area consist of two or three villages, which would have been logistically difficult to manage. But Bemni was in no way obviously unusual, and, although it was several kilometres' walk from the nearest road, it was close enough to the road head at Ghat to be able to travel from the village to Gopeshwar in a day. I rented a small flat in Gopeshwar, and settled into a routine of spending about three weeks in Bemni followed by five or six days in Gopeshwar to type up field notes.

Choosing the village was merely the start of it. Explaining myself was the next challenge. I appeared in the depths of winter, when snow makes many roads impassable and trekking routes are long since closed. I was married, and yet I travelled without my husband and suggested I stay for a year. I wore an acceptable *salwar kameez*, but it was paired with clumpy, foreign walking boots. I seemed happy to work in the fields or go to the forest, and yet at night insisted I sleep in a sleeping bag ('What happens to your farts?' worried one rather disgusted old woman). I was, indeed, a strange apparition. It was not simply that I was *videshi*, a foreigner, but, rather, that I came from beyond and beneath the Himalayas. Put simply, I was from *neeche* ('below'), a notion that encompassed a somewhat undifferentiated 'rest of the world', where things are done differently. My desire to conduct research in the village was therefore accepted on these grounds, and I was encouraged to stay.

I should not dismiss the ongoing tensions that ran through my research, however. For example, by virtue of originating from 'below', it was assumed – as well as being visibly obvious – that I was from a more privileged background. Both the hills people and those from the plains saw the region as 'backward', so the distinction between 'up here' in the mountains and 'below' also implied a socio-economic gap. While the children seemed unconcerned about my relative wealth, I struggled with men's enquiries regarding how much my husband and I earned. Given that I asked similarly sensitive questions concerning village incomes, I resolved to answer these queries truthfully, while seeking to contextualise our relative wealth with examples of the cost of living in the United Kingdom. I also sought to minimise obvious inequalities by reducing the amount of equipment I kept and dressing simply. I shared provisions, and villagers often called upon me for basic medical supplies. None of these tactics could squarely address the inequalities of standing, experience and prospects that marked me off from others in the village, and I often felt guilty being able to 'dip in and out' of a situation of considerable hardship, through being able to retreat from the village periodically to Gopeshwar, and ultimately through travel back to the United Kingdom.

The pressure of conducting research in an unfamiliar setting was considerable. I was often exhausted by the heavy physical labour required to conduct ethnographic research on children's work. Living conditions were also extremely basic; I shared a thin single mattress on the mud floor in a small room with no electricity. Outside there was a tap, but no latrine or private washing space. Day-to-day living took a long time. The process of getting going in the morning – going to the lavatory in a secluded field, heating icy water to wash hands and face, washing up the previous nights' dishes, cooking breakfast over a paraffin stove and washing up again – could take two to three hours. Our once-weekly bucket bath became increasingly hazardous in winter, when there were no crops in the fields to hide in and the risk of leopard or bear attack increased. Moreover, the isolation of the area also meant that reliable medical services were at least a couple of days away. I often had to balance my need to obtain medical attention against the exigencies of rural fieldwork.

Within the first month of beginning research in Bemni, I recruited a research assistant. It was considered odd for a young woman to be seen to be 'wandering around' alone in the village, and, besides, in the initial months, I needed some language help. I arrived able to speak good Hindi, and could communicate with little problem in the village. But the main language in Bemni was a dialect of Garhwali, which is related to Hindi. While I slowly picked up Garhwali in the village, I generally talked in a mixture of Hindi and Garhwali, with occasional help from my research assistant.

Bemni villagers encouraged me to recruit a female research assistant from the village, but I was concerned that such a move would draw me into village politics. I needed an 'insider/outsider': a young woman familiar with the mountainous environment but removed enough not to be associated with a particular local faction. HIMAD (the Himalayan Society for Alternative Development), a local NGO, recommended Anita, a twenty-four-year-old unmarried general caste girl, who had studied for a BA and MA in a private college in Gopeshwar and was fluent in Hindi and Garhwali (but, like other educated people in the area, knew only a smattering of English words). Anita's home village was substantially better connected than Bemni; it had a road, electricity and some commercial activity, and she was visibly shocked when she first arrived in Bemni after a very long walk. But she said that she would be willing to work with me, and quickly came to enjoy the research.

Anita became the subject of close scrutiny in Bemni, perhaps because of her simultaneous combination of a local background with outsider status. Many villagers in Bemni were concerned about Anita's caste. Friends took me aside during the first weeks, claiming that, by virtue of her slightly darker skin, Anita appeared to be SC. Anita's caste had implications for whose houses she could enter, and whose food and drink she could accept, so, given that we were already living and sometimes sharing food with a GC family, her assumed SC status caused considerable concern. But after three or four months many villagers changed their views quite radically. They praised Anita's competence in agricultural and forest work, and she soon earned people's widespread respect. This turnaround in Anita's relationships and reputation caused its own problems, however. The family with whom we lived became so attached to Anita that they insisted that she marry their eldest son. Anita flatly refused, and, until she claimed she was engaged to another man, she suffered good-natured pestering for several months.

Ajay Singh, a relatively prosperous and respected GC man in the village, invited me and Anita to stay in his family's house in Bemni. We later moved with them down the mountain to their winter settlement, where we renovated and occupied a tiny room above the donkey's stable. Ajay would not accept rent, but I regularly bought the family gifts and, when their prized buffalo died, I helped replace it. The living arrangement worked well. We retained a measure of independence but were otherwise integrated into many aspects of Ajay family's life, often eating together and helping around the household, perhaps preparing crops to dry in the courtyard, threshing grain with sticks or churning butter. Ajay's wife, who we called *tai-ji* (aunt), and his daughter, Saka, became close friends. On a daily basis we shared jokes, snacks and hardships, and we have remained good friends.

Anita and I spent the majority of our time hanging out, conducting participant observation, with fifteen key informant young people and their families. These children were chosen to cover a range of social differences, including age, gender and caste, in roughly representative proportions. For example, the number of SC children and young people roughly reflected the proportion of SC villagers in Bemni. The children and their families provided the core focus of my ethnographic enquiry. We spent lazy days herding cattle, or exhausting ones collecting lichen. We would set off in darkness to collect leaves from the forest, or join children and their parents in the fields harvesting wheat, weeding potatoes or lugging *gobar*. My participation in work was a source of constant bemusement, particularly to the ever-diligent women. I was relatively weak, and the baskets that I carried were always child-sized, and my hand blistered quickly after prolonged use of the sickle. Women thought I was *tard*, a word that means not so much lazy as being lucky to have easy work, and constantly asked: 'Ah, you are wandering around still?' Our status as 'wanderers' was devaluing in a place where a woman's reputation depends on her diligence. Children and adults were nevertheless pleased that I tried, and enjoyed teaching me, or teasing me when I got it wrong. Being a dependent, ignorant adult among a group of children often helped to redress asymmetries between us, encouraging them to be more confident, and to carefully explain their practices and perceptions of their work.

The research took on other forms, too. Thirteen of my KI children wrote daily diaries of their activities, including work, school and leisure. These diaries covered, on average, around fifteen days in each month, and were written in Devanagri script in a mix of Garhwali and Hindi. I collected and translated the diaries at regular (usually ten-day) intervals in the village. The diaries proved to be a valuable tool, providing insights into the full range of children's everyday activities. They tended not to include much detail, often omitting, for example, occasions when children carried out multiple tasks simultaneously, such as washing dishes while also cooking and looking after siblings, or collecting firewood while out herding the cattle. Their brevity provides a startling rawness, however. At other times, the detail might sound perplexing. For example, equal weight was often given to 'going to the latrine' as 'weeding a potato field'. These small details – reflecting the long time it took to walk to a suitably distant and private field in which to defecate – throw into greater relief the hardships of everyday life in Bemni. In practical terms, the diaries also provided the 'glue' through which we maintained contact with the children and their parents, helping build rapport and friendships.

There were drawbacks to the method, however. I felt uncomfortable about giving the children an extra task above their household chores and schoolwork, and regretted their feelings of guilt if they had not written their diaries. I tried to compensate by constantly giving them the opportunity to opt out or by encouraging them to adapt their writing according to their commitments. For example, when children spent the entire day collecting lichen in winter, they returned too shattered to write more than simply 'lichen', and the name of the forest they had visited. I also rewarded them for their diary writing with small gifts: sweets and biscuits, firecrackers for Diwali, jewellery and toys from the United Kingdom, and cricket bats and balls for collective use. At the end of the research period I gave a new *salwar kameez* to the girls, and shirts and caps to the boys; quite substantial gifts for children who otherwise only wore second-hand clothing.

I used a number of other methods too. I conducted several rounds of focus groups with the children and their friends, and two rounds of interviews with the parents of key informants. The first centred on children's work, and the second concerned details of household income, expenditure and agricultural output. I also worked at a broader village level. At the beginning of the research I conducted a full village census, documenting the age, educational background and occupation of every member of every household, as well as information about daughters-in-law, migrant relatives and remittances. I obtained information on household assets, including land, livestock and basic possessions. Towards the end I conducted interviews with a range of other relevant adults: local state representatives, including teachers; state farm workers; an ayurvedic doctor; a Forest Department guard; a Revenue Department officer; a *gram vikas adhikari* (village development officer); the village sarpanch (leader of the van panchayat); and a *chowkidar* (village forest guard). I also made extensive maps of the area using Global Positioning System (GPS) technology.

In representing the lives and perspectives of my KI children and their parents, I have been necessarily selective. The stories cannot capture the diverse characters of the children and young people with whom I worked. Moreover, I witnessed a number of shifts in the lives of my KIs. In some cases, these occurred in the children's households: people left, or new members arrived; income opportunities arose or dwindled. When large changes in context took place, and are important to my narrative, I have mentioned them. Less easy to handle or describe are the inevitable changes in the children themselves, particularly the marked changes in size, physical ability and confidence of individuals over my fifteen months in the village. Such transformations had implications for their role and status in their households, as well as for the everyday ways in which children spent their time.

Argument and structure of the book

The principal substantive argument of the book is that young people make crucial contributions to the agrarian economy in the high Himalayas. They are central players in the agro-pastoral regime, helping older villagers with agricultural tasks, caring for younger children and collecting materials from the forests surrounding the village. In documenting how they manage these tasks, the book offers a compelling picture of the resourcefulness and resilience of children and youth in an 'out-of-the-way' place (compare Tsing 1993).

Young people's ability to reproduce rural household economies reflects their determination, on the whole, to meet the expectations of parents and older villagers about how they should behave. They respected older villagers, performed the tasks assigned for them and often did so without the type of 'foot dragging' and non-compliance that Scott (1985) imagines as characteristic of subaltern workers in Malaysia in the 1970s. At the same time, young people were not the passive victims of local ideologies of work pedalled by those in power. Young people saw that their interests were best served by helping their peers and older villagers, and they consciously and deliberately chose to meet parental demands. At the same time, they breathed life into their labour, finding in things as apparently mundane as washing at the village tap and collecting dry leaves opportunities to improvise, laugh and learn new skills. They developed affective relationships to the environment in these spaces, and found opportunities to express ideas. More than anything else, work was a site in which people built social relationships, with each other, their parents and older villagers. Friendship, rather than kinship, was often the most important form of positive sociality. But I also show that friendship was a contradictory resource for young people, providing opportunities to fulfil difficult work but also reinforcing gender and caste inequalities.

The book also highlights the roles of geography, caste and gender more broadly in reinforcing inequalities among young people in Bemni. The remoteness of the village, and the limited means of most villagers, were important in constraining young people's opportunities to develop alternative possible routes through their pre-teen and teenage years. Standards of local education were poor. Few young people travelled beyond the Nandakini Valley in which Bemni is situated. Moreover, caste inequalities were such that higher-caste and low-caste young people rarely mixed. Similarly, dominant gender norms prevented boys and girls from working together beyond the age of about twelve or thirteen. Young people tended to reinforce gendered norms through their work, albeit often idiosyncratically and without working to any simple cultural script.

The next chapter of the book (Chapter 2) introduces Bemni village. It provides an introduction to the gendered and 'casted' political economy of Bemni that points to the continued force of much that is conventionally and locally imagined as 'traditional'. I introduce Uttarakhand and Bemni, focusing especially on the agro-pastoral system in the village. I then discuss the sociology of Uttarakhand and the village, with particular reference to caste and gender, and relate the chapter to the wider themes of the book.

Chapter 3 discusses young people's specific contribution to work in Bemni. It acts as an overview of young people's labour and a road map for the remainder of the book. I review, in turn, the work of children and youth in and around the home, in the field and in the forests. I discuss the process through which young people are drawn into work and how they juggle work with schooling. This chapter draws especially on the diaries that children wrote.

The remaining substantive chapters each examine a different aspect of young people's work. Chapter 4 focuses on herding and shows how young people are sometimes able to use work as a means to rest, play and socialise. Herding is a relatively undemanding task and provides many opportunities for casual conversation, song and reverie. I use notions of 'wayfaring' to understand the improvised ways in which young people engage with the environment while herding, and draw out the different meanings that young people attach to herding work.

Chapter 5 considers girls' leaf collection, a much more demanding task. I describe the mechanics of collecting leaves, the small teams in which girls worked and their close attention to meeting village expectations of what constitutes a 'good basket' of leaves. I also point to the importance of friendship as a basis for leaf collection and a product of girls' work. It was only through cultivating friendships that girls were able to carry out the gruelling task of leaf collection successfully, but these friendships excluded lower castes and tended to entrench dominant gendered ideas in the minds of many girls.

In Chapter 6 I focus on a type of work that did not emerge in Bemni until the 1990s: gathering lichen (called *mukku*), which is used to make dyes and other products in the plains. Higher-caste young people seized on *mukku* collection as an opportunity to further their goals, but they did so in ways powerfully shaped by gender. Boys saw in lichen collection a means to mark their potential future as male breadwinners. Girls perceived *mukku* collection to be an opportunity to achieve some respite from the demands of tiring labour, and also to transgress local notions of acceptable femininity.

Chapter 7 summarises my key arguments and draws the analysis back to the questions of agency, work and environment that underpin the book. I explain what has been learnt from focusing closely on young people in the high Himalayas, drawing out the importance of humour, improvisation and wayfaring. In emphasising that young people can be both 'active' and 'quiescent', I build upon other work on children's agency that stresses the social and interdependent nature of their action. I also show how caste and gender shape people's practices. Further, I provide a new way to think about the social construction of the environment, emphasising both the characteristics that young people attribute to the forest – as 'beautiful' or 'dangerous', for example – and also the social qualities that they attach to particular places, such as certain forest areas being described as 'secret'.

2 The high Himalayas

The journey from Delhi to Bemni took two or three days. It was laborious, long and uncertain, especially in the rainy season. First, one travelled by bus or train north from Delhi to Haridwar, a city whose name literally means 'gateway to the gods', and which marks the point at which the Ganges emerges from the Himalayas onto the north Indian plains. From Haridwar it was a nine-hour drive up a tortuously winding road through numerous riverside settlements and, eventually, to a small town: Nandaprayag. From there, one left the main road and headed east to Ghat along a rutted single-track road. Ghat is smaller than Nandaprayag but possesses a buzz not evident in the latter, perhaps because it plays a larger role as a market and administrative centre for surrounding villages. From Ghat, one's journey continued to Gaitna, now taking a local jeep along a precipitous path, dangerous in the dry season and ludicrously risky in the wet. Gaitna was a bleak spot, where mules huddled from the cold winds that tear down the valley, and a couple of wooden tea stalls provided temporary respite from the weather. In 2003/4 it was from here that one began the walk up to Bemni. It was an unremittingly uphill 8 kilometre slog, climbing over 1,000 metres, before emerging onto the windswept ridge, looking out over layers of mountains. Bemni itself appeared like a different world, lacking electricity, telecommunications or running water in people's homes. Many people dressed in black homespun cloth *chaddars*, speaking a dialect of Garhwali quite different from that found a few hundred metres lower down the mountain.

As this description might suggest, there was a chasm between the lives of the young people I came to know in Bemni and the lives of the young people who form the staple of textbooks on children and youth around the world. In the general literature it is hyper-mobility, spiralling ambitions, and information overload that are often key themes (for example, Bayart 2007; Davidson 2008). Even in India, one is regaled in the scholarly literature with examples of young people's increased exposure to new ideas and technologies (such as Dwyer 2000; Favero 2005; Fuller and Narasimhan 2007). In Bemni, it was remoteness, gruelling work and the predictability of seasonal change that were most prominent in young people's thoughts. Likewise, the mainstream literature on young people is full of references to the increasingly loose and non-determinate role of 'traditional' identities and inequalities in structuring young lives. But caste and gender powerfully shaped young people's practices in Bemni. Change, to the extent that it was occurring at this time, was halting, partial and reversible.

Bemni

Bemni is located in the inner or 'high' Himalayan part of Chamoli district in the Nandakini Valley. In the nineteenth and early twentieth centuries the Nandakini Valley played an important role at the junction of a cluster of trade routes. To the north, across the Kuari Pass, were the paths to Tibet. Heading southwards were two trails. One joined the Alaknanda Valley, winding its way to the Ganges and the markets of the Indo-Gangetic plains. The other took the path to the west, climbing over the dividing ridge into Kumaon and heading down to the western sectors of the plains. Villagers from the Nandakini Valley were themselves part of these routes, transporting goods by huge herds of goats, each animal carrying its own handwoven saddlebag. Men in their forties and fifties told stories of expeditions to trade local varieties of millet for 'black salt' from Tibet, or heading south to lower altitudes to exchange potatoes for wheat and rice. Bemni villagers took their goat herds up to the high Himalayan meadows (*bugyal*) to graze in the summer, and the village was often a point of convergence for herders from other villages and valleys, some far afield.

The Nandakini Valley has also long been the site of one of the most important Hindu pilgrimages of the region, the Nanda Devi Raj Jat. Held every twelve years, the pilgrimage draws tens of thousands of people from Uttarakhand and across India. They are responsible for escorting the goddess Nanda Devi away from her natal home, before leaving her at Homkund, from where she continues to the home of her husband, Lord Shiva, at Trishul (see Sax 1993).

Realising the importance of Bemni as an important halt for trade and religion, the colonial administration established a permanent camp in the village during the first half of the twentieth century. A group of missionaries were also active in the area in the first few decades of the century, establishing a small medical outpost. Known for their hardiness and resilience, the men of Bemni were coveted by the colonial army. Villagers I spoke to recalled the military actively recruiting young men from Bemni, and officials even travelled to the village to pick up young men who had deserted.

In some respects, Bemni became more isolated in the first few decades of independence. The post-colonial state did not maintain an administrative presence in the village, so the occasionally visiting forest officer and single resident primary school teacher remained, for decades, the only vestiges of the state. The 1962 Indo-China war also led to the closing of trade routes from Tibet, cutting Bemni's strong links with the broader Himalayan region. But

Bemni continued to be integrated into a system of barter with other villages in the nearby valleys, and herders continued their six-month migration to the high Himalayan pastures to graze their goats.

By the early 1980s livelihood patterns in Bemni were beginning to change more notably, however. The expanding road network made it easier to gain access to markets with direct road links to the plains. From the main trunk road that follows the river Alaknanda, a 20 kilometre tarred road was built in the early 1980s as far as Ghat, creating a burgeoning market within just 16 kilometres' walking from Bemni. The access to this market encouraged villagers to grow crops such as potatoes and amaranth for cash or barter. Mules, which are more easily maintained than goats, also offered a more efficient means of transporting goods to and from the market, and the population of goats declined accordingly.

In the late 1990s Bemni was brought further into the market economy when a dirt road was cut along the river Nandakini from Ghat, bringing the village within an 8 kilometre walk from the nearest motorised transport that led to the market. The road established stronger links between the traders in Ghat and Bemni villages, which led to the decline of the bartering system. It also generated a transport industry, as privately run jeeps serviced the link to and from Ghat along the dirt road and a number of villagers in Bemni began providing mule transport between the dirt road and Bemni. The barter trade and goat herd transport was almost entirely replaced. In addition, the road created a number of small markets even closer to the villages, as, for example, at Gaitna, where the Bemni path met the dirt road. By early 2004 rural people had established seven stalls in Gaitna, selling food, second-hand clothes and silver jewellery.

The village household survey that I conducted in 2003 showed that the total population of Bemni was 990, living in 188 households, a household being defined as a family cluster using a single cooking hearth. Of this population, 284 villagers were SC and 704 villagers were from the higher-caste Rajput group, including the sub-castes Bhist, Panwar, Negi, Rawat and Sahar, otherwise referred to as GC. There were no Brahmins in the village. The GC sub-castes in Bemni were considered equal in status to one another, and intermarriage occurred. In population terms, Bemni was larger than many villages in Uttarakhand, and SCs made up a relatively high proportion of the population (28.7 per cent, compared with the district average of 17 per cent: Ministry of Home Affairs 1991).

The agricultural regime in Bemni remained largely subsistence-based in 2003, following agro-pastoralist practices formerly typical of Uttarakhand but confined largely to remote areas in the early 2000s. This regime involved the complex integration of forest and livestock use into agricultural practices. Villagers relied on livestock for dairy products, transport, ploughing and manure for fertilising the fields. Livestock, in turn, depended on fodder from the forest and grazing lands, as well as from fodder crops and crop residues. Leaf litter from the surrounding forests also provided the livestock bedding, which, once soiled, formed organic compost.

Villagers grew potatoes, *chuwa* (a local species of millet sold for the manufacture of sweets) and soya beans for sale. But they continued to rely mainly on crops that were principally for their own consumption: wheat, barley, *cheena* (an indigenous variety of wheat), *manduwa* and *jhangora* (types of finger millet), rice, mustard seed, kidney beans and a selection of local pulses. There was some intercropping. Potatoes were usually grown with kidney beans, pumpkins, cucumbers and bitter green vegetables known as *kareli*. Villagers also tended vegetable gardens with a spectrum of spinach-like leaves, radishes and spices, including chillies, turmeric and coriander. A portion of privately owned land was also left aside for grass, which was harvested for winter hay for livestock.

The fields in Bemni were sown on a two-yearly rotation, following one of two patterns. In the larger, flatter fields, wheat or barley crops were followed by soya or kidney beans in the first year, before being left fallow for four months, then sown in the second year with either *manduwa*, *cheena*, *jhangora* or *chuwa*. In the smaller, terraced fields, where wheat and barley were generally not grown, *manduwa*, *cheena* or *jhangora* were rotated with *chuwa* crops. Villagers also grew several varieties of beans and lentils. Those villagers who owned land at the lowest altitudes grew rice in small quantities. Potatoes were grown as the sole crop in high-altitude fields, which would not otherwise support crops. There were two especially busy times in the agricultural calendar. From mid-April until the end of June villagers had to harvest wheat and barley, weed millet and potatoes and plough fields in preparation for new crops. From early September until the end of November they harvested potatoes, millet and hay and ploughed the fields.

Villagers referred to the crucial importance of mutual assistance in ensuring that agriculture was successful. On numerous occasions people would help one another on an informal basis. Slightly more formally, villagers often assisted households experiencing a shortage of agricultural labour under a system known as *boliya*. In return for helping a labour-poor household, people received a midday meal, and sometimes some local alcohol. Those receiving labour felt bound to reciprocate at a later point in time.

Bemni's agricultural regime depended on seasonal, small-scale transhumance. Transhumance had been largely abandoned in the more accessible parts of the region, even in villages downstream of Ghat, where agriculture was more commercialised. But in Bemni there was a coordinated small-scale system of transhumance that entailed villagers shifting between three settlements at different heights (see Map 2.1). In a typical year villagers would move four times. In the cold winter months between December and April most villagers lived in the lower settlement, Gwar, at an altitude of about 2,200 metres.

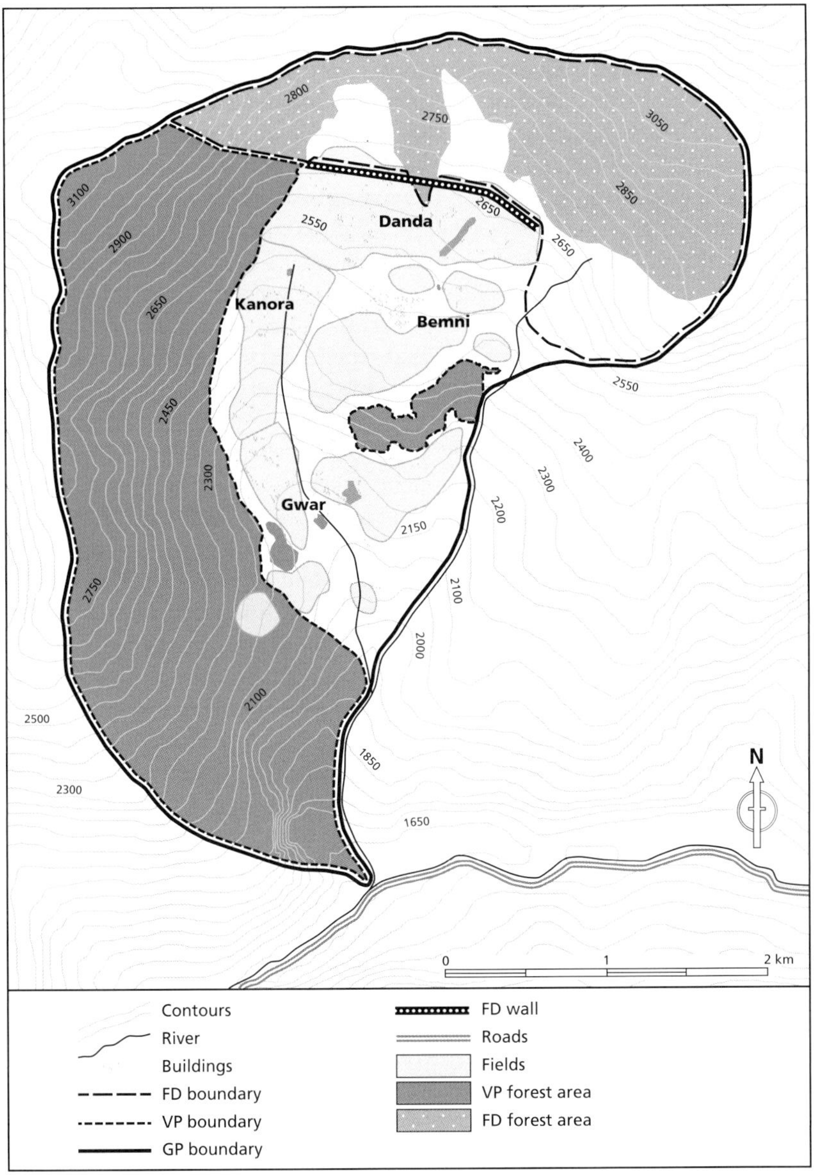

Map 2.1 Bemni gram panchayat, showing field, forest and village areas

Gwar was relatively clement and provided some shelter from fierce winds and heavy snowfall. At this time the fields lay fallow or had been sown. Livestock provided manure to the fields, and grazed freely in Gwar. Sometime between the beginning of April and June villagers would pack up their possessions and move with their livestock to the middle settlement of Bemni, at an altitude of 2,500 metres. I participated in the shift from Gwar to Bemni and other moves between settlements, and remember being surprised by the speed and efficiency with which villagers moved their homes. Shifts were largely made in a single day, with preparations for the move and minor repairs to the new location being carried out some days in advance. Household members made several trips to and from the new house, carrying baskets on their backs full of bedding, clothing and cooking pots, as well as food supplies for the family and livestock. Infants and the very elderly were carried in baskets or on the backs of family members.

It was crucial for villagers to be based in Bemni during the intensive month of June, when they would work all day in the fields, harvesting grain or potatoes, ploughing fields and spreading manure in preparation for the next crop. They were also busy threshing grains and tending to livestock. The work became less intense during the humid monsoon season, from mid-July to September. During this period most villagers relocated to the upper settlement, Danda, where houses were dispersed between 2,550 and 2,650 metres. Livestock provided the manure for the uppermost fields, where they also had access to lush grazing.

In the succeeding months villagers moved in two steps back down the mountain. In October villagers returned to Bemni to oversee the harvesting of millet. Livestock draught power was needed for ploughing after harvesting, and for the provision of manure on fallow or newly seeded fields. In November the winter hay harvest began, and livestock grazing was restricted until all the hay had been cut. In mid-December, with the hay harvest over and the increasing likelihood of snow, villagers returned to Gwar for the winter.

The majority (76 per cent) of GC households lived in three or more locations (three households lived in four locations), and all households had a house in Bemni. Of the 24 per cent of GC households without a house in Gwar or Danda, many borrowed a dwelling temporarily from a member of their extended family. SC villagers lived slightly separately from the GC population, on the west of the village in a area named Kanora (see Map 2.1). Their patterns of transhumance differed slightly, involving moving between settlements that were located more closely, and often between fewer settlements. Just over 74 per cent of SC households lived in only one or two locations. In the winter months only five SC households lived in Gwar, in a cluster of houses immediately above the most northern of the GC households.

In spite of the recent construction of a few large stone homes in Bemni, most of the housing was in the basic low *gosaala* (cow stall) style, in which all

Figure 2.1 One-roomed *gosaala*-style house in Bemni

household members and livestock shared a single room (see Figure 2.1). Few households had their own outdoor tap and only two had an outdoor latrine for personal use. Bemni lacked electricity or telecommunications.

A gram panchayat (the lowest level of elected government), led by a pradhan, administered Bemni at the local level. State policy dictates that the pradhan position is reserved on a rotational basis for women and lower castes. When I first arrived in Bemni the pradhan was a woman, who, at the end of her tenure, handed the position to an SC man. (The following term was not reserved, and a GC man was elected.) In 2003, however, the meagre state involvement meant that the pradhan was less influential at the village level than the sarpanch, the head of the village forest committee, or van panchayat. The VP, with its seven other members, imposed a series of rules concerning transhumance patterns, forest use and livestock grazing at different times of the year. These rules were designed to conserve forest resources and prevent livestock damaging crops. Specific areas of the forest or grazing lands were either 'open' or 'closed' at different points in the season. For example, small sections of forest were opened on a five-yearly rotation to allow the cutting of green leaves for livestock fodder, and subsequently shut to enable regeneration. Similarly, on an annual scale, the sarpanch shut the entire Gwar area at the beginning of June to allow the grass to grow and provide the livestock with hay for the long winter months. Those villagers who had not yet moved to their higher Bemni house were then forced to do so by these VP rules. Villagers, including children, quickly developed a keen knowledge of local regulations. Those who did not abide by the rules were fined, and the village employed a watchman (*chowkidar*) to check for violations. The very real and immediate impact that these rules had on villagers' lives thus meant that it was the sarpanch, rather than the pradhan, who held the power in Bemni, and he was regularly called upon for more general administrative duties.

There was very little commercial or government activity in Bemni. The seven shops in the village were tiny, cramped spaces selling only basic foodstuffs: rice, flour, some *daals*, sugar, salt and a few spices, for example. The government had built two tourist bungalows and two village government offices, but these were very simple constructions without facilities. There was an ayurvedic doctor in the village, a trained nurse who visited from Ghat, but otherwise no other functioning clinic or medical staff in Bemni or any of the seven neighbouring villages.

Bemni children were served by a single primary school (BPS), which was established in the late 1940s and offered education up to class five. Children who continued in education had to walk for forty-five minutes to the government-run Sunti Senior Basic School, which covered classes six to eight and was opened in 1992. Alternatively, small numbers of those from more prosperous households attended Sunti Private School, which covered classes six to ten. Wealthier villagers from Bemni and Sunti had established SPS in 1995 in response to a perceived need for better education in the area. For classes nine and ten, a handful of boys walked more than 5 kilometres to Kurra village, a distance away from the village that was considered inappropriate for girls to travel. Otherwise, pupils attended classes nine to twelve at the high school in Ghat, living either with relatives or in private lodgings. In 2003/4 government school fees were very low, just Rs. 2 per month at BPS and Rs. 5 per month at SSBS. But books, pens and uniforms were expensive, and many households struggled to keep their children in education. Those at SPS paid considerably more, at Rs. 150 a month.

Bemni households' expenditures typically ranged from Rs. 500 to Rs. 2,000 a month, which, at 2004 exchange rates, was equivalent to between US$12 and US$48. This was spent mainly on basic food items, including rice, sugar and salt, as well as soap, cigarettes, clothing, schooling (uniforms, books, pens, private school fees) and medicine. Households also typically spent between Rs. 1,000 and Rs. 4,000 each year on wedding gifts. Every ten to twelve years households expended Rs. 10,000 to 20,000 on repairing buildings. Buying livestock – Rs. 15,000 for a milking buffalo, Rs. 10,000 for a milking cow and Rs. 35,000 to 40,000 for a mule – also represented large, occasional outlays.

Most households could not keep cash savings to cover irregular expenses, and only those men in state employment used bank accounts. Without accounts, villagers could not apply for bank loans. Instead, villagers sought lump sums from extended kin and friends, usually within the village. Households could typically borrow between Rs. 200 and Rs. 4,000 from individual households, and there were no interest payments. They also claimed that they would be willing to lend the same amounts to others when it was available. The poorest households, however, said that villagers avoided lending to those with no obvious means of income for repayment. Some had pawned pieces of jewellery or plots of land as repayment guarantees.

With Bemni's increasing contact with the market, notions of wealth and patterns of conspicuous consumption had changed somewhat. Houses continued to be built from local materials, but richer villagers were increasingly adding a layer of cement plaster to the house front. Clothing and jewellery styles had also changed. Older girls and married women in the village typically wore black *chaadars*, a blanket-like garment that was gathered and held around the waist with a brightly coloured strip of cloth and pinned at the shoulder with a large silver safety pin that used to form part of the wedding jewellery. These heavy *chaadars* used to be spun and woven in the village from goats' wool. By 2003, with the decline of goat herds, lighter, factory-made models were often bought in the market. My impression was that, in roadside villages in Chamoli district, *chaadars* of all kinds were considered symbols of backwardness and had been altogether replaced by plains-style saris. In Bemni some younger women had begun to follow the trend by wearing brightly patterned cotton saris during the warmer summer months. Meanwhile, all but a handful of men had opted for Western-style clothing rather than the handwoven blankets and baggy trousers of the past.

Another sign of change was in the sphere of marriage. The vast majority of marriages in Bemni were caste-endogamous (within their own caste) and arranged by the parents of the bride and groom. The wedding system was undergoing a transformation from a system of bride price, wherein the parents of a groom provide money to the parents of a bride shortly before the marriage, to a system of dowry, in which money and other goods pass from the bride's family to the groom's family at the point of engagement and again when the couple are married – a system common on the north Indian plains (compare Fanger 1987). Although this shift had already taken place in less remote areas of the hills, the Bemni system was in a transitional phase between these two regimes. The major expenses, particularly the bride's jewellery, were roughly shared between both families. But villagers were under increasing pressure to augment the customary gifts of a dhoti, blouse, plate and cup with expensive consumer goods and cash. Several older people suggested that the overall cost of weddings had increased sharply between 1983 and 2003. One SC villager described how his own wedding seventeen years previously had cost Rs. 2,500, but that he expected to pay up between Rs. 40,000 and 60,000 for his own daughter's wedding in 2005.

Social inequalities

In the popular imagination, the high Himalayas are not characterised by caste and class differences. It is place of social as well as natural 'tranquillity', as tourist brochures are wont to put it. Such images reflect in part the continued resonance of colonial stereotypes of people in the region as 'backward', genial and egalitarian. Several scholars have also argued that class, caste and gender discrimination is less marked in Uttarakhand than in plains north India (for example, Berreman 1972; Guha 1989). In his classic ethnography of a village in Garhwal, Gerald Berreman (1972) refers to a relative lack of hierarchical practices among rural people. Likewise, Ramachandra Guha (1989) attributes the success of the Chipko movement in part to the capacity of people to come together across caste, class and gender boundaries.

Most studies of rural Uttarakhand suggest that the last four decades of the twentieth century witnessed a marked decline in the *jajmani* system, in which lower castes performed services for higher castes in return for cash or kind payments (see also Raheja 1988). Some scheduled caste individuals were able to migrate in search of work and were in a wide array of jobs, many of them not related to their traditional occupation.

But other scholars point to marked caste inequalities in Uttarakhand in the 1990s and early 2000s (see, for example, Mawdsley 1998; Jayal 2001; Klenk 2010). SCs continued to live on the periphery of many villages and towns and suffer from higher-caste harassment and sometimes violence (for example Jayal 2001; Kumar 2001; Klenk 2010). Moreover, in rural and urban Uttarakhand class often overlaps with caste. As many commentators have observed, however, they are not coterminous. Within the GC category there are substantial differences in landownership and access to non-farm incomes; many GCs are poor. But GC households are typically richer than are SCs, such people possessing superior social contacts outside the village, and having higher educational qualifications. Moreover, GCs tend to own more land than do SCs, benefit to a greater extent from remittance incomes and have superior contacts outside the state. Social and economic differences between GCs and SCs tend to militate against the erosion of caste discrimination (see Kumar 2001; Klenk 2010).

My research in Bemni bolsters these general points. There was some evidence of a decline in caste discrimination in Bemni in the last few decades of the twentieth century. Several older SC men and women said that, in the 1960s and

1970s, rules regarding contact between castes were more strictly observed than they were in the early 2000s. But notions of purity and pollution continued to shape how castes related to one another. Villagers typically disapproved of cross-caste friendships, and they were unanimous that people should not marry across caste. I also observed a great deal of everyday caste discrimination. GC villagers frequently referred to SC families as 'backward' and 'dirty'. SC villagers were also said to be 'greedy' and 'short-sighted', thinking only about immediate gain, particularly their stomachs, rather than long term benefits such as education or building a good house. GC villagers highlighted SC's alleged darker skin and lighter build as evidence of their inferiority. The 'backwardness' of SC women was similarly discussed by GC women, who criticised SCs' old-fashioned clothes, their 'gaudily' coloured hand-embroidered waistcoats and their preference for home-made jewellery, including necklaces strung with coloured beads and with old coins rather than the more 'civilised' shop-bought gold chokers. In Bemni, caste was deeply inscribed in what Pierre Bourdieu (1984 [1979]) terms the 'habitus': durable dispositions inscribed in people's prejudices, movements, reflexes and tastes.

As well as being subjected to social prejudices, SC villagers were restricted in their spatial mobility. SC families lived on the outskirts of the GC-dominated village, or in separate SC-only clusters, thus avoiding the sharing of water sources and defecation areas. Some aspects of the *jajmani* system survived in Bemni (compare Raheja 1988; Lerche 1999). SC villagers could not provide food or drink to GC villagers because of their assumed 'polluting' influence. Besides the everyday spatial reinforcement of caste differences, there were also seasonal rules that restricted the movement of SCs around the village. For example, throughout most of April until early May, when the wheat and barley crops were ripening in the fields immediately below Bemni, no villagers were allowed into or across the fields between 10 a.m. and 4 p.m. SC villagers were also banned from entering any part of the GC-dominated village between 10 a.m. and 4 p.m. These rules were upheld until having conducted the *puja* to celebrate the start of the harvest (on 9 May in 2003). If SC villagers did not abide by these rules, GCs believed that their crops would be damaged. A harsh hailstorm that destroyed large portions of the ripening wheat and barley in May 2003 was said to have been a result of God's anger when an SC person broke the rules by entering the ripened fields at the 'wrong' time.

An especially troubling further dimension of caste discrimination was that it continued to exist in schools (compare Nambissan 2003). There were no formal rules regarding where GCs and SCs should sit, but low castes commonly sat apart from their peers – among both girls and boys. It is also likely that the GC teachers paid less attention to SCs, as has been found in many other schools in Uttarakhand (Klenk 2010) and neighbouring Uttar Pradesh (Jeffrey, Jeffery and Jeffery 2008), although I was not able to investigate this point in detail.

Caste discrimination became especially obvious to me in Bemni during the course of my daily interactions with Ajay Singh and his family, with whom we lived. As with other GC households in Bemni, Ajay Singh and his family held deprecating views of SCs. They were annoyed and confused about our spending time with SC children. Ajay Singh and his wife *tai-ji*, in particular, made references to our becoming 'overfamiliar' with SCs. Sometimes these criticisms were more open. *Tai-ji* complained that we had allowed SC children past the threshold of our door, and that in her house we should abide by her caste rules. On another occasion, we took a packed lunch to accompany a group of SC children herding, but when the children decided to leave early we returned to our house with our uneaten picnic. We were about to eat it when *tai-ji* announced that, since our food had been in the presence of the SC children, it was now impure. 'You cannot eat food from "those people",' she said.

These observations suggest that open forms of discrimination perpetrated against SCs, which were being undermined in plains India as early as the 1960s (Mandelbaum 1970), continued to mark the social landscape in Uttaranchal in the late 1990s and early 2000s. To a greater extent than in parts of plains north India in the early 2000s, higher castes in Bemni publicly expressed the aversion to contact with SCs that was inscribed in their habitus. They sometimes openly ridiculed lower castes in public settings, and referred proudly to their observance of perceived caste rules. These differences reflect the political isolation of people in Bemni relative to their peers on the plains, and the relatively low population of SCs in most parts of Chamoli and the region more broadly. In addition, GCs in Bemni had not absorbed the types of public anti-caste rhetoric that has become a common feature of higher-caste discourse in the plains and Delhi (compare Jeffrey 2002).

Caste and class overlapped to a large extent in Bemni. This point should not be exaggerated. No GC household in Bemni was 'rich' in comparison to rich households in Patricia and Roger Jeffery's (1997) study of a village in western Uttar Pradesh, for example. The wealthiest GC household in Bemni owned only three hectares, and even those households receiving a remittance income from a son in the army were still much less wealthy than moderately prosperous businesspeople in local towns or rich farmers on the plains of western UP to the south. It is also important to note that there were some GCs who were very poor. Eight GC households owned less than 0.1 hectares, and many in this group struggled to meet their daily subsistence and complained about their inability to buy food, pay for children's education and acquire necessary healthcare.

But the point remains that GCs were, viewed as a whole, substantially better off than SCs. In 2003 46 per cent of the 137 GC households in the village owned more than 0.5 hectares, whereas the equivalent figure for the fifty-one

SC households was just 4 per cent. GC households were therefore better able to feed their families. They were also relatively well placed to profit from the sale of cash crops. All households tried to sell a portion of their cash crops each year. *Chuwa* was the most reliable crop for sale: prices were fairly steady and the crop could be grown fairly easily on all parts of the Bemni mountainside. Potatoes were a riskier cash crop, because the market price tended to be quite volatile. For example, in 2002 the potato price was Rs. 5 per kilogram in Ghat, but this dropped to Rs. 2.5 in 2003, and Bemni farmers could hardly cover their transport costs. One GC farmer went to some lengths to investigate the possibility of making potato chips in Bemni, but, without the necessary contacts or knowledge of the best technology, this project was left unrealised. Soya beans were another significant cash crop. Prices were fairly stable, but only farmers with land at low altitudes could grow soya beans. Because they had more land, especially at lower altitudes, GC households made substantially more money from cash crops sales than did SC households.

GC and SC men benefited from government development programmes that provided occasional daily wage labour, usually on the relatively good wage of between Rs. 70 and 100 a day. This work flowed, especially through the Sampoorna Gramin Rozgar Yojana (SGRY), a scheme established by the state to provide employment to the poor and improve village infrastructure. There were also occasional opportunities for both GCs and SCs to work on a government farm fairly close to the village. Yet GCs and SCs were unequally placed in their search for non-farm incomes. GC men had been much more successful than had SC men at migrating out of the village, which meant that GCs benefited much more from remittances than did SCs. Of the eighteen- to thirty-five-year-old men born in the village, 46 per cent of the 125 GCs were living and working outside Bemni in 2003, compared to 11 per cent of the thirty-seven SC men. Despite reservations for SCs in government employment, GCs had been much more successful in acquiring lucrative and secure state employment, all in the army or police, than had SCs, reflecting patterns common in other parts of north India (see Jeffrey, Jeffery and Jeffery 2008). GCs also monopolised the relatively lucrative local business of mule transport. A mule cost between Rs. 35,000 and 40,000, but people could earn the locally sizable sum of Rs. 120 (nearly twice the typical daily agricultural wage) carrying goods or crops between Bemni and local markets. Several men took their mules on their annual migration to the pilgrimages sites of Kedarnath and Bedrinath, where they could earn even more from carrying Indian tourists to the temples. SCs often owned ponies, which they could occasionally hire out for local marriages, but this was less profitable than mule transport.

Several SC men drew on their respective 'traditional' caste occupations to earn a cash income in the village. Yet this work was less remunerative and secure than was that performed by taking on migrant work outside the village. The main trades among SCs were carpentry and house building. Carpenters contributed to house building, and also made furniture, agricultural implements and small items, such as combs. A number of men made bamboo baskets, producing a range of shallow round bowls and the carrying baskets worn on villagers' backs. Two men in the village ran small tailoring businesses. Two worked as blacksmiths, forging cooking pots, agricultural implements and mule shoes. And five men gained a less regular income as musicians, particularly drummers and bagpipers, at religious celebrations or weddings.

Gender also powerfully shaped life in Uttarakhand and Bemni. Men usually expected their wives to play a subservient role within most public and private settings and to conduct the majority of household, agricultural and forest-related work. The emigration of men, and the shift to an increasingly commoditised economy, was also altering patterns of labour allocation in the 1990s and early 2000s, placing additional burdens on women, who had to assume responsibility for a greater range of tasks (Mehta 1995; Bose 2000; Chopra and Ghosh 2000). While women may effectively become household heads in the absence of husbands who had migrated away, research by Manjari Mehta (1995) in an area of rural Garhwal suggests that they continue to be discredited as capable managers and enjoy little control over the returns of their labour.

The gradual integration of Uttarakhand into plains north India in the 1990s and 2000s was having other detrimental effects on women's autonomy. The new system of dowry restricted women's capacity to escape from abusive marriage arrangements. Within the bride price system, it was possible for a woman to be married more than once, and to be relatively active in her choice of partner. A young woman could often annul a recent marriage if she found that her new husband was abusive, and a second husband would typically then pay some compensation to the women's previous family to cover the cost of marriage expenses and bride price. The dowry system, with the additional financial burden placed on the girl's family, made it more difficult for women to exercise agency and choice within marital relationships (Rana 1996).

Two points must be set against this evidence of gender discrimination and inequality. First, increasing numbers of girls were being enrolled in school in Uttarakhand in the 1990s and early 2000s. In ethnographic research on schooling and development in Uttarakhand, Rebecca Klenk (2010) points to girls' enhanced skills, confidence and capacity to participate in society on the basis of their education. Second, the seventy-third amendment to the Indian constitution called for a 33 per cent reservation for women as members and chairpersons of the three-tiered panchayati raj institutions, the system of local government. The seat for the pradhan, the head of the gram panchayat, or village committee, became reserved on a rotational basis for women and scheduled caste village members. But these educational and political shifts were not significantly undermining structures of patriarchy in Uttarakhand. With respect to education, Klenk also points to the continued marginalisation of girls from school, relative to boys, and the manner in which some aspects of the educational system reproduce gender norms. In the sphere of local representative politics, women and SCs who obtained the pradhanship in Uttarakhand in these positions rarely acquired effective control of the institutions, and often seemed to become 'puppet heads'.

Gender relations in Bemni reflected the broader Uttarakhand scene. Strong patriarchal norms existed in the village. Men and women occasionally said that they lived in a society of *purush pradhaan* (male dominance). Men were usually considered to be the head (*maalik*) of the household and took all major decisions concerning land management, finances, including healthcare and children's schooling, and employment. Men's superior standing was reinforced and elaborated in numerous ways within the home. Men ate first at meal times, dominated household conversations and expected their wives and children to treat them with deference and respect. Men also dominated discussions outside the home, usually on matters of religion, politics and development. Women lacked access to land in Bemni, and they rarely worked outside the home. Their non-farm activities were confined to low-paid work making ghee or, more rarely, collecting lichen for sale in local markets. When they did earn money in such ways, they almost always passed their income to a male head of the household.

Notions of gendered and sexual difference were also embedded in the manner in which agricultural tasks were organised in Bemni. Women conducted the majority of the most common agricultural tasks performed in Bemni (shown in Figure 2.2) and tended to work more intensively than men. They were almost solely responsible for forest-based work (collecting leaf litter, green leaves and firewood), as well as weeding, winnowing and threshing crops. Women were also more involved than were men in harvesting crops and spreading them out to dry. The one area in which men assumed primary responsibility was ploughing. Men guided the draught animals, while women moved behind them breaking up clods of earth. The prohibition on women relates to religious ideas: women should not 'penetrate' and fertilise the mother earth. There is also a patriarchal explanation: it gave men control over land (compare Agarwal 1994). A widowed or unmarried woman had to pay relations or labourers to plough for her, thus reducing her autonomy.

The ubiquity of gender difference and inequality was also evident in how women, in particular, responded to my own presence in Bemni. Some female researchers have discussed using their outsider status as a means of circumventing local rules about gender and propriety (Razavi 1992; Robinson 1994). I could have capitalised on my foreign status in this way. Instead, though, I tried to adapt my demeanour to be consistent with village ideals of married

(a) Ploughing

(b) Harvesting barley by hand

(c) Pounding and winnowing

(d) Carrying winter hay

Figure 2.2 Common agricultural tasks

women. By remaining relatively demure in public settings and avoiding public discussions with men, I gradually earned the respect of men, women and young people in the village. At the same time, women often chided me for being lazy. The compliments and the criticisms both strengthened my understanding of gender norms in the village.

Conclusions

This chapter has set out some of the structural factors, especially the physical distance from India's urban centres, that were important in shaping the lives of young people in the village. Much has been made in the literature on young people and globalisation of increased mobility among children and youth, of their increased exposure to multiple media and of the growing influence of the internet (for example Nisbett 2009; Bayart 2007). Such accounts sometimes unwittingly generalise from the experiences of a small section of the world's youth population to young people around the world. It is therefore important to remember that, in Bemni, young people not only lacked computers or televisions in the early 2000s, they did not have electricity or running water in their homes. Few had even seen a telephone, and most teenagers had never left the Nandakini Valley. The substantive point is that 'time-space compression' (Harvey 1989) has its own uneven geography.

Caste and gender inequalities, as well as geographical ones, influenced the lives of young people and adults in Bemni. Caste discrimination was endemic, and patriarchal norms were entrenched. There are therefore good reasons for stressing the limits to young people's capacity to rethink and change local structures in the region of the high Himalayas in which I worked.

At the same time, Bemni had been opened up to many of the changes occurring in modern India, for example through the flow of remittance incomes into the village. Moreover, Bemni was in a state of 'transition', from a settlement characterised by low education and early marriage via a bride price system to a regime in which children remained in education for longer periods and marriage occurred later via dowry. It was perhaps in a state of transition, too, towards a more cash-crop-based economy and greater reliance on off-farm work. The theme of continuity and significant change recurs over the following five chapters, colouring my account of how boys and girls work, play and relate to one another.

A question that arises in this context is the extent to which Bemni is representative of other villages in the region. My travels in Uttarakhand suggested that Bemni was markedly different from many roadside villages in the high Himalayas and from villages in the middle and lower Himalayas (see also Klenk 2010). At the same time, Bemni was in no way obviously unusual among villages in the Nandakini Valley and surrounding areas. It is therefore probably sensible to note that processes evident in Bemni were likely to be occurring in other villages located a moderate distance from the road in the high Himalayas of Uttarakhand, but that my account of children's lives cannot be used to intuit processes occurring in well-connected parts of the state.

3 A delicate dance: young people's work

Lalita was a tiny, twelve-year-old GC girl, narrow-shouldered and with owl-like eyes, who lived in the centre of Bemni. She usually rose at 5 a.m., lit a fire, made tea and woke her brother. She washed her hands, and made bread for the family. After eating a few pieces of bread and some left-over potatoes from the night beforehand, she would change the livestock bedding, run up to the fields to cut some fresh grass for cattle fodder and then run back down the hill to go to school. After finishing school, she might collect several more loads of fodder for the cattle, sweep the house, replaster the mud floor, cook rice, wash up and look at her schoolbooks. In the whole day she would probably find just half an hour to sit in the house talking to her family, and even then she would most likely be knitting a jumper or comforting a younger sibling on her knee.

Children's seemingly constant absorption in different forms of work was one of the most remarkable aspects of the social life of Bemni. Much recent research in the global South has pointed to a shift in patterns of work and responsibility between the generations. Sara Berry's (1985) classic account of cocoa farmers in Nigeria charts a process of slow transition from a period in which sons worked for their fathers to one in which 'fathers work for their sons'. Cynthia Lloyd's (2005) survey of children and development in the global South makes the more general point for Asia, Africa and Latin America that modernisation and urbanisation have ushered in new forms of social reproduction. Parents have increasingly withdrawn their children from paid employment and unpaid household work in favour of enrolling them in school.

In Bemni, however, children were centrally involved in household reproduction. Some of the recent African literature anticipates this argument (see Ansell 2008). For example, Elsbeth Robson (2004) has shown that, in the context of the HIV/AIDS crisis in southern Africa, children – some very young – have been compelled to assume responsibility for the basic tasks of household reproduction. In Bemni, children's involvement in household work was not the result of an external 'shock' but reflected the precarious and gruelling nature of life in the high Himalayas and the constant need among most households for extra hands.

Many other scholars have noted the importance of children's labour in processes of economic and social reproduction (Schildkrout 1980; Elson 1982; Maharatna 1997; Riley 2009). In south Asia, with notable exceptions (Nieuwenhuys 1994; Gold and Gujar 2002), this work has focused on paid labour and the contradictions between such labour and children's schooling needs (Ennew 1994; Kabeer, Nambissan and Subrahmanian 2003). My research points to the crucial significance of children's unpaid household work in the economic and social life of Bemni village. This labour did not necessarily compete with education, in the manner that other scholarship might lead us to expect. Children often successfully balanced their commitment to household work alongside primary school education, at least up to the point that they had obtained the rudiments of literacy and numeracy. At the same time, caste and gender powerfully shaped the capacity of children to negotiate unpaid work and balance their household labour with school responsibilities.

This chapter builds on the last one by providing a thicker sense of the constraints under which young people operated while living in Bemni. I show how adult expectations around work and maturity influenced young people's agency. But I also demonstrate that young people were able to fulfil family obligations through building relationships of mutual dependence with their parents and older villagers more generally. The manner in which young people coordinated their work with other young people and adults amounted to a type of 'improvisation' or 'dance', in which the moves were powerfully shaped by the rhythms of season and school. The chapter provides an overview of this delicate dance.

Children's household work

Adults spent whole days in the fields during many periods of the year, especially in the months immediately before and after the rainy season, when agricultural work was most intense. In June parents were under great pressure to harvest pulses, wheat and barley. They needed to plough the fields, fertilise them and sow the next round of crops. In September, October and November villagers harvested potatoes, millet, kidney beans and soya beans. They also ploughed, sowed pulses, wheat and barley, and harvested the winter hay.

Reflecting the intensity of parents' work, children were often left at home, where they were expected not only to look after themselves but also to care for younger children, tend livestock, make food and maintain the physical infrastructure of their dwelling. Children said that they felt a type of internal compulsion to work during most of their young lives, saying that 'we must work' ('*kaam karnaa hai*'), and they referred to work in and around the home as arduous activity: 'home work is hard work' ('*ghar ka kaam mehnat ka kaam hai*'). 'Toil' (*mehnat*) was a powerful theme of children's narratives, just as it features strongly in other accounts of everyday labour in India (Parry, Breman and Kapadia 1999; Chari 2004; Gidwani 2008).

Of course, the range of tasks performed by children varied according to age and gender. There is substantial debate among those who conduct research with working children on when precisely children become 'economically productive' (for example Corbridge 1993; Bissell 2003), in the sense that their contribution to the household outweighs the burden they place on their parents financially and in terms of consumption – a debate that stretches back at least as far as Karl Kautsky's analysis of farm size, family size, productivity and class reproduction (see Goodman and Watts 1997). My research did not aim to quantify children's work in this way. But I became aware of how children's activities develop over the first two decades of their lives. By the age of seven or eight, children were crucial to the material and social reproduction of the household.

Children actively contributed to household reproduction at a very young age. By the age of five, children – boys and girls – could often look after younger siblings and prepare water for washing their face and hands. They could pick nits out of younger children's hair, carry or watch babies and attend to younger infants. By seven, children were able to clean the house and surrounding yard and collect water or wash dishes at the nearest tap.

By the age of ten, most children could conduct a wide range of household tasks (see Figures 3.1 and 3.2). They could hand-wash their own clothes, light fires, cook, clean dishes and deliver meals to other family members outside the home. They could keep the house, cattle stalls and courtyard clean. I also saw many children aged as young as ten resurfacing the mud floor of their houses, a complicated task that entailed carefully mixing earth, cattle dung and water together in large piles and then spreading the mud out evenly to dry over the floor, walls and hearth.

There were many other tasks that pre-teen and teenage children conducted more intermittently throughout the year, including preparing for religious events, decorating homes in advance of local festivals, repairing clothes and fetching medicines. They also ran errands for relatives to the post office or local shops, and ground spices using enormous pestles and holes dug into the ground. Children also played an important role in assisting their families' moves between settlements. These shifts usually occurred on a Sunday, to coincide with a school holiday. Beyond work for the household, children sometimes engaged in labour that was beneficial for the village as a whole. They cleaned village drains (Figure 3.3), repaired sporting equipment that belonged to the village council and occasionally improved paths around the village. This work was typically unpaid and carried out by children belonging to relatively 'labour-rich' households, often at the insistence of parents, but sometimes on their own initiative.

Figure 3.1 Ashish sweeps his courtyard

Figure 3.2 Saka prepares baskets of *gobar*

Figure 3.3 Young children wash clothes and dishes at a communal tap while one boy unblocks the drain

Parents were reluctant to allow very young children to participate in agricultural tasks. But they did expect children to feed and supervise cattle. By the age of ten, many girls and boys were given the responsibility of looking after livestock, and, by twelve, most children had become competent in this activity. They collected green grass, hay, crop residues or fresh oak leaves to feed their cattle. Children also removed soiled leaf bedding from cattle's stalls, laid down fresh leaves and carried away soiled leaves to nearby fields, where they were used as fertiliser.

Children learnt how to conduct these various activities through what Jean Lave and Etienne Wenger (1991) term 'legitimate peripheral participation'. They watched their parents or older children, then tentatively tried to carry out the activity themselves. Through a process of trial and error, they slowly became proficient. It was very difficult to get children to reflect on this process of learning. They said that they just 'picked things up as they went along', or they said that tasks were so easy as to not require any type of formal instruction.

Young people sometimes carried out household tasks alongside a relative or neighbour. In many instances, they were able to chat to siblings or older relatives while working in the home. In particular, many girls worked alongside older brothers' wives. Scrubbing pans, collecting water at village taps or washing clothes in the river offered children opportunities to chat to other children and older villagers – meetings that were always caste-segregated, since SCs and GCs used different taps. I often heard children using the task of washing up or washing clothes in the river to catch up on village news, sing songs and tell jokes. These social work tasks contrasted with other more lonely work at home or in the fields. One fifteen-year-old girl described a winter's day taking her family's clothes to the river to wash as a 'holiday', in spite of the freezing water in the river and the exhausting nature of the work.

Yet much of young people's work in and around their homes was solitary in nature. The degree to which they were in earshot of neighbours and able to converse with them while carrying out tasks depended on whether they were in Danda, where houses were dispersed and conversation was unlikely, Gwar, where houses were positioned in small clusters and so it was more sociable, or Bemni, where houses were the most tightly packed. For the most part, however, children and youth were screened from neighbours while cooking, cleaning and tending livestock. These tasks were not group activities and did not afford opportunities to chat, laugh or play. The unsociable nature of the work partly explains why young people regarded labour in and around the home as burdensome – a form of 'toil' (*mehnat kaam*), as many children put it.

Young people had developed a wide array of micro-tactics to evade household responsibilities. Children and youth often gave excuses (*bahaana*), such as having schoolwork to complete or being unwell. In other cases, they tried to persuade or compel a younger sibling to stand in for them. In still other cases, they delayed their return from an errand, or simply wandered off to distant parts of the village, hoping that their parents would not track them down. Young people joked with me that wandering was a good tactic for avoiding work, mentioning the Hindi word *ghoomna*, and drawing out the long 'oo' sound to suggest a lengthy period of aimlessness.

Children's daily diary entries give a sense of the variety of work that they conducted in and around the home. The diaries also provide a feel for how activities were sequenced through the day. There was no typical diary entry, because children's responsibilities often varied, for example, according to the health and availability of family members, and family structure. But the following account penned by Sarita, a fifteen-year-old GC girl, of a working day in winter is indicative of the type of diary entries I collected. Sarita writes:

13/01/2004 Got up, lit a fire and warmed water. Went to the latrine [in a distant field] and washed my hands and face. Washed up the plates and made food. Ate food and went to wash clothes. Came home and lit a fire. Warmed water and washed my sister. Took the buffaloes out of their stalls, secured them outside, and gave them grass. Took dung out [of the cattle stalls] and made food. Ate food and washed up the plates. Secured the buffaloes inside. Fetched water and took three baskets of dung to Nandoli. Came home and lit a fire. Made tea and made food. Ate food and knitted part of a sweater. Slept.

Children's blunt recounting of a day's tasks does double duty. It reflects both the grind of conducting successive tasks throughout the day and children's typically pragmatic attitude towards their work. Household work was simply what one had to do. 'Well, it is just work,' is the type of response I received several times when I asked children to comment on their activity.

The range of tasks was roughly similar for SCs. Papita, a ten-year-old SC girl, offers an example. Papita managed most aspects of maintaining the family home while also looking after her young sisters, aged two and four. The following two diary entries in autumn 2003 give a sense of the diversity of her tasks:

23/10/03 Got up, went to collect leaf litter. Came home and ate bread. Cleaned plates and fetched water. Took dung out [of the cattle stalls] and bathed my sisters. Then I lit a fire, made rice and cooked green leaves for vegetables. Then I had a bath and washed my clothes. I ate rice, washed up the plates and fetched water. Then I went to fetch grass from Gwar. I came home, drank tea and washed up the glasses. I gave grass and water to the cattle. I cut up vegetables and ground masala. Studied my book, ate food, and slept.

16/11/03 Got up, lit a fire, made tea and drank tea. Then I kneaded dough, made bread and ate bread. Went to fetch grass and came back home. I swept room and re-surfaced room [with mud]. Washed my hands and face and took dung out [of the cattle stalls]. Lit a fire and made rice. Ate rice and cleaned plates. Fetched water and lit a fire. Drank tea and studied books. Ate food and went to watch *Panch Pandava* [a religious festival]. Slept.

Devendre, a twelve-year-old SC boy, carried out a similar range of tasks, leaving his siblings and mother free to engage in other work:

6/2/04 Got up, went to the latrine [in the fields], and washed my hands and face. Made tea and drank tea. Kneaded dough, made bread, and ate breakfast. Went to send the cows to graze in Kanora [a grazing area near the village]. Took dung out [of the stalls] and washed my hands and feet. Washed up the plates, fetched water and lit a fire. Made food and ate food. Washed up the plates and went to fetch the cows and secured the cows. Fetched water and lit a fire. Made tea and drank tea. Studied for one hour. Ate food and slept.

Some of the diary entries of Sanjay, a fifteen-year-old GC boy, offer a sense of the particular demands placed on children's time when households were moving home between settlements:

1/6/03 (Sunday) Got up, went to the latrine, and took a basketful of clothes from Gwar to Bemni twice. Came back to Gwar and went with cows to Charra [another grazing ground near the village]. Then ate food and washed plates. Then took one more load of clothes and the cows to Bemni. Then night fell. Secured the cows inside and made tea. Drank tea and kneaded dough. Ate food and slept.

Later, when moving back down from Danda to Bemni, Sanjay mixed agricultural work with moving house, while caring for his twelve-year-old disabled brother, who was unable to walk after contracting polio.

12/10/03 (Sunday) Got up and went to the latrine [in the fields] and drank tea. Took one load of clothes [to Bemni]. Returned to Danda and washed my brother's hands and face and ate breakfast. Went to the fields, and broke up earth clods in half a field then ploughed half a field. Came home and drank tea. Ground masala and fetched one bucket of water. Ate food and took one basket of plates from Danda to Bemni. Returned to Danda and took my brother with me [carrying him in a basket]. Night fell by the time I got to Bemni. I washed potatoes and cut them. Studied for half an hour. Ate food and slept.

Sanjay's caring responsibilities for his disabled brother mirrored those with duties towards younger siblings, and his diary entries are similarly representative of the type of work conducted by children in moves up and down the mountain.

Parents largely expected children to be able to perform a range of tasks in and around home. Boys and girls unable to do so were often scolded or regarded as having become 'behind' (*peeche*). In some cases, children, most usually boys, were beaten by their parents if they repeatedly refused to work, remonstrated with their elders or carried out tasks in a shoddy manner. Parents said that they had had to conduct similar work when they were young and that it was the 'duty' (*farz*) of children to help parents in any way that they could.

Gendered norms in Bemni influenced the work that children performed in and around the home and also parents' attitudes to their sons' and daughters' labour. Villagers believed that girls were, in essence, obedient, diligent and conscientious, and therefore obeyed their elders and performed household tasks with good grace. Girls were associated with particular activities, such as knitting and cooking. Parents argued that girls were especially suited to these activities and forms of work because of their innate patience, dexterity and tenacious attention to detail.

By contrast, parents considered boys errant, lazy, suggestible and rebellious, and therefore likely to remonstrate with parents and elders, avoid all forms of work and be swayed by bad influences. Villagers said that boys were often bad (*gunda*), naughty (*shetaan*) or argumentative (*tu tu mein mein karte*), that they rarely settled to work and were incessantly playing cricket or volleyball. The following statement by a GC man in his forties is typical:

> Girls do good work. Boys just wander around, play games, and play cricket. They think that when they get service work [*naukri*], they won't have to work at home later, so they don't do it now. They think it is girls' work. Girls do all the work; they clean plates, and go to the jungle.

Reflecting these gender stereotypes, parents usually expected daughters to play a more significant role in performing household chores than their sons. In particular, girls usually carried out tasks relating to the cleaning and resurfacing of the hearth and the management of livestock, including taking dung out of stalls and replacing leaf litter bedding. These gender differences should not be overstated, however. Parents assumed that boys would make some contribution to work in the home, and boys were always expected to take care of personal tasks such as washing their own clothes. But there was frequently a large gap between the degree of pressure placed on boys and girls in terms of completing work in or around the household. Moreover, girls often started to conduct specific tasks, such as tending to livestock or cooking food, a year or two earlier than did boys.

The gendered differences in children's obligations to work related largely to notions of the future. Parents did not expect boys to engage in household work during adulthood. But girls were imagined as future daughters-in-law and were expected to continue undertaking these tasks. In preparation for their role as daughters-in-law, mothers said they had no choice but to ask daughters to take on many household tasks.

As a result of these gendered notions of work, boys found it easier than did girls to avoid household tasks in negotiations with their parents. Manoj (SC, fifteen) told me openly that he refused to work when the work was troublesome (*parishaanee*): 'I hate taking manure to the fields, so I often refuse to do that.' He would refuse his mother's requests to work by claiming he had school homework to finish, or needed to wash his school uniform or leave for school earlier than usual. Manoj was aware of his parents' strong belief in the importance of his education, and knew that he could negotiate time for himself by pitting his responsibilities to his educated future against his parents' more immediate desire for his labour.

Janki (GC, twelve) tried to deploy similar tactics to those of Manoj. She said that she often told her parents that she had pressing schoolwork to complete. She also tried to offload work onto her nine-year-old younger brother. But Janki was generally unsuccessful in avoiding household work, in large part because her parents did not value her education as highly as they did her brothers' academic achievement. In addition, Janki said that her sixteen-year-old older brother forced her to do his work. Janki concluded bitterly:

> The boys sit around and play, while we have to work. Older people get angry with us [as girls] if we don't work, but not with the boys. Sometimes I feel angry when my brothers do little and I do a lot. But we can only think these things. We can't say or do anything.

Other factors also influenced children's negotiations with their parents. For example, first- or second-born children in a sibling group often had to shoulder greater responsibilities than did their younger brothers and sisters. One boy once commented: 'Being an eldest son is like being a father.' Many parents also cited their greater affection for particular children as also shaping their attitudes towards their children's work. But it was gender that was of paramount importance in determining the degree to which children were involved in household work and intergenerational bargaining.

Children's agricultural and forest work

Agricultural work was largely considered to be an adult domain. Most children and their parents claimed that children and young people did not generally participate in work in the fields. But children were involved in such tasks. Most children began agricultural work from the age of around seven years old, when their main task was taking manure to the fields in small baskets on their backs. Slowly, children started other chores, such as making bundles of harvested crops and carrying a backload of crops from the fields. By the age of around ten, children took on relatively physically demanding work, such as breaking up earth clods with large wooden clubs in a freshly ploughed field, or threshing harvested crops with long sticks. Around this time children tried out more skilled jobs such as harvesting, involving the use of a sharp sickle (*daranti*), and weeding, using a hoe (Figure 3.4). Weeding or taking dung to the fields was generally perceived to be girls' work, reflecting broader gendered assumptions about agriculture in Bemni. On the other hand, ploughing was a

Figure 3.4 Parwati weeds potatoes

male task, and so, by the time boys were ten or eleven, fathers began to teach their sons to plough.

Some of the diary entries of Parwati, a fifteen-year-old GC girl, give a sense of her heavy involvement in field work during the busy summer month of May:

24/05/03 Got up at 4am, went to the latrine, cleaned up the room, washed my hands and face and washed up the plates. Made a fire and made tea. Made food and ate breakfast. Got ready for school and left at 6am. Arrived at 7am. We prayed, studied, then had break from 10–11am. We studied again until 12pm and went home. Went immediately to Gwar to harvest barley. Made three trips bringing barley from Gwar to Bemni. Then took dung out of the house. Made four trips to take baskets of dung to the fields. Ate food and went to harvest barley. Made two trips to the house with harvested barley. Made rice and tea. Made *daal*. Kneaded dough and made bread and ate bread. Wrote two pieces of homework and slept at 10pm.

25/5/03 Got up at 4am, made tea and made hot water. Washed hands and face. Cleaned up the room and made bread and ate food. Went to Gwar to harvest wheat. Made two trips bringing basket loads of wheat. Came home at 12pm. Ate food and bathed. Washed clothes at the tap and came home. Took dung out of the house and took two basketfuls of dung to the fields below Bemni. Then threshed barley and put it in a big bag. Then I went to the fields in Norla to harvest barley. Then came home, made a fire, made tea and drank tea. Made *daal* and ground spices. Kneaded dough and made bread and ate bread. Slept at 10pm.

Sarita, also a fifteen-year-old GC girl, helped with the weeding and harvesting in June.

7/6/03 Got up, went to the latrine, and washed my hands and face. Kneaded dough and made bread. Ate breakfast and went to weed potatoes in village fields. Came home and ate food. Took cows out of the stalls and took dung out [of the stalls]. Went to wash clothes at Norla. Came home and ate food. Washed plates and went to harvest wheat in village fields. Came home and fetched water from Norla. Lit a fire and made tea and kneaded dough. Made bread and ate food and slept.

Even eleven-year-old GC Janki participated in the harvesting during the busy October period.

18/10/03 Got up and went to fetch grass [from where it had been cut]. Came home and washed my hands and face. Washed up the plates and went to school. Came home and ate rice. Went to harvest *chuwa* and came home and fetched water. Washed plates. Lit fire and made tea. Made vegetables and kneaded dough. Made bread and ate bread and slept.

Sanjay, a fifteen-year-old GC boy, describes doing field maintenance work, in this case building a wall and, later, breaking up earth clods after a field has been ploughed:

28/05/03 Got up and went to the latrine, washed my hands and face, made tea and ate breakfast. Went to Nandoli to harvest wheat. Came home and took dung out [of the stalls]. Made food. Washed up the plates and bathed. Came home and swept and cleaned the room. Ate food and washed plates. Came home. Went to make a wall in our field. Came home. Fetched water, made tea and drank tea. Cut up vegetables and made vegetables. Kneaded dough, studied, and ate. Went to watch a *Devtar* [dancing *puja*] for four hours then slept.

26/10/03 Got up, washed my hands and face, and ate breakfast. Broke up earth clods in three fields. Ate food and harvested one field of *chuwa*. Rain fell and came home. Night fell and changed clothes. Went to the shop to buy *beedis* [country cigarettes – for his father]. Came home and ate food and slept.

Ashish, also a fifteen-year-old GC boy, describes two other crop processing tasks undertaken by children: the rather lonely job of grinding wheat at the watermill (*chukki*), and threshing *chuwa*.

10/6/03 Got up and ate breakfast. Went to grind wheat at the *chukki* and stayed there during the day. I was so hungry it was difficult to come home carrying the flour. Then I ate leftover rice. Washed up the plates and fetched water. Fetched wood [from the store], made a fire and made tea. Cut vegetables and made vegetables. Washed hands, ate, and went to sleep.

30/11/03 Got up, drank tea and went to Gwar. Sat a while and then pounded *chuwa* (with feet). Then washed some clothes. Ate rice and washed up the plates. Then pounded *chuwa*. Came home at 3pm. Fetched wood [from the store] and played *carrom* [board game]. Made tea and drank tea. Studied book and slept.

Some young people sometimes helped other villagers as well as their own parents. Here, Manoj, a fifteen-year-old SC boy, helped bring in the winter hay.

8/11/03 Got up, went to the latrine, drank tea and washed hands and face. Fetched water and ate breakfast. Went to cut grass. Ate lunch and rested. Then cut grass and made three trips to bring backloads of grass home. Also brought plates back home from there [grass cutting area where they had cooked lunch]. Met someone on the road who asked me to take their grass, so I took their grass too. Then took the plates. Warmed water and washed hands and face. Studied and wrote my homework. Ate bread, sat a while, and slept.

These diary entries offer further insight into the diversity of children's tasks and the sequencing of particular activities during the day. The diary entries also point to the matter-of-fact manner in which children evaluated their agricultural labour.

As well as conducting multiple agricultural tasks in the fields, children also spent long periods working in the forest. Children engaged in three main activities in particular: herding cattle, collecting leaf litter for livestock's bedding, and gathering lichen (*mukku*). I discuss these activities in detail in the next three chapters, but the main points about this work are easily summarised. Herding was the most common activity for boys aged six to seventeen and for girls aged six to thirteen. Parents regarded herding, which involved mixed-gender contact, as inappropriate for girls beyond the age of puberty. They carried out herding throughout the year, but it was especially common during the busy months of May and June, when children were often required to add herding to the long list of other summer tasks.

Leaf litter from the forests surrounding Bemni was used as bedding in livestock stalls. Once soiled by cattle, the *gobar* was spread as organic fertiliser on the agricultural fields. Girls were mainly responsible for collecting leaves, although boys sometimes helped out too. Girls began to collect leaves at about the age of eight and were carrying very large loads, equivalent to those carried by adult women, by the age of fifteen. Leaf collection occurred throughout the year, but especially in the period immediately before and after shifts between settlements.

Collecting *mukku* was a newer form of household work and entailed children travelling to relatively distant forests, bagging up the lichen they collected from tree branches and taking it to Ghat, where it was sold on for the production of dyes and other products in the plains. Boys and girls conducted this work. They began to collect lichen at about the age of nine and continued until their middle or late teens, except in the case of SC girls, who often carried on harvesting lichen into adulthood. Lichen collection was one task that was differentiated according to caste. GCs tended to make day trips to nearby forests, mainly during periods of relatively low labour demand in the agricultural cycle, such as the winter months of December and January. SCs tended to travel to distant forests for several days at a time and at a greater range of times throughout the year.

The great variety of work that children conducted, at home and in the fields and forests, highlights the crucial importance of their labour to the economic life of Bemni. Children not only covered for their parents while they were out of the home working, they also provided surplus agricultural labour that could be deployed flexibly, quickly and without having to go to the expense and difficulty of negotiating with other households.

The roles that young people played within agriculture were fairly predictable year after year. Parents knew when they were likely to face a labour shortage. But there were also a range of imponderables that lent unpredictability to the manner in which children were called upon to help. Emigration, marriage, illness or quarrels, for example, often changed households' labour needs from one year to the next. At a finer level, a wide range of events – from the arrival of unexpected guests to unusual weather conditions, from an outbreak of disease among cattle to a spate of wild animal attacks – could result in agricultural and forest-based tasks being rescheduled. Villagers therefore had to improvise throughout the year in order to ensure that the complicated system of labour, livestock, and crop rotation described in Chapter 2 proceeded smoothly, and children were centrally important in this dance of life.

Schoolwork

Recent literature on children's work in the global South has raised the crucial issue of the extent to which and how children navigate school and work (for example Nieuwenhuys 1994; Gold and Gujar 2002; Orkin 2012). It is broadly possible to identify three arguments on this topic. First, there are commentators, many of them within development studies and the policy world, who argue that any form of work is harmful to children because of its detrimental impact on their education (for example Weiner 1991). Those making this argument have often focused on the most dangerous and exploitative forms of work, such as children's involvement in factory labour. There is good evidence that in some parts of south Asia and Africa, for example, the pressure to earn money or engage in household labour prevents children from acquiring even rudimentary literacy and numeracy skills in school, and may impact very badly on their health and well-being. This is an understandable cause for concern among academics, activists and policymakers (see Nieuwenhuys 1996, 2007; Swaninathan 1998).

A second set of studies have countered the first set in part by offering a critical perspective on formal education. This work has pointed to the common irrelevance of school curricula in poor countries to the future lives of children (for example Heissler 2011). Rather than learning skills relevant to the local job opportunities available, schools often provide knowledge suited only to an elite of metropolitan children. Indeed, Peggy Froerer (2011) shows that in the village in which she worked in Chhattisgarh, central India, many parents and children perceived formal education to be 'deskilling', in that it prevents children from learning through apprenticeships, work and friendship networks. Gareth Jones and Sylvia Chant (2009) have made similar observations in urban west Africa. Moreover, the infrastructure and teaching in most schools in the global South is often of poor quality (see, for example, Lloyd 2005). In north India teacher absenteeism is common, and many government schools lack even the most basic teaching equipment and facilities (Jeffrey 2010). Other scholars have referred to the tendency for education to instil pernicious social ideas and inappropriately lofty ambitions (Chopra 2005). Where there are no jobs for high school matriculates or graduates from degree colleges, young people may become frustrated and reflect negatively on the time that they spent in school.

The problem with the argument as set out in this way is that it counterposes work and education as if parents and children are necessarily compelled to choose between these as alternative 'paths'. But research from different parts of the world shows that children and young people, even very young children, can often combine school and work in their everyday lives. This is a point that emerges forcefully in Swanson's (2009) ethnography of begging in urban Ecuador. The child beggars at the centre of her study use the money they earn on the street to fund their education, balancing the need to make cash and study on a daily basis. Hannah Hoechner (2011) makes a similar observation in her work with Muslim children attending Islamic schools, while also begging, in the city of Kano, Nigeria. In Asia, Nieuwenhuys (1994) has described how children in south India can combine school and work. In these studies, parents and children typically operate with a pragmatic view of schooling as something that has a place in their children's futures without being a 'silver bullet'.

My material resonates with this third line of argument. Parents in Bemni were beginning to place emphasis on the importance of formal schooling for their children. 'Education is a huge thing' was the type of statement I heard many times. There was a marked increase in school attendance in the 1980s and 1990s in Bemni. Tables 3.1 and 3.2 show that there was a particularly sharp rise in school participation among girls. Girls tended to leave school by the age of thirteen (SCs) or fifteen (GCs), whereas most boys remained in school until seventeen. By 2004 a handful of students had been to Gopeshwar to take degrees.

The standard of education in BPS and SSBS was poor. There were four teachers for the roughly 110 pupils formally enrolled in BPS and four for the 150 students in SSBS. One or two of these teachers were regularly absent, so

Table 3.1 *Parents aged forty to forty-four who had reached class five, 2003/4*

		Reach class five
Women	Average (SC and GC)	3.9% (N = 26)
	SC	*0 (N = 9)*
	GC	*5.9% (N = 17)*
Men	Average (SC and GC)	60% (N = 20)
	SC	*50% (N = 4)*
	GC	*62.5% (N = 16)*

Source: Village survey.

Table 3.2 *Girls and boys aged fifteen to nineteen who had reached class five, 2003/4*

		Reach class five
Girls	Average (SC and GC)	76.8% (N = 56)
	SC	*16.2% (N = 17)*
	GC	*86.1% (N = 39)*
Boys	Average (SC and GC)	91.9% (N = 62)
	SC	*90% (N = 20)*
	GC	*92.9% (N = 42)*

Source: Village survey.

that in practice the schools failed to meet the government-mandated target of one teacher for every thirty pupils. When they did turn up to school, teachers often adopted a rather detached approach to their work, issuing instructions to children and then spending long periods chatting or drinking tea. Most children could barely read or write by class five. Many GC and SC parents complained bitterly about the teaching in the BPS and SSBS. For example, a GC parent told me:

> The teachers are not afraid . . . nobody comes to check up on them as they do in the plains or in villages near the road. So they go away to their homes and don't stay at school and teach. But what can we do?

In addition, the physical infrastructure of BPS and SSBS was woefully inadequate. There were very few teaching aids, aside from a blackboard and a stick to beat children. In both schools there was no furniture and children had to sit outside on thin mats. The facilities at SPS were much better than they were at BPS and SSBS. But only a few relatively well off families could afford the fees of Rs.150 per month at the SPS. Many parents said they would like to send their children to the SPS and cited teachers' relative diligence as a major draw.

In 2003 the BPS received money through the World-Bank-funded Sarv Shiksha Abhiyan scheme to build latrines, a tap and a water tank. Under this scheme, free textbooks and lunchtime meals were also provided for primary school children to encourage higher rates of school attendance. The scheme also offered an honorarium for shiksha bandhas, local temporary teachers or 'para-teachers' who were employed to take up vacant positions in government primary and senior basic schools in remote areas. The government's Social Welfare Department also provided every SC family with education grants of Rs. 30 per month for ten months for each registered child, to help towards buying uniforms, pens and exercise books. These provisions encouraged parents to educate their children in school, but they did little to improve the facilities and teaching in BPS and SSBS.

Parents frequently discussed the value of school education through reference to their own ignorance and lack of skills. The majority of parents were illiterate. In Bemni, 64 per cent of men and 88 per cent of women over the age of twenty had less than five years of schooling, and 52 per cent and 76 per cent, respectively, had never attended school at all. One GC parent told me, 'We are not educated. What do we know? But our son will be educated, so he will know everything.' In some cases, parents appeared to engage in forms of self-denigration, wryly reflecting on their own lack of knowledge and inability to read medicine bottles and signs (compare Jeffrey, Jeffery and Jeffery 2008). 'Those words you are writing down might as well be buffaloes,' one old woman quipped during an interview.

More commonly, parents focused on the future lives of their children in discussing the benefits of education. One GC man said:

> Education is very important these days. It is good. If you are educated, you can know everything. If you are uneducated, you can't know anything. Like you [looking at Jane Dyson] . . . ; you know everything and we don't know anything.

This man's wife added, 'If you are educated, you can live happily.' Some parents referred in particular to the capacity of education to raise people's awareness. A GC woman said, 'Education will open my daughter's eyes. She will be able to write . . . and know what things are.' Another said, 'We are in the dark because we are not educated. My son must be educated.' Karuna Morarji (2010) notes similar discourses in a study of social change in a village close to the Uttarakhandi town of Mussoorie. The parents with whom she spoke tended to equate formal schooling with opportunities for young people to acquire secure employment and travel outside the village, as well as seeing education as having a more general transformative power.

Local assumptions about gender powerfully shaped parents' choices around school (see also Klenk 2010). In line with patriarchal norms prevalent across north India, parents wanted to ensure that their daughters behaved in a demure and restrained manner; they wanted them to be and appear 'homely', in the language of Indian middle-class newspaper marriage advertisements. They hoped that their daughters would become competent workers, but they did not want their daughters to enter paid employment outside their homes. As a result, parents and villagers more broadly imagined education for girls as a basis for consolidating girls' feminine accomplishments, providing a measure of self-assurance and improving their capacity to be effective mothers, wives and household workers. Any deviation on the part of a single girl from this normative vision of schooling and gendered social reproduction could have implications for the reputation, and therefore the marriage prospects, of all girls from the village. The last thing anyone wanted was for Bemni to obtain a 'bad name' (*badnaam*) for its young women.

By contrast, parents and villagers linked boys' schooling to the economic advancement of the household. In discussing their sons' futures, GC villagers made a three-way distinction between secure, well-paid and prestigious jobs within government service (*sarkari naukri*), insecure and poorly paid private 'business' (using the English word) and demeaning, exploitative and gruelling manual wage labour (*mazdoori*). Parents were aware of the rigours of the physical tests required to enter the military. Parents therefore put a particular emphasis on the need for boys to be brave (*bahadoor*) and strong (*taaqat*). It followed that parents tended to be particularly tolerant of boys' naughtiness (*shetaanee*) when they were developing skills that might improve their bravery, strength and competitive spirit. SCs were generally less confident of their sons obtaining government service. In discussing their sons' futures, SC parents distinguished between work based on skilful entrepreneurship usually in the village (often also termed *naukri*), relatively undesirable work as daily wage labourers or the possibility of their sons not obtaining work at all and therefore remaining poor (*gareeb*).

I often heard parents discuss sons' education as being more important than that of their daughters. For example, a GC woman said of her daughter, 'She's a girl, so she won't get salaried employment anyway, so she will only go up to class eight.' Many girls complained about being compelled to leave school, and looked enviously on as their brothers were allowed to continue in education.

Children tended to make similar statements to their parents when discussing education. Several recent analyses point to children's relative disinterest in school in north India. In a study of education in rural western UP, many Muslims and Dalits said that they are better off learning in the workplace – 'learning through blisters', as one labourer put it – than attending school (see

Jeffrey, Jeffery and Jeffery 2008). In research on children's work in rural Rajasthan, north India, Ann Gold and Bhotu Ram Gujar (2002) point to a generalised antipathy to school and formal education among children. The children in their research village perceived household and agricultural work to be more meaningful than was schoolwork. Household and agricultural work was fulfilling and social and led to immediate rewards in the form of gratitude from elders and successful household reproduction. By contrast, schoolwork was unfulfilling, tedious and associated with a lack of tangible awards.

My findings in Bemni provide some further support for these arguments. I also heard students refer to schoolwork as unrewarding, in comparison to relatively engaging household and agricultural work. The poor standard of government schooling in and around Bemni dampened students' interest in formal education. In addition, students could see the social and economic benefits of working hard for their families in the home and family. Moreover, some children spoke of harsh punishments that had been meted out on them. They had been 'made into chickens', a punishment that involves bending double, putting your arms between your legs and holding your ears. Boys also referred to painful beatings that they had received in school. One boy aged ten joked that he regularly had 'two strikes for breakfast', and several boys who had left school told me: 'Now I only get beaten in one place [home] rather than two.'

Indeed, several children tried to avoid school by persuading teachers and their parents that it was necessary for them to conduct work in the home, fields or forest. Some children simply did not turn up to school. Many others developed elaborate excuses, communicated usually through siblings, friends or letters. Prema (GC, thirteen) specialised in writing notes of absence to her teachers, in which she often claimed that the burden of household work prevented her from coming to school. Prema would often turn up at school a day or two later and show off her blistered hands as evidence that she had been working. After failing class six three times because of her low attendance, her father sent her to a private school, in which teachers issued fines of Rs 5 for absence. But Prema continued to devise excuses, and she failed her examinations again shortly after I left the village.

These observations might usefully inform NGO pronouncements about moving children from work into school. Development practitioners rarely probe in sufficient detail into the quality and content of the education that young people receive. But children's criticisms of school and their efforts to skip school must be read in context. As mainstream writing on development primes us to expect, children typically expressed great enthusiasm for the idea of becoming 'educated' (*parhe likhe*). Children said that education makes one 'alert' and 'skilful', and boys, in particular, perceived education to be a route out of the village into salaried employment. Children also said that they liked school, even in unguarded moments when they were not trying to impress obviously 'educated' outsiders, in the shape of Anita and me.

Irrespective of their attitudes towards formal education, children were highly adept at managing the twin burdens of accomplishing household tasks and keeping up their school attendance, at least to the level in which they could acquire basic educated skills. Their efforts to juggle school and work varied according to the season. The month-long summer holiday in June allowed them to relieve their parents during one of the busiest agricultural periods. The numerous official holidays and Sundays also enabled children to work for their families. On a more everyday basis, children fitted their work around a shifting school timetable. In the summer timetable, when school ran from 7 a.m. to 12 p.m., children had a full afternoon to work. When the winter timetable (from 10 a.m. to 4 p.m.) was in effect, children were more constrained. In October and early November it was light enough for them to accomplish some tasks in the morning and evening. Anita and I often accompanied children running up and down the mountain to collect winter hay from the fields, or leaves from the forest, before school in the late autumn. But, when the days became shorter and villagers moved down to Gwar, children had little time for work outside school hours.

Children's diary entries give a sense of how children negotiated their dual commitment to school and household work. Ashish (GC, fifteen) writes:

> 26/05/03 Got up at 4am, lit fire and made tea. Washed hands and face and ate food. Went to plough a small field then went to school. Came home at 12pm. Ate one piece of bread. Went with cows to Chapra. Brought home a backload of wood. Night fell. Fetched water and lit fire. Made tea and cut vegetables. Ground spices and made vegetables. Kneaded flour and made bread. Ate bread and slept.

On seven consecutive days in November Manoj (GC, fourteen) helped bring in the winter hay harvest, both before and after his school day. He writes:

> 10/11/03 (Monday) Got up and went to fetch a backload of grass. From there, went to latrine [in the fields]. Came home and fetched water and warmed water. Washed hands and face and ate breakfast. Put on school clothes and went to school. At school, cleaned classroom and did prayers. Studied for two hours and had break. Then studied for two hours and left school. Came home and ate food. After eating, fetched one backload of grass from Kanora. Then went to fetch cows from Ankur. Studied for two hours and ate bread. Went to watch the *Panch Pandava*. Came home at 2am and slept.

Children and youth also tried to combine school, work and leisure. Some were able to play before or after classes, while others would meet and chat with friends on the journey to and from school. Groups of boys used particularly flat areas on school journeys for short games of cricket. Young people also talked about their school break times as valuable leisure periods. They similarly snatched short opportunities between work tasks to have their own fun. This diary entry of Manoj (SC, fifteen) is suggestive:

> 6/11/03 Got up, went to the latrine and studied for half an hour. Drank tea and washed my hands and face. Fetched water and ate breakfast. Played some games. Then I put on my school uniform and went to school. I sat for a while on the path [to school] and chatted with friends. Studied at school. Left at 3.30pm and came home and ate food. Changed clothes and went to fetch grass from Kanora. Brought it home and fetched water. Studied for two hours. Ate bread and slept.

Conclusions

Children in Bemni were engaged in a wide variety of forms of work in the home, local forests and fields. This work did not seriously undermine their schooling, since most children could combine household tasks and educational work. Moreover, household work provided children with opportunities to acquire skills useful in later life, and some activities offered a means of socialising outside the home. In a study of Muslim weavers in the north Indian city of Banaras, Nita Kumar (2000) observes that many weavers did not send their children to secular schools in the 1970s and 1980s in part out of fear that they would abandon the family trade. In contrast, Bemni parents were eager to provide their children, especially sons, with educational opportunities. Bemni children likewise valued schooling as well as their household work. These conclusions provide a counterpoint to the negative evaluations of labour that are offered by some critics of children's work in the global South. They are also at odds with the argument that formal education is irrelevant to children in poor rural settings.

The energy and productivity of young people in Bemni provides a vivid example of agency defined in terms of the capacity to act effectively and exercise power. The diaries in particular offer a window on the bewildering variety of tasks conducted by children. 'Youth', those aged over twelve, carried out a still greater range of activities, many of them complex and requiring considerable local knowledge. A key empirical point here is that young people were valued over and above their role as embodiments of future value (compare Anagnost 2008). They were not just 'becomings'. Instead, they were important workers in their own right, integral to the successful reproduction of the household and village economy (compare Punch 2001).

Young people's agency also emerges in the manner in which they negotiated with parents over their work and balanced school and work commitments in ways that varied throughout the year. Their developing agency was sometimes oppositional; there was a considerable amount of 'foot dragging' (compare Scott 1985). But they generally acquiesced in assisting their parents within and outside the home. Nor was their agency primarily about establishing 'independence', except in the sense that they were able to conduct a greater array of tasks independently as they got older and matured. Rather, young people's agency was performed through their participation in a programme of work wherein people, livestock, energy, crops and fodder are marshalled carefully up and down the mountain. Gender powerfully shapes this dance. Boys tended to have more room for manoeuvre than did girls, and it was not anticipated they would carry out quite the same range of activities as that performed by their female peers. What also lends young people's everyday unpaid work its predictability is the time–space organisation of the agro-pastoral system. Just as Bemni's remoteness influences the nature of village life, so too, at a smaller scale, the particular geography of the mountainside influences how people live and work.

The next three chapters develop these key arguments in new directions. I demonstrate more clearly the manner in which young people express agency through building mutual dependences, and highlight the improvised nature of such practice. Not only do I refer to space as a container for action, but I show how materials and representations of space and place become entangled in young people's opportunistic work and play.

4 Herding, fun and difference

On a sultry June afternoon three friends, Jaivir, Pradeep and Sunil, coaxed their cows across the rocky, still-dry riverbed before the final steep climb up to Changeri. Whistling and harassing their cows with thin sticks and the occasional hurled stone, they picked their way up a narrow path. Once up on the open meadow, the boys looked back down onto the village, beyond it to the steep slopes of the forest and far down the valley in the other direction. A pair of eagles circled noiselessly overhead. It was the school holidays, so it would soon be busy with other young herders and their livestock. But the boys were the first to arrive, and they enjoyed the peace.

Sunil, being the youngest, was sent off to see to the cows, to make sure they had found fresh grass and were far from the precipitous edges. Meanwhile, Jaivir and Pradeep went straight into the tumbledown building that had been the home of American missionaries in the 1940s. While made in the same local stone as the rest of the village buildings, the layout was totally different. They pointed out the multiple rooms, high ceilings and grand fireplaces, so different from their own low one-roomed houses, which were more suited to the harsh Himalayan winters. The boys mentioned, as they always did, that *Issai-log* (Christians) ate cows and buffaloes. With shudders of disgust, they wondered if the house was full of ghosts.

They returned to the open meadow, each carrying a couple of stones from the crumbling walls, and set up a cricket pitch, tall stones as wickets. Sunil came running back from checking the cows, bringing with him a chunk of wood, which he fashioned quickly into a cricket bat. By the time they were ready to play, two more boys had arrived, and the game began.

Within an hour there were fifteen boys and girls milling around Changeri, some sitting in small huddles chatting and playing with stones, others hanging from the branches of a tree, while the remainder of the boys joined the cricket game. Intermittently the smallest children would be called upon to check on the livestock, and they would race off, jumping over hummocks of grass and shrieking to the cows. And so it continued, until the dipping sun reminded them to make their slow, reluctant return to the village, to the chores that awaited them.

The supervision of livestock was one of the most important everyday work activities in Bemni. Most households owned cattle, and they were greatly prized possessions. Indeed, many people perceived their oxen, cows and buffaloes to be part of their family. In the *gosaala*-style houses, people shared a single room with their livestock at night. During the day they were let out to graze in pastures, some close to the village and some a trek of an hour or two away. Villagers were intensely concerned about the safety and health of their livestock, and so cattle had to be tended to while out of the village rather than left to their own devices. Moreover, cattle had to be kept away from ripening crops, and there were village van panchayat rules about where cattle could graze at different times of the year.

Herding was relatively easy work, and one that was, when possible, left to children. During my research I developed a close knowledge of where and when children herded and became centrally interested in how they herded livestock. Herding was a chore, but hardly laborious. It allowed children a great deal of time to engage in other, fun, activities. Understanding young people's activities while herding therefore places in sharper focus the creativity of young people and their potential to make 'fresh contact' with their surroundings (Mannheim 1956 [1923]).

Young people's engagement with the environment in Bemni occurred through movement. Walking through fields, meadows and stands of forest while herding was an important means by which young people developed a sense of their own relationship to nature. Anticipating this point in certain respects, Ingold (2007) makes a useful distinction between 'transport' and 'wayfaring'. For him, 'transport' is simply the movement of a body or bodies across space from one destination to another. The route is usually known in advance, and the traveller does not engage with his or her surroundings. In addition, in this hypothetical vision of pure transport, the movement occurs without the body or mind of the traveller being transformed by the action. In Ingold's schema, 'wayfaring', by contrast, is not a process worked out in advance; it involves people in making a series of tactical decisions (see also de Certeau 1984; McFarlane 2012). Wayfaring typically results in a path that is sinuous rather than straight, the speed and nature of the journey often varies, and stopping points, U-turns and digressions are the norm. Ingold also stresses the physical, mental and affective engagement with the environment associated with wayfaring, and the close contact it often entails with the weather, animals, plants and the terrain. Affective and emotional engagement is in turn a source of knowledge. 'Knowledge' in this optic is not simply additive – deposited straightforwardly in a person's mind as 'content' – but resides instead in what Bourdieu (1977 [1972]) terms the 'habitus': durably inscribed dispositions that reflect histories of experience and acculturation. Jaivir and Pradeep were expert 'wayfarers', in this sense. But wayfaring is not a transcendental capacity innate in all human beings, as Ingold sometimes implies: it has to be understood with reference to people's social background, and especially their gender, caste and age.

Herding, seasonality and gender

Children herded cattle in different places, at different times and with varying levels of attention. There were several reasons for this seasonality. The van panchayat imposed rules about where cattle could graze at different times of the year to ensure that pastures were not denuded of grass and that ripening crops were not damaged. The availability of household labour, the organisation of the school timetable and even the movement of wild animals also shaped herding patterns.

Herding practices can be divided into four broad 'seasons'. Summer (May and June) was the main 'herding season' for children, especially June, when there was a month-long school holiday. Adults were busy harvesting grain crops and weeding potatoes, so young people would assist their parents by herding cattle to designated pastures and keeping them away from the crops. Children often started work at 5 a.m., spending the early morning in the forest collecting dry leaves for cattle bedding before helping in the fields with the wheat and potato crops. They would then take the cattle out to graze in the early afternoon, returning to the village around 6.30 p.m. In relatively 'labour-rich' households, children often herded all day during June, setting out to the grazing areas at 8 a.m. and returning between 5 and 6 p.m. These children tended to travel to more distant herding areas, often taking a packed lunch with them.

During the monsoon, from July to September, cattle grazed above Danda, the highest settlement. People were less concerned about supervising livestock here, as it was largely situated above the line of fields, and cattle posed little threat to their crops. Children had less time to herd during this season because they attended school in the morning until midday. Besides, they hated monsoon herding, because of the relentless rain, and the snakes and leeches that lurked in the long grass. They often showed me craters on their legs more than 2 centimetres in diameter, where leeches had sucked and caused infections. The children therefore usually led cattle to pastures and allowed them to make their own way back home in the evening, around 5 to 6 p.m. This was a somewhat risky strategy, as cows did occasionally get lost, sometimes for as long as three days.

Villagers moved back to their homes in Bemni at the beginning of October, and the period from then until early December was one of the most difficult seasons for herding. Adults were really busy, harvesting potatoes, millet and mustard seed crops and, later, cutting winter hay. The children attended classes on the winter school timetable, from 10 a.m. to 4 p.m., which left no time for herding. But this labour shortage coincided with a period when cattle needed the most supervision to prevent damage to crops or hay. Owners of cows that caused damage were fined Rs. 20 per cow. Cattle also needed protection from leopards, which – having spent the monsoon at high altitude – now returned to the village and found cattle easy prey. In 2003, in the first week of November alone, leopards killed two cows, a bull, a mule and a goat, and I heard of several more occasions in which herders interrupted attacks that would have resulted in livestock death. Young people therefore combined their journeys to and from school with sending and collecting their cattle from grazing areas, often making a larger than usual loop to school. During some particularly busy times children missed school for days at a stretch in order to herd.

In the first week of December villagers would move for the winter from Bemni to Gwar, the lowest settlement, where the previous season's pressures eased. By December the crops had been harvested and the winter hay cut, so cattle offered little threat and were often left to graze by themselves. The cold weather and short days meant that cattle grazed outside only for a few hours each day, and were stall-fed when snow lay on the ground. This pattern continued until around the end of April.

There were, therefore, two intensive periods of herding for children: June, when they had their days relatively free, and October and November, when they herded intermittently around school attendance, or sometimes by simply skipping school. The ways in which young people engaged with their environment and carved out spaces of fun were shaped by these seasonal dimensions of the agricultural cycle.

Young people's herding also changed over their early life course. Boys and girls began to herd at the age of around five, often working alongside older siblings. By the time they were six or seven, children took their cattle to graze in areas close to home. By eight or nine years of age, children were capable of herding in more distant grazing areas and for longer periods. At this age girls and boys gathered together, but, after the age of about thirteen, gender started to shape their herding activities. Gendered codes of behaviour dictated that a young woman's demeanour should be shy and demure, and that she should interact minimally with men outside her family. Herding in mixed company did not accommodate these social restrictions. Moreover, herding took place in socially rather 'risky' places, in the hinterlands of the village but in full view. Herding locations were public spaces, and yet were simultaneously on the cusp of privacy, occupying a place from where to escape to the more secluded forest. When young people talked of illicit affairs, lovers were always said to have met in the forest. Herding areas, by straddling the village and the forest, were therefore rather ambiguous spaces for teenage girls, offering the potential both for private liaisons and public appraisal.

The example of Saka (GC, sixteen) illustrates the gendered nature of herding and the social forces that prevented her from herding after adolescence. Saka said that until the age of eleven she had been part of a mixed-gender group of friends who always herded and played together. Saka talked wistfully of this time, which she remembered as the best and most carefree period of her life. By the age of thirteen, however, Saka began to understand that there were 'rules' (*neeyam*) about the ways in which girls and boys were expected to behave while herding or working and playing together in other mixed-gender contexts. She realised that soon she would no longer be allowed to play in public, particularly with her male friends. By the age of fifteen Saka reluctantly began to separate herself from the group, and herded less frequently. When she did go out with her cattle she carefully chose her company and the location. She remained with other girls and joined mixed-gender groups only when the boys were members of her extended family (*rishtedaar*). Saka recalled, 'I would only go with those boys I call "brother", and, if other men or older boys came along, we would move away or stay silent.' She also chose to herd in areas where she was always visible, usually in the spaces as close to the village as possible.

Saka understood that to contest these gendered ideas around herding would create a bad reputation: 'If we don't act like that, people would say dirty things (*gundee cheez*) about us.' Aged nearly seventeen in 2003, Saka no longer regularly herded cows except on rare occasions in conditions of extreme labour scarcity, such as during the November harvests. She made an effort to remain alone, and found it boring, lonely work.

Parents played a key role in enforcing gender norms around herding. Saka once told me, 'You wouldn't see it, but my mother tells me all the time what to do or not to do.' Saka's mother was open about her lectures to Saka: 'We worry about our daughters. I can't stay with her all the time, so I have to teach Saka how to work and behave properly.' Saka was also under considerable pressure from her older brother, Mukesh, to maintain a good reputation. She said that Mukesh and his male friends discussed which of the village girls were good (*atchchee*) or bad/dirty (*gundee*). If Mukesh's friends thought that Saka was bad, however, they would not have told him directly. Worried that his friends might gossip, Mukesh therefore carefully monitored Saka's behaviour. He ordered her not to laugh too much in public or to stay too long in the forest when taking the cows to graze. Before Mukesh left for his long army training, he threatened Saka: 'If I hear any bad stories about you, I'll throw you in the river!' Saka laughed as she imitated Mukesh: 'If he had not been in such a rush as he left, he would have told me more; then I would have got the whole lecture!'

Saka was not alone in receiving constant advice from parents or older siblings. Other similarly aged girls acknowledged the pressures they were under to adhere to gendered expectations of how young women should behave, and norms around herding were an especially common topic of conversation. In a group discussion with Saka and her friends, one girl said: 'We used to play when we herded at Simgaita but we can't now because we are grown up. We can't play anywhere at home, because adults will see us.' Thirteen-year-old Prema was equally aware that her herding days were limited. She explained:

> We herd cattle and play now, and when adults pass us and see us playing there is no problem. But when we grow up a bit, then we will be afraid of what village people think, and we won't play in front of them.

Gender norms influenced how young women such as Prema and Saka reflected on grazing pastures around the village. They stressed that many of the areas where young people gather to herd were ambiguous: they were neither situated in Bemni, under the watchful gaze of older villagers, nor were they hidden sites far from the village. Moreover, in the presence of young men, they perceived these pastures to be socially precarious: places to be avoided during their daily movements about the village. 'Wayfaring' was not as free and careless a process as Ingold's (2007) work might suggest. Herding groups therefore tended to contain only young girls; there were very few older than fourteen. By contrast, boys continued to herd throughout their teenage years and, when there were no children available to take over the task, into adulthood.

Herding and fun (*mazaa*)

It would be mistaken to imply that herding is a wholly 'easy' activity, a straightforward cover for children to 'have fun' (*mazaa karna*). Herders had to prevent livestock from grazing outside designated zones, and they were responsible for ensuring the safety of the animals. The characteristics of both these duties changed throughout the year, as grazing availability and threats to livestock varied with location and season. The slippery rainy season conditions, for example, and the hidden gullies along some paths were perilous. Herders also had to account for the presence of monsoon leeches, which could kill cows if they grew inside their nostrils, and later for the threat of leopards and snakes. The change in diet in different seasons and locations occasionally led to livestock poisoning and death.

Children had to recognise their livestock in a group of others, and account for the vulnerabilities of specific animals. For example, small calves were easy prey for leopards. Buffaloes were clumsy on rocky ground and their digestive systems were susceptible to poisons. Some pairs of oxen tended to fight while out grazing, increasing the risk of fatal injury through falling. Some children prided themselves on keeping the peace between oxen and scolded those who could not. Thirteen-year-old Bimla, for example, claimed that she alone had the skill required to herd her family's oxen safely, and that her twelve-year-old brother Devendre naughtily encouraged the oxen to fight. Even when livestock were docile, as they were most of the time, children had to ensure that they kept to the paths on their way to grazing areas. Children prepared long fine branches with which to whip and chide the cattle into moving. It was skilled work, requiring patience and sometimes strength. Herding also involved physical stamina, as I found during treks to the more distant grazing areas.

Children therefore required considerable, and up-to-date, knowledge to herd well. They needed continuously to appraise their information on seasonal conditions by discussing where to herd with their parents or peers. An especially slippery path, a leopard sighting or a rock fall might all be reasons for children to need to alter their planned route, and they had to keep abreast of news regarding such incidents. Here, too, children needed to 'improvise' (*jugaad*).

But it remains true that herding was usually much less burdensome than agricultural labour or most of the other tasks performed by children. In many cases it involved spending long periods doing very little at all. 'Doing nothing' can itself often be a form of labour. In a classic piece of work, Paul Corrigan (1979) writes of the boredom and frustration that teenagers experienced simply 'sitting' on street corners in Sunderland in the 1970s. All they could do, he writes, 'is sit on the pavement and smash milk bottles on the ground'. Ross McKibbin (1990) similarly argues that unemployed youth in inter-war Britain had a profound sense of lost time. In McKibbin's example, youth had a sense of bearing only a distant relationship to their surroundings. For example, they could not afford to watch football matches themselves, and had to hang about outside the stadium. Life was lived, as it were, 'second-hand'.

In the Indian context, several authors have written recently of the problem of 'boredom'. For example, Craig Jeffrey (2010) has written of young men studying in the north Indian city of Meerut who spend very little of their time attending classes. Instead, students spend much of their time hanging out engaged in 'timepass', the term they use for passing the time. Chris Fuller (2011) has written of similar 'timepass' among women in middle-class households in south India. Perhaps more closely related to my own study is the work of Jonathan Parry (1999) on timepass in a central Indian steel factory. Employing participant observation methods similar to my own, Parry describes the boredom associated with some jobs in a steel factory, in which supervisory workers are sometimes called upon to do a particular job only for a few minutes every hour, or even for a few minutes in an entire day. Parry describes the culture of passing time that evolved to cope with long passages of dead time, such as card playing, joking and simply sitting around 'doing nothing'.

Teenagers sometimes complained of boredom while herding. For example, when girls aged over fifteen were occasionally pressed into herding under conditions of labour scarcity, gendered norms prevented them from wandering too far from the village or joining in with games and fun activities. Instead, they had to sit quietly, with few interactions with others. Like Saka, these girls sometimes complained simply of loneliness, but they also bemoaned the long passages of unstructured time associated with herding. In a somewhat similar vein, many young men over the age of sixteen were no longer able to enjoy the company of younger boys, and often complained of being bored while herding. Instead, they preferred to spend time with similarly aged male friends in or close to the village, chatting and playing *carrom*, a board game. These boys and young men would sometimes enlist the help of younger relatives to take care of their cattle, often with their parents' disapproval. For example, seventeen-year-old Mahvir occasionally made time for himself by sending his two cows, two oxen and a buffalo with his twelve-year-old cousin Bina, who already had her own two oxen and a buffalo to supervise.

More generally, children sometimes complained of boredom during October and November, when children were pulled out of school on an individual basis. The grazing areas were highly regulated then, with small pastures scattered across the landscape, so children were less likely to be able to gather together. They were regularly alone all day, and went rather reluctantly. Children frequently told me that while herding in the autumn they had experienced feelings of boredom and restlessness, mixed with a sense of loneliness. 'It is no fun to herd alone', one twelve-year-old boy told me.

But the complaints of older children and occasional grumblings in the autumn about boredom should not be overstated. I never heard children using the term 'timepass' or any similar term in Garhwali. Children – especially boys, who were relatively free to wander – perceived herding as fun (*mazaa*). Children told me that herding was their favourite household chore, certainly better than working in the home or helping in the fields. Basanti, a thirteen-year-old SC girl, said, 'My favourite work is herding the cows, because then I can sit around and play.' Bina, a GC girl aged twelve, independently agreed: 'I like going with the cows most of all. You stay close to the house, and I can play and it's not like work.' Fifteen-year-old SC Manoj said, 'The best work is going with the cows. I can play and sing and be with my friends and it doesn't seem like work.' His SC contemporary, Devendre (aged twelve), similarly explained, 'I prefer going with the cows, because then I go with friends and stay in the jungle all day.' One young man, Mohan Singh, also compared his herding work to the tyranny that he had experienced at school. He had decided for himself to drop out of school two years previously, and now, aged seventeen, his days were regularly spent with his family's cattle. He said emphatically that being with the cows was better. 'With the cows,' he said, 'I sit. All day I just warm my backside. At school, I would just get beaten.' There was a consensus among young people that herding is 'good work' (*atchhcha kaam*), because it often provides a certain amount of free time.

Parents were not very concerned about what children did while they were herding. Parents themselves had herded while they were young, and they remembered the activity as relatively fun. Bina's mother said, 'Going with the cows was better than staying at home. I was with my friends and we laughed and played.' Basanti's mother similarly remembered her experiences: 'I liked taking the cows to the forest when I was a child. I went with my friends and played and everyone was together.' Other parents empathised with children's wish to escape from parental supervision. Saka's mother remembered: 'I liked going to the forest. I didn't want to stay at home, because I would be told to do this work or that work. In the forest I got away from that.' Nor did villagers in general try to police the activities of children when they were herding. There was a general acceptance in Bemni that herding was in some sense 'children's time', in which it was possible for them to relax with friends.

I became especially aware of the range of activities in which children engage while herding on a warm clear morning in June 2003. Anita and I had breakfasted early. Two SC boys – Manoj and Chotu – had told us that they would be happy for us to accompany them on a trip herding cattle, and we were eager to set off. Zigzagging our way between the ripening crops, Anita and I soon spotted Manoj and Chotu, cajoling their cows along the path to the Chapra pastures. We caught up with them quickly, exchanged greetings and then ambled slowly behind the cattle as they stumbled along the rocky paths. Chotu pointed out the hundreds of lizards (*chipkali*). He explained that they bask in the sun during this season and that he was afraid of them. The bite of a *chipkali* was said to be like an electric shock and be able to kill a person. Chotu said that, while most children avoided Chapra on hot sunny days when *chipkali* abound, some boys, such as Manoj, were brave and played with the *chipkali*. Manoj willingly proved this and threw a stone to surprise a lizard. As it turned to re-enter a crack between two stones, Manoj swiftly grabbed the end of its tail, and dangled it triumphantly in front of his awe-struck friend.

When we had finally reached Chapra, Manoj and Chotu pushed their cows up the hill towards the forest to graze. With the cows safely out of the way, the boys climbed to the top of a vast oak tree, where they sat singing Garhwali songs at the top of their voices. Manoj had a reputation for his strong voice and for knowing more songs than other boys. He rolled one song neatly into the next, as Chotu giggled at the stories he told. In one song, the narrator complained of his stepmother's mistreatment. Another was the tale of a Garhwali bus conductor who, having migrated to the city, reminisced about home and his mother's food. The subject of another was a Nepali migrant who said he liked Garhwal so much he wanted to stay for ever and not return to Nepal.

The boys abruptly stopped singing when Chotu announced that he had found a bird's nest in the tree canopy. He knocked the nest, and a tiny egg fell to the ground and smashed. The boys hurried down to look, finding a foetus among pieces of shell. They laid it gently on a rock, expressing sorrow and regret.

But the boys were simultaneously fascinated, and spent some time debating the function of various body parts.

When their concentration flagged, Chotu and Manoj briefly checked on their cattle before wandering up the hill to a pipeline that supplied water to the neighbouring village of Lungi. Despite knowing its function, and that Lungi perpetually suffered from water shortages, the boys tampered with a join in the pipe so that water came spurting out into a growing puddle. Delighted when a rainbow formed as the sun beamed through the spray, the boys made a bigger hole in the pipe to allow more water out. They positioned a rock just in front of the water jet, sending it up into a huge arc across the path. The boys stood laughing as they marvelled at their creation. Suddenly worried that a passer-by might discover the damage they had wrought, they struggled to close the hole with a piece of wood.

With a makeshift block shoved into the pipe's leak, the boys ran on along the path towards Lamsori. Here the oak forest became thicker again, and, although this part of the van panchayat was officially closed, the boys decided they would cut some fresh oak leaves. Their parents had asked them to bring cattle fodder home with them, and lopping branches of oak was considerably less time-consuming than the legitimate cutting of green grass. The boys said the *chowkidar* alternated his daily patrols in this area with the northern parts of the forest, and that he had patrolled the Lamsori area the previous day. They therefore knew that, in his absence, they could safely steal what they wanted from the forest.

When the boys eventually emerged with their baskets of fresh oak leaves, they explained how they would cut green grass to stuff into the top of the basket to hide the oak leaves. But they would wait until just before returning home before cutting the grass, for it would otherwise wilt and reveal the leaves underneath. Besides, cattle needed fresh rather than wilted grass. In this way, the boys could avoid a fine for breaking van panchayat rules while satisfying their households' fodder needs. By 3 p.m. the sky had blackened, threatening rain. We decided to race home, leaving the boys to slowly collect their cattle and follow on later.

There was no common pattern to such days in the forest, herding cattle. Children often went with different friends to herd. They found different opportunities to play, and their days followed different types of rhythms. While not explicitly citing the Hindi term for improvisation, *jugaad*, these boys found ingenious ways of making the most of their free time while herding. They shrewdly assessed their material environment, took account of the friends who happened to be at hand and found ways to have fun.

The variety in children's activities while herding and their capacity to take advantage of opportunities became obvious to Anita and me when we met up with Manoj again some days after the incident with the water pipe. We were climbing up the hillside the next day when we saw Manoj sitting on a low-slung branch of a tree at the start of the Chapra path, the meeting point where he waited for his friends. Manoj's friends, twelve-year-old Mukesh and fifteen-year-old Sohan, soon appeared, and we decided to set off with the cattle towards Chapra.

As we walked, Manoj excitedly told us his news. He had found a parrot's nest and had taken a chick home to teach it to talk. He said that parrots have the same tongues as humans and can say anything. Mukesh was thrilled by this idea, so Manoj promised to help him find one on this trip.

The boys had also decided that, rather than take ready-cooked bread to the forest, they would cook their own food there. Manoj had secretly taken bagfuls of rice, pulses and spices from his home, and Mukesh described how he had smuggled out his mother's pressure cooker. They tied the carrying bags together and slung them like saddlebags across the backs of their cows. As the cows loped along the rocky, eroded path, the bags knocked into boulders, and the metal of the pressure cooker made resounding crashes (and, undoubtedly, dents). In endless fits of giggles, the boys ran constantly behind the cows, rearranging the bags as they were knocked out of place.

After an hour's walk we arrived at a large oak tree, where we sat in the shade. When the boys had sent their cattle off to a safe grazing area, they climbed the tree and cut branches with which to build a fire. Although no cutting of oak was allowed at that time, the boys said that the *chowkidar* was again patrolling the other side and they were in no danger of being caught. Having collected enough wood, the boys lit a fire, put rice, *daal* and spices into the pressure cooker, covered it with water and placed it over the flames. With the food cooking, the boys wanted to fetch more fuelwood from the nearby forest. But, as we looked towards the forest ten minutes later, we spotted the three of them huddled together smoking *beedis*.

Having returned from their secret smoking session with barely any extra wood, Manoj hurled a rope up over a large branch of the tree to make a swing. Mukesh tried first, but, because the ground sloped away from the tree, he was too short to climb into it. Sohan, although tall enough, was too scared to climb onto it and declined. Manoj shrugged, leapt into the hoop of the rope and made an exaggerated show of swinging. He swung in such precarious circles, so narrowly missing the tree trunk, that even his friends' looks of admiration were tinged with concern.

As the food was nearly ready, the boys ran to search for improvised plates. They found a couple of large flat slates, onto which, once rinsed, they served the rice and *daal*. They asked if I could take a photograph of their meal, and sat proudly in front of their heaped plates (Figure 4.1).

Figure 4.1 Manoj (right) and his friends eat a meal prepared in the forest while herding

Having eaten and washed up their pan, the boys briefly checked on their cows. Manoj saw a couple of bright green parrots, so they all ran off to find the nests and catch a chick for Mukesh. We tried to follow them for a while but soon lost them in the Lamsori forest. When we did finally find them, Manoj, Sohan and Mukesh had climbed to the top of a massive, dangerously leaning tree. They sat smoking another shared cigarette and pointing out parrots as they glided past. We left the boys enjoying their private moments and wandered back to the village.

SC boys tended to engage in playful activities in separate spaces from those occupied by GCs. But my experience of spending time with Manoj in June 2003 gives a sense of the broad type of activities in which all boys engaged while herding: messing about in the forest, playing games, foraging and eating food. Running through these activities was a sense of mischief, humour and horseplay. Verkaaik (2004) has argued that young men in urban Pakistan were often motivated to join political movements or 'resist' adult institutions not as a result of some type of deeply held ideological vision but simply in a search for 'fun'. Verkaaik characterises fun as an abiding, everyday concern of urban youth. I observed a similar preoccupation with fun among teenage boys in Bemni, where the term *mazaa* had also become part of daily conversation. But in Bemni the quest for fun was channelled into a range of social activities rather than overt political action.

Gender, caste and play

Boys' playful activities while herding took a bewildering variety of forms. They often spent hours of their herding time simply chatting. Depending on the herding location and the company, these chats could be among larger groups of mixed-aged boys, or groups of two or three boys huddled under the shade of a tree or sharing an umbrella during the monsoon. On other occasions a boy would surreptitiously leave home with a radio to listen to a live cricket match and relay a broken commentary to the surrounding group. Larger groups of boys chatting were generally open to my presence. But conversations among pairs of boys were more difficult to follow. In other circumstances, boys became restless and found other things to do. They constructed swings, washed their bodies and hair in icy mountain streams, threw stones at targets, climbed trees and ran races. As in the case of Manoj and his friends, boys also organised picnics at grazing areas. They occasionally foraged for food, but more commonly brought items from home.

In addition, boys often staged pranks or got into playful fights while herding. They rarely caused serious damage to each other or property, but their 'hanging out' in the pastures had a boisterous, ebullient and sometimes rebellious quality. The 'naughtiest' activities tended to only occur in the grazing areas that were distant from the village, and opportunities to visit these areas usually occurred only in June, when children were on school holidays and had long periods free to herd their cattle.

Boys also played team games while herding. The choice of games varied according to the season, the availability of other herders and the location. For their favourite team games – cricket, *kabaddi* and *puria* – the boys needed lots of participants, and sufficient space with a flat surface. The June school holiday period, when all the boys were regularly herding, was the best time. Cricket was their favourite game, and was typically played with pieces of wood for the bat and stumps and a tightly bound length of cloth for the ball. For GC boys, in particular, their reputation as proficient cricketers was an important marker among their peers, and their hours spent herding allowed them to practise. Cricket continued outside school holidays, however; boys would often spend their time walking home from classes organising where to meet up with their cows for the afternoon's game of cricket.

Kabaddi is also a nationally recognised game, although faster and more aggressive than cricket. Two teams occupy different ends of the court, while one team member is sent to 'raid' the other team, winning points for touching team members before retreating uncaught to his own team. All the while, he holds his breath and repeats '*kabaddi, kabaddi, kabaddi*' rapidly. It is a game in which agility and daring are the key requirements – skills that are essential and well respected in other more agricultural settings in the village.

There are also a number of less well recognised games, of which *puria* is perhaps the most popular. In this game two teams compete to either protect a pile of stones or dismantle it by throwing stones. Since the game involved no direct physical contact, girls also occasionally joined in, and, hence, it was the only team game that was ever mixed-gender. The boys also had a large repertoire of other semi-improvised contact games, such as human pyramids. Two boys stood side by side while another clambered up to sit on their shoulders. Another two boys stood opposite them, again with a third boy balanced precariously on his friends' shoulders. The two teams of pyramids then tottered towards each other, locked together and wobbled in mock battle. The boys just about had time to shout their slogans – '*Yudu kha salaam hai*', loosely meaning 'Come and fight' or 'Welcome to war' – before they toppled to the ground, giggling.

Boys' activities while herding tended to occur in similar places at similar times of the year, and thus, over time, particular grazing areas around Bemni had come to be understood locally as 'children's areas' (*bachche ke ilaqe*). For example, the flat, plains-like, area at Changeri was perfect for organised games such as *kabaddi*, *puria* and cricket. This area had become so strongly associated with children and their herding practices that, when Anita and I returned from our regular afternoons with children at Changeri, we were often teased by adults for having spent time at the 'children's place'. Adults laughed that we had become 'childlike' (*jaise bachche*) as a result.

Herding practices also served to reinforce local masculinities. The forms of naughtiness and spirited competition that boys undertook while herding bolstered their claims to be becoming successful men. Their non-work activities typically emphasised strength, bravery, agility and balance, all skills that were important for other work performed by men in the village. Fighting games, in particular, consolidated notions of boys as rough, errant and 'naughty' (*shetaan*). Consideration of boys' games also underlines the spontaneous character of their actions while herding. The passage of the seasons lent a certain level of predictability of herding, but children nevertheless improvised within this pattern, creating for themselves opportunities to forage, eat, play and chat. At a finer level, boys rarely set out with the intention of, say, playing *puria* or having a play-fight. Rather, they improvised opportunistically according to the people, time and material resources available. Indeed, this very inventiveness itself appeared to be an aspect of how people defined young masculinities.

Youth masculinities in Bemni were shaped by caste, however. GCs had a longer tradition than did SCs of entering the army, in which toughness, bravery and a certain type of male camaraderie were highly prized. Moreover, GC adult men tended to be a little more prominent in village cricket games than SC men.

The most important caste difference in boys' herding practices in Bemni related to song. Although GC boys could sing a wide range of Garhwali songs, they tended to restrict their singing to specific events. For example, young people, including GC boys, regularly put on music evenings and plays, and rehearsed acts for the big fair (*mela*) in September. There were also several village-level ceremonies – for example, during the wheat harvest in June – as well as household religious ceremonies (*pujas*) in which young people sang and danced, and in which GC boys took part. While all families enjoyed singing Garhwali songs at celebrations and listening to singers on the radio, singing was not an everyday practice for GC boys outside these events. Singing was accorded no real value among GC boys or adult men, and those with gifted voices received no specific attention. By contrast, there were several SC men in the village who were professional musicians. All the musicians regularly employed in the village – drummers, bagpipers, accordion players and the singing trainers for school dramas – were men from musical schedules castes. For SC boys, therefore, becoming a skilful singer carried with it a reputation, and the possibility of future employment – the real marker of successful masculinity. Moreover, the singing of local Garhwali songs was an entertaining means of storytelling and comedy, and the rather static task of herding provided an ideal opportunity to practise the latest songs of regional singers.

SC boys' singing constituted a type of herding 'subculture'. Their songs typically celebrated aspects of the natural environment in Garhwal. They sang about the mountains' resources, such as the water, said to be beautifully cold and fresh, the grass, which was plentiful but which grew on dangerously steep slopes, and the abundant and life-giving forest. Some songs praised the local area, including Bemni village itself and the high peaks of Trishul visible from the village. Other songs were more cosmopolitan in their subjects, with frequent reference to the struggles of migrant Garhwali men in faraway cities or army regiments. Yet others were concerned with the role of external agents in local settings. These included a song about the ski resort at the nearby town of Auli, in which a man beseeches a woman to join him in seeing the 'five star hotel' and the 'trolley car'. In another song, a man urges his sister-in-law to defy her mother and participate in a Special Security Bureau weapons training course, a programme implemented by the Indo-Tibetan Border Police in border villages, including Bemni, to prepare civilians for the possibility of Chinese invasion.

SC boys enjoyed competing informally over the number of songs they could recite and the skill with which they sang. Especially good singers received great respect from their peers and were given prestigious nicknames of famous Garhwali singers. Ashish was a particularly talented singer, and would regularly weave together a mix of several songs, linking them seamlessly into a rendition that lasted fifteen or twenty minutes. One such example began with a plea to pray for the health of their forest, imploring villagers to plant trees to ensure clean air and plentiful water. It merged into a lament about the river Ganges, complaining that the people in the north Indian plains were poisoning the water, which is now inferior to their mother's milk. The next song told of a girl who wore lots of make-up, and whose eyes seemed to be looking for someone through the kohl. The final song, again merged without a break, was a muse on the trials of the seasons, asking ‘How can we live through these long cold nights, or through the sunless days of cloudy July?’. Groups of children also organised team singing competitions; one team would start singing a few lines of a Garhwali song, and the word on which they ended was the word that the other team had to begin their extract of another Garhwali song. This would continue back and forth between teams until one team could not match the word with a new song.

The masculinities produced by SC boys singing in the pastures were therefore similar to the masculine styles of GC boys in their emphasis on showmanship, talent and rivalry. Indeed, many SC boys both sang and played many of the games associated with GC boys. But SCs’ emphasis on singing lent a specific character to their vision of young male accomplishment.

Girls were also heavily involved in herding, and in finding ways to use their work to have fun and pursue their own ends. The following vignette of a day spent herding with a small group of GC girls gives a sense of the range of activities in which girls (including SCs) engaged.

On a dull, chilly day in late November, Anita and I wandered towards Silgwani, a forested grazing area below Bemni village where for the past few days several people had gathered with their livestock. We soon came across Deepa (aged fifteen), Manju (aged fourteen) and Chaita (aged sixteen), who had been herding every day for a couple of months. They had arrived around 9 a.m., when the schoolchildren had also dropped off their cows on their way to class. Despite the real threat of leopards in the area, those families were forced to risk leaving their cattle to graze alone while the children were at school, relying on the goodwill of the present herders to keep half an eye on them. We sat to chat with Deepa, Manju and Chaita for a while before two other girls, Savitri (aged fourteen) and Sutti (aged sixteen), arrived. They both had cows, and Savitri also had a goat. Sutti had long since dropped out of school, while Savitri was still in class six but had been asked to miss school to look after the goat and cows. We sat chatting for a while; the girls took turns to run off to look after their cows. Deepa, Manju and Chaita decided to move to a sunnier patch where they could also see their cows.

Anita dozed off while Deepa took over her knitting. Deepa claimed that she was an expert knitter, and liked to learn new designs. She admired Anita’s headscarf, and planned to make a similar one. Manju told how her sister-in-law had brought back an excellent design for a sweater after visiting her natal home recently. They began to talk about school. Chaita explained that she had dropped out of school last year. She had spilt boiling tea on her leg in October and the burns had become infected, taking two months to heal, during which time she could not walk. She missed so much school that, by the time she was better, she was so behind she dropped out. She laughed that she was sixteen but did not even have a class five pass. Manju and Deepa had both dropped out two years ago, aged twelve and thirteen, respectively.

Deepa suddenly shivered, and wanted to get warm. She suggested they construct a swing. They first tossed a rope high into the branch of a nearby tree, but decided the branch was not strong enough and moved to another tree. Here they made two swings, so Deepa and Manju sat on one each. Then, in fits of giggles, they faced each other and stretched their legs out in front of them, resting their feet on each other's laps so that they swung together like a boat.

After a few minutes the girls then ran off to gather up the cows again, ushering them towards a more open area, before collapsing on the ground again in the sun. They complained about the cold, the clouds just letting through glimpses of sun. Deepa mentioned all the recent leopard attacks, reeling off whose animals had been killed or attacked. The cow that had been killed on the road to Chapra had been quite young, with a calf about to be born in two months. The girls spoke in hushed tones about its beauty: 'It was totally white.' Deepa continued:

> The leopard attacked it on the road but dragged it above the path, where it was eaten by vultures. The same man who owned the cow also had a goat killed in Gwar recently. He was leading it by a rope when the leopard attacked it from behind. The man turned and frightened it away but the goat bled to death. Oh, and did you hear about [X], whose cow was killed by a leopard? The leopard left it and would have come back to eat it at night. So, to punish the leopard, he covered the carcass with poison from the shop. But the leopard was too clever and didn't touch it, so it didn't die. But then the vultures ate the carcass and they will die instead.

The other girls' eyes widened, and they looked scared.

Deepa changed the subject to weddings, especially the impending marriage of Mohan Singh. They discussed the rumours of his fiancée's beauty and competence as a worker, and the merits of her natal village. Their concentration waned, so we sat cross-legged for a game of *garra* using stones found nearby. They threw and caught stones in a sequence of embellished moves, the stones landing on the back of their hand or between their fingers.

The girls broke off to shoo the cows away from a prickly plant. When they returned to throwing stones, they began to fling them in a rather desultory fashion at a rock in the grass. They discussed what they would do if a leopard came now, and Deepa tickled the others because she knew they were scared. 'You'd be so scared,' she joked, needling the others with her words and digging her hands into their ribs.

As this story of Deepa and her friends suggests, girls, like boys, found many opportunities to 'play' (*khelna*) while herding. I participated in numerous similar herding trips with GC girls and SC girls during the course of my fifteen months in the village. But girls' activities differed from those of boys in certain respects, being less oriented around naughtiness and more concerned with structured games, conversation and 'productive' activities such as knitting.

Girls often used their herding time to collect wild fruits or nuts. In July girls foraged for tiny wild strawberries in the forests of Bengana. We made delicious feasts by mixing the miniscule fruit with parcels of freshly ground chilli and coriander brought from home. From August to October girls spent hours beneath walnut trees, throwing stones to knock the nuts to the ground. When they had collected a pile, we sat chatting as we crushed the kernels beneath rocks and prised out pieces of nuts with a pin. Later, while herding during the cold winter days in Gwar, the girls took small picks with them and dug tubers known as *chiuna* from the ground. These were often rubbed clean of the mud and eaten immediately, raw and crunchy. At other times they gathered up their hoard and took them home, where they were cooked as a rather slimy vegetable and eaten with bread. On frosty winter days the girls would build a small fire, usually not big enough to give out any real warmth, but nevertheless offering a focus around which to huddle, while regularly rearranging the sticks or jumping up to gather more.

SC and GC girls also occasionally sang, though I never witnessed the kind of competitive singing in which the SC boys engaged. Rather, girls tended to sing in casual groups, and for shorter periods. The songs of SC girls and GC girls did not differ noticeably in terms of their content and form. Girls' songs often concerned the natural environment and how it helped or hindered their work, as well as the cruelties of mother-in-laws. Many of the songs also incorporated girls' fears – be they about the forest or the social pressures in the village. For example, I heard a GC girl sing about a woman in the forest who meets a government Forest Department officer on patrol. He asks her why she has come so far into the forest, warning her that a leopard or tiger might come. He wants to confiscate her sickle as a punishment for coming so far. But she pleads with him, 'My mother-in-law will be very angry. They are bad and will beat me.'

On other occasions girls' songs were full of the pleasures of mountain life and the particular advantages of Bemni as a place to live. 'In my village everything is beautiful. There are no steep cliffs from which to fall. The water is fresh and very cold,' one girl sang. Another girl sang of how the sun shines in Bemni while the steep mountains cast dark shadows on less fortunate villages nearby.

As the vignette of Deepa showed, girls spent a great deal of time knitting while herding, especially in the winter. They would take their work everywhere, knitting as they walked closely behind the cows, somehow managing not to trip on the uneven rocky paths. Girls talked about how the cold weather suddenly made them want to start, and that during the hot weather they 'just did not feel like it' (*man nahin lag raha*). For the young girls, their efforts were never destined for wearable garments; their skills did not warrant the use of new and expensive wool. Instead, they would unravel old and unusable knitted clothes, using the wool to make simple squares that were later unravelled and reknitted endlessly. They knitted at other times, too, but the long periods of free time while herding provided the rare privacy for girls to swap techniques and teach each other new patterns. Older, more skilled girls discussed the latest fashions in headscarf design or sleeveless sweaters. Knitting was a respected skill and one that formed part of a suite of desirable feminine attributes that could be physically displayed.

As among boys, girls' activities while herding tended to reflect and deepen prevailing gendered norms. The ways in which girls multi-tasked while chatting and herding were different from the kinds of activities in which boys engaged, more often having a 'productive' element. Girls simulated their mothers, who always seemed to be engaged in a task and rarely did nothing. Moreover, girls' activities while herding provided a basis for developing skills, such as dexterity, keen eyesight and coordination, that were perceived to be valuable for women, particularly by potential in-laws.

What is also striking about the herding activities of children in Bemni, especially boys, was the extent to which they improvised creatively to fashion opportunities for pleasure from the local environment. They learnt, too, about the countryside they inhabited. They tested themselves: who could climb the highest? Who would be the bravest with a lizard in his hands? And they applied and developed their practical sense through such antics as erecting a swing or playing with a pipe. The term 'wayfaring' (Ingold 2007) nicely captures the extent to which children were constantly in conversation with their environment while herding, even while it is important to remember that not all young people were equally capable of engaging in such meaning-filled travel across the local landscape.

A herding *puja*

Alongside the everyday trips to herd cattle were occasional 'special events', in which young people's intimate relationship to local environments was thrown into stark relief. These special events included games organised in advance involving both boys and girls, and religious acts of worship of various types. The most notable incident was an annual event when a group of children built a small temple and organised a *puja* (act of worship).

Religious celebrations were an integral part of the seasonal rhythm of life in Bemni. Villagers celebrated a number of 'official' one- or two-day *pujas* that occur in the Hindu calendar, such as Diwali, as well as locally salient longer events, including the Pandav Lila (see Sax 2002) and the Nanda Devi Yatra in September. Individual households also performed *pujas* at different times of the year, such as in late April before the first major harvests of the year. In between the large festivals and household rituals were several collective village-based *pujas*. One of these *pujas* occurred in October, when villagers thanked the gods for protecting livestock, particularly during the slippery monsoon conditions that could claim livestock lives, and when swelling leeches caused havoc in the noses of cattle. They also asked for the future protection of the livestock and their herders from forest-dwelling ghosts, wildlife and tough conditions. Although the *puja* was conducted by a small handful of adults, it was attended predominately by children, as the major herders. This autumn herding *puja* was Bemni's only adult-led *puja* in which children were the key recipients and which related directly to children's work. Rather than simply being oriented 'upwards' to the gods, the *puja* marked and sustained the relationships of mutual dependence between adults and children upon which the successful reproduction of Bemni's household economy rested.

Since 1993 young people had also organised their own 'herding *puja*', mirroring the one held by adults. The young people's *puja* was held in June, during the children's school holidays. Young people said that their own herding *puja* was important in order to protect them and their cattle from the deprecations of the jungle, the wild animals, foul weather and the dangers of the steep mountain landscape. They also talked of the dangers posed by malevolent spirits and retold stories of people who had seen ghosts in the forest: foxes with human heads, old women who disappeared as you watched. In addition, they sometimes discussed the dangers of being possessed by a 'bad ghost'. Young people said that a herding *puja* would protect them from occasional attacks from ghosts as well as keeping their cattle safe.

In June 2003 young people expanded their herding *puja* by building a temple for the first time. The decision to build a temple seems to have been taken on the spur of the moment. We were at Changeri, a pasture relatively close to the village, and some boys were playing around with some loose stones at the derelict missionaries' house ('Izzai Bungla'). 'Let's build a temple,' one boy said cheerfully, and we were all quickly shepherded into action. The children's roles varied according to their age and gender. Older boys (thirteen to seventeen years old) guided the construction, while the girls and younger children (aged six to twelve) of both sexes did much of the manual labour. Seventeen-year-old Mahvir, in particular, organised the workforce and allocated roles. He and some other boys drew up the lines of the walls and smashed stones into shapes that they shuffled and squeezed into neat, densely packed walls. Meanwhile, the younger boys and girls went tirelessly back and forth collecting stone slabs from the old house (Figures 4.2 and 4.3).

It took the children three afternoons to construct the temple, combining their building work with their herding responsibilities. Once finished it was an impressive sight. It was small, but painstakingly finished, with tiny alcoves for placing incense and offerings to the gods. Located just in front of the 'Izzai Bungla', it commanded striking views over the village and the surrounding

Figure 4.2 Children collect stones from a derelict building to make their temple

Figure 4.3 Making the temple

Figure 4.4 Cooking the feast for the herding *puja*

forests. The children said the temple would be dedicated to their special god, Krishna. They claimed a particular affinity with Krishna, for he was said to have spent his own childhood herding cattle and playing with his friends.

It was some days before the children could find time to conduct the inaugural *puja* at their temple; the start of the rains had prompted a sudden rush of leaf collection that cut into their herding time. When a suitable day arrived, Mahvir called other children to attend and told them to bring contributions of flour, rice, *daal*, spices, sugar, oil and whatever large cooking pots and water containers they could find.

By 11.30 a.m. Mahvir, Rakesh (aged sixteen) and Mukkar Singh (aged sixteen) had lit a fire and sent ten small boys between the ages of six and ten to collect wood. All the children had been granted their parents' permission to bring food contributions, and piles of plastic bags were neatly arranged under a nearby tree. Mukkar began by kneading a huge ball of dough, and asked Anita and me to make *puri*. Mahvir made a second fire while Rakesh was sent to grind the *daal* using a large round stone and a flat slab found nearby. Mahvir washed the *daal* and put it on to boil. With the *puri* finished, Mukkar and Mahvir used the left-over oil to make *halwa*, which, once ready, was put aside and replaced on the fire by a huge pot of rice. By 1.30 p.m. the rice was cooking and the *daal* was almost ready (see Figure 4.4). Meanwhile, the young children ran to obey Mahvir's orders to collect more wood or water, wash plates or sweep the area in front of the temple. Once the food was ready, Mukkar Singh began to organise the samples of food neatly in the temple. He laid out five *puri*, each with dollops of *halwa* and ghee, and sprinkled pinches of turmeric over them. He then lit five incense sticks and spoke words of praise to Lord Krishna, son of Nanda Babu.

The young children were told to sit cross-legged in a line on the ground. Mukkar smeared turmeric *tikkis* on everyone's foreheads, and each of the children was handed a *puri* with *halwa* as *prasad*. The older boys washed plates, the lids of pans and *parath* (a large plate for kneading dough) for the children to eat from and served them vast piles of rice and *daal*. Once the children had finished (and many returned for a second helping) the plates were washed and Mukkar, Anita and I ate. Having adopted the role of chief chefs, Mahvir and Rakesh ate last.

When everyone had eaten, the *halwa* and *puri* were divided and packaged into plastic bags for everyone to take to their siblings who had not come. As other young people continued to arrive, they too were handed helpings of leftovers. Any remaining rice was given to the cows, and the large pots left to soak. Within minutes the entire set-up had been packed away, and Mahvir called everyone together for a mixed game of *puria*.

The children's *puja* was planned to a greater extent than most other non-work activities carried out by children when herding. But there was also an important spontaneous – *jugaad*-like – element to the children's practices. They had not constructed a temple in the past, but the crumbling missionary's house sparked them to build. Beyond its importance as a means of warding off danger, the temple construction and *puja* offer a compelling example of the capacity of young people to improvise spontaneously while herding. The particular form the temple took, its structure and the materials employed were issues worked out in practice as young people collaborated with each other. The work also served to inscribe meaning in that environment; some villagers now refer to the area in front of the missionaries' building as 'the place of the herding temple', and it is reconstructed each year by new generations of young people. Moreover, young people often pointed out the site of the temple to Anita and me, and to older villagers, as a type of visual reminder of their developing maturity, knowledge and ability to shape the local environment to reflect their own goals.

Boys' work on the temple and their engagement in the *puja* ceremony reproduced gendered expectations of young people's behaviour, especially the notion that boys would be future leaders in the village. Although boys or adult men did not generally cook at home, it was always men who organised and directed the preparation of feasts at large village occasions, such as weddings and the October herding *puja*, or feeding the participants during the Pandav Lila. On these occasions, women were usually brought in to make *roti* and *puri*, but men made the *daal*, rice and other large dishes. This was similarly the case at the children's *puja*, when Anita and I were asked to make *puri* while the boys, under a male leader, prepared and organised the rest of the food. The *puja* ceremony thus provided a context in which boys rehearsed and reproduced local notions of appropriate masculinity.

The children's annual *puja* celebration demonstrates that children not only engaged in games understood as 'childish', they also simulated practices usually considered 'adult'. Children and parents did not understand the *puja* as 'play' (*khel*) but as an important activity that helped to prepare them for later life. In her writing on children's lives in rural Sudan, Katz (2004) coins the terms 'playful work' and 'workful play' to suggest the mutual imbrications of labour and enjoyment. But these formulations do not fully capture the seriousness of some of young people's everyday practices in Bemni.

The *puja* also shows that the subtle gradations that exist in terms of what work young people do (see Chapter 3) were also evident in the sphere of many of their non-work activities. The three sixteen-year-olds lit the fire while the younger boys collected firewood. Mukkar served as master of ceremonies during the preparation and serving of the food, while the younger boys played peripheral roles. Similar peer hierarchies emerged in other ways during children's activities while herding. Older boys were able to 'pull rank' to avoid work. I often witnessed an older boy order a younger boy to herd his cattle away from a restricted area while the older boy continued to chat or play with friends. On one occasion, when ten-year-old Diraj complained that he did not want to be left out of a cricket game to look after the cattle of an eighteen-year-old player, the older boy tossed Diraj a Rs. 1 coin and said that he had no choice. Peer hierarchies also emerged in child-only games. GC boys who were particularly good cricketers received respect and enjoyed a position of relative power and leadership among peer groups. SC boys similarly competed for respect by being the best singer, and, to a lesser extent, valued expertise in team games such as cricket, *puria* and *kabaddi*. Younger children rarely complained about their subordinate position within age hierarchies. For example, young boys recognised that their own future place at the centre of cricket matches and the *puja* depended upon their playing subordinate roles earlier on (compare Lave and Wenger 1991).

Conclusions

Although some young people performed a particular type of youthful 'rebellion' while herding livestock, most used herding to assist their parents with livestock-related and other household work. In the process, young people tried to thicken and strengthen the ties that bound them to other villagers. This was especially clear among girls, but also in the games and *puja* organised by boys.

Children's herding therefore had the double significance of being important for the reproduction of the household economy and key to young people's attempts to develop useful working relationships with each other.

At the same time, children could use the relatively undemanding work of herding as an opportunity for enjoyment and means of engaging closely with their local environment, practically and imaginatively. There is a rich literature within social science, especially youth studies, on work as a site of cultural production (for example Willis 1977; Joyce 1987; Gidwani 2001). As Willis (1977: 52) notes, work cultures 'are not just layers of padding between people and unpleasantness. They are appropriations in their own right, exercises of skill, motions, activities applied towards particular ends.' The complicated range of activities in which young people engaged while herding, including playing games and singing, highlights young people's capacity to appropriate herding for their own ends, and also offers a complement to the stark rendition of daily life in the diaries that I described in Chapter 3.

Herding also offered young people the chance to engage closely with their local environment. Commentators on urban youth have examined how environments mesh with people's social and cultural lives. Literature on street children around the world, as well as work on older 'youth', is full of references to young people's complex engagement with the materiality of the city, including their knowledge of the properties of 'the street', their circulation within urban space and their capacity to rework urban locations to reflect their own goals. For example, David Driskell, Carly Fox and Neema Kudva (2008) show that neighbourhood spaces served as a resource for youth in New York City keen to improve their locality. Young people acquired experience and confidence in the city through such simple acts as installing garbage cans on a street corner or improving a playground – successes that, once inscribed on the landscape, could provide the inspiration for future political acts. Jeffrey (2010) describes the manner in which educated but unemployed young people in urban north India recovered a sense of self-respect and mitigated hardship through forming into small groups at tea stalls, which in turn became spaces for social mobilisation.

My account of herding extends these studies through focusing on precisely how young people utilised and imagined their everyday work in the field and forest. The materials of the forest – everything from small pebbles to large trees, from birds' eggs to water pipes – were constantly being drawn in to young people's games and activities while herding. Moreover, young people frequently discussed the nature of the fields and forest while herding, imbuing them with particular qualities, such as 'danger' or 'beauty'.

Young people interacted with their environment while on the move, and the idea of 'wayfaring' (Ingold 2007) is instructive in its emphasis on how people can construct meaning out of environments in a spontaneous manner.

But in Ingold's hands the term risks distracting from the important inequalities in people's capacity to journey through local environments. Young people's capacity to herd in Bemni was closely circumscribed by gender. Young men had greater freedom to roam than did young women, who had to make careful calculations about where it was socially 'safe' to remain. For girls beyond the age of fourteen, the herding pastures took on a new and 'risky' significance, where, in the company of men of all ages, their reputations were open to scrutiny. Moreover, gender shaped the manner in which young people engaged with the environment while herding, especially in the case of older 'youth'. After the age of thirteen, boys tended to engage in rough games and forms of 'naughtiness' that aligned with gender stereotypes of boys and young men, while girls engaged in the more demure, patient and dexterous activities associated with femininity. Caste also influenced herding practices. GCs rarely encountered SCs while herding, and there were few opportunities for high-caste children to develop friendships or relationships of empathy with low castes.

Two further important points emerge that are not explicit in the existing studies of youth and the environment. First, young people's engagement with nature's materials – stones, sticks and lizards, for example – was more intense and intimate than it is typically for youth in urban areas; the Bemni case offers an especially compelling insight into how the environment can be entangled in young people's individual and social lives. Second, seasonal shifts in Bemni shaped these engagements profoundly. Herding patterns were closely linked with the agricultural and forest management cycle, shifts in the availability of grazing areas, the system of transhumance and fluctuations in labour availability. This seasonal cycle structured children's role in herding practices by shaping where and when children of different ages and castes could herd their livestock. Children's school timetable also influenced who herded cattle and when.

The manner in which social structures and the pressing demands of the agro-pastoral system shaped young people's work and room for manoeuvre was even more evident in the case of girls' efforts to collect leaves. The next chapter charts girls' efforts in this arena, while also further developing the overall point that young people built social agency through their engagement with the local environment.

5 Friendship in practice: collecting leaves in Bemni

A remarkable aspect of working in Bemni was the frequency with which young people talked about friends (*dost*, *duggree*) and friendship (*dostaana*). Friendship was important in all the tasks that children performed in the village. For example, boys and girls often established friendships while herding, and they preferred to go out to herd with other young people whom they considered to be 'friends'. Yet friendship was especially crucial in the case of the most gruelling task performed by girls in the forest: collecting leaf litter for cattle stalls. A close investigation of how girls collected leaves in Bemni in 2003 and 2004 offers an opportunity to reflect on friendship as it is conceptualised in contemporary social science, as well as to further address the issues of youth agency and young people's relationship to their environment.

Michel de Montaigne (1972 [1603]) famously defined friendship as a relationship between equals that expresses free choice and is founded on affection rather than calculations of individual gain. This definition has influenced much recent scholarly thinking on the topic (see Santos-Granero 2007 for a review). For example, Ray Pahl (1998: 113) conceptualises strong friendships as relationships 'detached from the fixtures of social role, status, and custom'. But many other studies of friendship have shown that it is bound up with people's interests and questions of power (Allan 1989; Bell and Coleman 1999). Rather than imagining friendship as primarily a personal matter and one characterised by free choice, as per Montaigne (1972 [1603]), scholars now are emphasising how friendship is inserted into the processes through which inequalities are reproduced and contested. The few existing studies in India certainly point towards the importance of pragmatic, utilitarian considerations in the emergence of friendships (Sangtin writers and Nagar 2006; Jeffrey 2010; compare Allan 1996).

Recent research on friendship and power has two strands. First, there are a set of studies, many of them ethnographic in nature, that present friendship as a means through which marginalised sections of society counter situations of powerlessness. Much of this work considers the links between friendship and public activism. Friendship may generate or sustain political protest, as David Featherstone (2008) has argued in his work on transnational anti-capitalist demonstrations in the 1990s and early 2000s. Friendship may also provide a basis for critiquing dominant power constructs at a more covert level (Sangtin writers and Nagar 2006). Alternatively, friendship may be a means for the poor to escape or mitigate poverty. For example, Tilo Gratz (2004) demonstrates that friendship plays an important role among poor artisanal gold miners in west Africa, allowing them to engage in mutually helpful behaviour in a threatening social environment. While not centrally concerned with friendship, much of the burgeoning literature on social capital within development studies makes a parallel point. The poor may be able to harness the social capital associated with relations of acquaintance and friendship so as to organise collectively and improve their lives (Coleman 1990; Putnam 1993; see Harriss 2002 for a critique).

A second strand of scholarship emphasises friendship as a medium of unequal social reproduction. This point is evident in recent research on patriarchy and friendship (for example Santos 2008), but comes across especially clearly in literature on class inequalities (for example Savage 2003). Most notably, Bourdieu (1984 [1979]) argues that the middle and upper classes in French society in the 1970s tended to possess a more influential and therefore 'useful' set of friends than those possessed by lower classes. Building on their social contacts, the rich were typically better placed to compete in various fields of social struggle, for example to enrol their children in prestigious schools, acquire secure employment and influence political decisions.

In this chapter, I combine the insights of these writing about friendship as a form of empowerment with research on the pernicious aspects of friendship so as to conceptualise friendship as a contradictory resource for young people. Friendship provides girls in the Indian Himalayas with social and cultural possibilities but also draws them more tightly into certain systems of dominance. In making these points, the chapter also advances the more general thesis that young people's agency in Bemni – their capacity to 'act effectively and exercise power' (Durham 2008: 175) – is expressed primarily by nurturing intimate ties within their home area rather than asserting independence. What also emerges strikingly from my account of friendship among girls collecting leaves in the Himalayas is the extent to which social relationships are forged through processes of environmental engagement. People nurture friendships through material practices that involve such things as gathering leaves, cutting twigs, building baskets and shouldering loads.

Leaf collection in Bemni

'Leaf litter', known as *suttoor* in Garhwali, refers to the leaf litter covering the forest floor. In Bemni it was used as bedding in livestock stalls, and, once soiled, the mixture of dung and decomposing leaves, known as *gobar*, was scattered across the fields as organic fertiliser. The leaf litter was typically made up of oak and rhododendron leaves, and collecting these leaves absorbed a great deal of girls' time in the village.

Leaf collection was highly seasonal. Although leaf litter was needed for cattle bedding throughout the year, villagers in Bemni had developed a pattern in which leaves were collected in intensive phases to fit around the agricultural cycle and the system of transhumance. The main leaf collection periods occurred around the time of each shift between settlements, either just beforehand or immediately afterwards, depending on the expected workload before or after moving. Once collected, the leaves were stored, usually to last throughout the period spent in each settlement, Gwar, Bemni and Danda. This pattern, which had emerged in response to fluctuations in labour availability, drew on the labour of both adults and children, usually at different times. Children played a crucial role in providing adjustable labour during times of peak agricultural activity.

In villages depending to a lesser extent on agriculture, and where the system of transhumance was no longer practised, leaf collection tended to occur on a regular basis throughout the year. In such cases, children's contribution may not have been so critical, and stores of leaves were not required. A 'punctuated' pattern of leaf collection was followed in villages, such as Bemni, where small-scale transhumance was practised.

Leaf collection in Bemni fell into four main periods, coinciding with the four yearly transhumant shifts. Leaves were collected from forest areas nearest to the settlement where leaves were stored, so reducing the distance people had to travel carrying heavy loads. The first period occurred in late March and early April, at the time of the shift from Gwar up to Bemni. This period was relatively quiet in the fields, so adults did most of the collection. The children attended school on the winter timetable from 10 a.m. to 4 p.m., so, with the days still short, there was insufficient time in the morning or evening for children to make the long journey to the forests.

The second period of leaf collection began in June, in preparation for the July shift from Bemni up to Danda. This was a particularly busy period in the fields, and the children, who were on school holidays for June, bore the brunt of the leaf collection. The children sought to create a sufficiently large store to see their families through much of the period in Danda. If supplies ran low, children would replenish their stores during the afternoons, when they herded the livestock after their mornings spent at school (from 7 a.m. to midday).

The third phase of leaf collection started in the middle of September in anticipation of the early October return from Danda down to Bemni. It was a busy time for adults harvesting potatoes, and leaf collection fell largely to the children. The school day had returned to the winter 10 a.m. start, so, if they set off at 5.30 a.m., the children had just enough time to collect leaves before school. They usually dropped off their baskets in Bemni on their way to class. Children could also collect leaves at weekends and during the two-week long Divali holiday, which falls in October or November.

The final period of leaf collection occurred between December and March. In early December households returned to the lower settlement of Gwar. Households were no longer busy in the fields, and so women, often accompanied by girls, could collect leaf litter as well as wood. The short winter days, and the longer uphill walk to school, meant that children could no longer collect leaves on school days. But weekends and holidays provided opportunities for them to help.

The collection of leaf litter for livestock bedding, and of fresh green leaves and green grass for fodder, were all part of the woman's domain (see also Shiva 1989; Mehta 1996; Gururani 2002). When boys did become involved in leaf collection, it was typically for short periods and in a more lackadaisical manner than that of girls. Gender differences in propensity to engage in leaf collection also reflected the relative bargaining power of children within the household. Parents tended to regard sons as inevitably 'naughty' and wayward, and this allowed boys some room to manoeuvre in disputes about whether they should collect leaves. Moreover, parents tended to value the education of their sons over the education of their daughters. As in the case of tasks in the home (see Chapter 3), I frequently watched boys being able to negotiate with their parents to avoid leaf collection using their studies as an excuse. For example, Sanjay (GC, fifteen) was occasionally called upon to help with leaf collection. He was happy to work during his summer school holidays in June, but he was reluctant to go when their leaf supplies dwindled in the autumn and the weather was damp and cool. I witnessed two incidents in which Sanjay steadfastly refused to collect leaves, saying it was too cold, citing the need to do homework and complaining that he could not go without his friends. Sanjay's mother was philosophical: 'If his friend isn't going, we can't force him to go to the forest alone. And when he refuses to collect leaves because his hands are too cold – well, we can't force him.' Few girls were able to provoke such a forgiving response in their parents.

Among girls, caste and class influenced their bargaining power – a point that emerges through a comparison of the experiences of Bina, a twelve-year-old GC girl from a relatively prosperous household, and Papita, a ten-year-old SC girl from a poor family. In 2003 Bina went to live in her paternal uncle's household, where she provided valuable extra labour. Alongside her uncle's two daughters-in-law, Bina's additional contribution to dry leaf collection helped ease the household's forest work. On an almost daily basis in September, Bina collected leaves before school, in preparation for the shift from Danda down to Bemni. Sometimes, however, Bina did not want to go to the forest, and would excuse herself from leaf duties by claiming she had homework to finish and stressing the importance of her studies. Her uncle was a keen advocate for girls' education. Sometimes he would compel Bina to collect leaves, but on many other occasions he allowed her to stay at home.

In contrast to Bina, Papita, the oldest of three daughters in a SC household, could not avoid collecting leaves. As the only working daughter, Papita made a vital contribution to her mother's forest and agricultural work. In September Papita, like Bina, went almost daily to the forest for leaf litter. But Papita accompanied her mother rather than friends, leaving nobody at home to prepare their breakfast. In order to be home in time to cook, change and allow Papita to reach the Bemni Primary School on time, mother and daughter set off early. Leaving in the dark, at 3 to 4 a.m., they travelled with other SC women and children, returning home around 6 to 7 a.m. Although these early morning trips left Papita tired even before her school day began, she had little power to resist. Papita's mother insisted that, despite the impact on Papita's schooling, she needed her help. 'I am forced to send Papita to work,' she stated simply.

Reflecting gender differences, I focused my research on girls' leaf collection work. It was difficult for me to accompany SC girls to collect leaves. Anita was reluctant to participate in these trips, and I had not built up the level of rapport required to ensure that SC girls and women would trust me on these expeditions. As a result, this chapter concentrates on the practices of GC girls (labelled simply 'girls' henceforward).

Village expectations

Girls usually collected leaves in the early mornings, when the ground was still dew-soaked and the softened leaves were easier to handle. They would set off before dawn, travelling to the forests surrounding the village in groups of between two and ten. Their journeys, like the meanderings of young people while herding, were forms of 'wayfaring'. On the steep climb, girls would often stop to talk to other small groups. They had to keep abreast of where other parties had been gathering leaves so as to avoid well-raked areas denuded of leaf litter. They often swapped information on where thorny plants had emerged, since these made the hand-raking of leaves painful. Still more important was knowledge of the changing conditions of leaves in different parts of the forest. Leaf litter had to be slightly damp. When very dry, the leaves became slippery and difficult to stack above the level of the basket. Although heavier, damp leaves stuck to each other and were more easily secured. The spikes on the edges of some leaves were also pliable when damp, but hard and sharp when dry, painfully piercing the skin when the girls were finger-raking. Dry, slippery leaves could also be hazardous while working on steep gradients; I frequently slipped and fell down the slope while collecting leaves.

Choosing a forest site to collect leaves often required a trade-off, however, between a collector's current knowledge of leaf availability, quality and general conditions with other factors, such as time. Those children who collected leaves before the school day were restricted to visiting the lower forests closest to their houses, irrespective of their yield. The children acknowledged that, although they would find a greater supply of leaves in higher forests, they had enough time only to collect lower down given that they had to reach home in time to eat, change and run to school before the 10 a.m. school assembly. Girls often spent several minutes on the hillside discussing these dilemmas with members of their own 'leaf collection team' and with other groups travelling up the mountain.

Having reached their chosen forest site, usually at least an hour's walk from home, the girls' leaf collection entailed their moving through a series of closely choreographed techniques. They began by raking the leaves from the ground with their fingers, walking backwards downhill and bringing the growing pile of leaves with them. After gathering several piles in this way, they threw the leaves into woven baskets, interspersing this activity with efforts to tamp the leaves down. Younger girls, up to the age of about eleven or twelve, typically stopped collecting once their basket was full to the brim. They slung the basket onto their backs and used string straps to carry it back to the village like a backpack.

The mechanics of leaf collection for older girls was more complex. Once they had filled their baskets to the brim, the girls would then set about constructing supports to enable them to carry an even greater load. They would find four flexible, 2-metre-long branches. They wove the thicker end of one branch through the side of their basket so that the thinner, leafier end stood proud above the top. They repeated this process with the second branch, placing it next to the first, before twisting the two branches together to make one strong branch. They then repeated this process on the opposite side of the basket, so that it now had two long twisted branches protruding from the top, like horns (Figure 5.1). The girls then cut two long sturdy branches with V shapes at the end to support the two branches sticking out of the basket, and returned to leaf collection. They raked the leaves against their ankles so that they formed dense packs and then placed these packs carefully on top of the basket, in each case using the basket's long horns to prevent them from slithering to the ground. Once the girls felt that the tower of leaves on their baskets was as high as possible, they brought the two twisted branches on opposite sides of the basket together, and knotted them together across the top of the piled leaves. Finally, as if that were not enough, the girls piled extra bundles of leaves on top of their colossal load, and secured them with sprigs of rhododendron, the radial leaves acting like hairpins to secure the bundles in place (Figure 5.2).

Leaf collection was a key means through which girls could establish a reputation for conscientiousness and competence in Bemni. Villagers tended to

Figure 5.1 Parwati threads side branches into her basket of leaves

have clear ideas about the quantity of leaves that should be collected by children of different ages. They typically felt that girls of twelve should carry baskets with leaves protruding well over the rim, and that by fifteen they should collect almost full-sized baskets by securing dense packs of leaves using branches looped across the top of the load. By the time girls were eighteen, their baskets should match those of adult women (Figure 5.2). These generalised 'standards' for girls of different ages were institutionalised in the village, although there were individual variations. Specific household circumstances, such as labour availability and sibling birth order, often influenced when girls began leaf collection, and their subsequent skill.

Parents did not monitor closely their own children's work in order to enforce village standards. They trusted that their children did as much work as they could manage, or as their experience allowed. Bina's mother was typical in her explanation: 'I am happy when Bina brings lots, but I don't say anything. It doesn't really matter if she brings lots or a little.' Prema's father spoke similarly, claiming:

> Whatever Prema brings, we think it is good. If she brings less, we don't say anything. We respect whatever she does. What can we do? She is only a child. We must give our children the right training.

Figure 5.2 Savitri (aged eighteen) carries a full sized basket, secured with branches and rhododendron twigs

Other parents said that they actively discouraged their children from carrying more than was expected of them. Parwati's mother used the never-ending nature of forest work to warn her against collecting too much. She would tell her that, no matter how much she brought from the forest, she would always have to go again. Similarly, Janki's mother said that

> Janki brings as much as she can or as much as she wants. If she brings less than usual, I say nothing. If she brings lots [more than usual], I say: 'Don't bring too much; you'll get ill if you bring too much.' She brings as much as she wants to, so we don't say anything.

Girls agreed that it was not parents who pressured them to meet village standards but, rather, 'other villagers' (*gaon ke log*) outside the family. There was a general tendency among adults to comment critically on the leaf collection abilities of other people's children, while keen not to put their own children under pressure in this regard.

Rather than engaging in a sustained way in the types of foot dragging and non-compliance described by Scott (1985), girls sought to meet or exceed adult expectations regarding appropriate standards of leaf collection. A ten-year-old girl said:

> When I meet other people in the forest, I think I should bring back as much as they do. I'm not shy of what my mother thinks, but, if I bring less, I become ashamed of what village people will say about me.

Similarly, a fourteen-year-old girl told me:

> If we collect just a little, village people will laugh and ask, 'Why did such a big girl bring so little?' If I see my friend has more [leaves in her basket] than me, I feel angry in my stomach. Then I have to collect more. I don't mind if older girls have more, but I don't want girls of my age to have more than me.

These types of statement were repeated on numerous occasions. Girls said that failing to meet village expectations would undermine their reputation as workers – they would be labelled 'lazy' (*sust*) or 'careless' (*laparwah*). By contrast, girls believed that those who met village standards acquired a reputation for hard work (*mehnat*) and, more broadly, for being 'good' (*achchhee*) and 'straight' (*seedha*).

In my own attempts to participate in leaf collection, I experienced the same pressure to conform to these social expectations. While I usually sought to carry baskets of leaves back from the forest, many villagers, including young people, were aware of my relative weakness and insisted that I carry only the tiny baskets usually reserved for small children. The sight of me carrying such baskets was the cause for much amusement, however, and opened me up to ridicule. I was a head taller than most adult women, and yet carried a fraction of the load that even a fourteen-year-old girl could manage. I was frequently met with laughter and comments about the ludicrous ratio between my height and the weight I carried. Although I knew my status did not entirely depend on my ability to perform such tasks, I found myself increasingly concerned about my reputation for 'incompetence'. The girls I accompanied during these trips often empathised with my concerns. Although they reassured me that, as an outsider, I was not subject to such assessment, they frequently sought to protect me from teasing. For example, on one occasion, as we neared the village on our return from the forest, two girls in their mid-teens repeatedly urged me to allow them to carry my small basket of leaves as well as their own huge baskets, thereby sparing me from jibes. At other times, when out of pride I attempted to carry larger baskets, the girls pleaded me to stop, citing my physical weakness. It was in these circumstances – caught between a desire to share the work, while knowing I was incapable of doing so, and a fear for the consequences of my meagre harvests on my reputation – that I came to understand parents' reluctance to monitor their own children's progress. Parents actively discouraged their children from carrying too much as a means of protecting them from excessive pressures to over-perform in the face of village scrutiny. I also became painfully aware of the demands that older villagers placed on Bemni girls.

Achieving leaf collection standards by friendship

Efficient leaf collection, and adherence to village standards, were founded on girls' relationships within leaf collection teams. These teams often consisted of groups of sisters, cousins or near neighbours. Sisters and cousins had grown up in close proximity and had often developed a working relationship. Among non-kin, near neighbours were favoured team-mates, because forest trips required early morning starts, and children found it easier to set off with those living nearby. Yet girls exercised a degree of choice about whom they accompanied to the forest. Moreover, notions of friendship tended to be more important than kinship or residence in how girls talked about their working relationships with peers. With the exception of sisters, who called each other by the kinship term *bahn* or *didi* ('big sister'), girls tended to label cousins, more distant kin relations or neighbours with whom they collected leaves as 'friends' (*dugriyan*). The relationship between friendship and leaf collection came across most strongly during participant observation. In ten separate instances, I watched teams of two or three girls of similar age and ability cooperating in the forest. The example of Bina (twelve) and Gita (thirteen) is instructive.

Bina and Gita were near neighbours in the highest of Bemni's three settlements. In September they went almost daily to the forest before school. Gita and Bina had similar leaf-collecting skills, and had both recently learnt to tie up their baskets. Anita and I accompanied Gita and Bina on a leaf collection trip on a rather grey September morning in 2003. We started from the house as a group of four, but soon saw a number of other leaf collection teams tramping up the mountainside. We soon joined the others to form a large group of about twenty-five, mainly girls but also four or five older women.

Once fairly high up the mountain, the women and children stood about to debate where they should all go to collect leaves. Bina and Gita talked first as a twosome. Bina had a good knowledge of the relative merits of different sections of the forest at this time of year. Gita had recently heard where good, damp leaves were to be found. Their combined knowledge, which emerged during conversation, served as a basis for selecting a suitable site. They then augmented their knowledge through listening to the points made by other women and girls. Statements about the forest – 'No, that area is too thorny'; 'That part of the forest has been plucked clean of leaves'; 'There were bears seen in that part' – filled the air. After a few minutes the debate died down, and the different leaf collection teams set off on their different paths.

When we reached the area that Bina and Gita eventually chose, the girls immediately set to work raking leaves and stuffing their baskets. Having piled high her basket, Bina was struggling to fill it with the last bundles. Gita suggested that, rather than work alone, Bina should first help her to finish her basket. Bina held the twisted tying branches in place while Gita raked the leaves into small and uneven flat packs and placed them between the sticks. The girls took a branch each and jointly tied the leaves on top. With one basket finished, they turned immediately to Bina's load. Gita nimbly climbed to a nearby tree to cut some flexible branches, which they wove into each side of the basket. Again, Gita raked and made flat packs of leaves while Bina kept them in place with the twisted branches. Soon, with their combined efforts, both baskets were tied and secure. They helped each other to launch the heavy baskets onto their backs and scampered down the hill towards home.

This episode was similar to many other occasions that I observed, and highlights the importance of friendship and reciprocity. Friendship seemed to operate at two social scales. First, there was a generalised type of friendship among the girls and young women in the group of twenty-five that climbed the mountain together. This relatively diffuse camaraderie was important in allowing different teams of leaf collectors to obtain up-to-date knowledge about where to collect leaf litter. A second and more important dimension of friendship, however, was represented by the intimate relations that characterised the small leaf collection teams, in this case Bina and Gita. Had Bina and Gita not helped each other, they would each have failed to tie their baskets. Through assisting each other in the forest, the two girls were able to negotiate collectively village norms that dictated the productivity and skill with which they should collect leaves. They emerged from the forest with baskets that met social expectations.

The types of friendship that existed between Bina and Gita in September 2003 constituted a frequent topic of discussion among my informants, and we often discussed friendship when we went to the forest to collect leaves, while conducting other tasks or during brief periods resting in the village. Although I was careful not to frame these conversations in the context of forest practices, most girls instantly related good friends to notions of peer support during forest work. Bina said a 'firm friend' (*pukkee dugree*) is someone 'who doesn't leave me alone in the forest. We collect leaves and wood for each other.' Similarly, a thirteen-year-old girl told me independently that friends 'go to the forest together to collect leaves. If I've not finished collecting my leaves, but my friend has finished, she'll come and help me collect leaves.' As these statements suggest, girls imagined friendship not as a static 'thing' but as the lived product of how certain peers worked in the forest, their commitment and skill, and their regard for the activities and needs of team members. More broadly, it is evident that there was a dialectical relationship between friendship and leaf collection. The idea that it is valuable to possess 'friends' was crucially important in the formation and maintenance of leaf collection teams.

The manner in which collecting leaves both reflected and reaffirmed friendship was often evident among girls with different skill levels, as the example of the work of Parwati (fifteen) and Sarita (fourteen) demonstrates. Parwati's parents had long-term health problems, and she was therefore compelled to assume primary responsibility for leaf collection from a young age. Parwati was consequently more skilled at this task than Sarita, who had not started leaf collection until much later. In spite of their unequal abilities, however, Parwati and Sarita collaborated while collecting leaves for much of 2003 and considered themselves 'firm friends'. Their friendship became especially evident during a trip to collect leaves late in September 2003.

Parwati and Sarita walked up the mountain in a group of about twenty-five girls and women on a fresh day that month. Spirits were high, and the large group of girls and women were chattering noisily on a wide range of subjects. When we reached a large rock, the group of twenty five began debating the different places in the forest in which they might work. Parwati and Sarita listened attentively, voiced a few of their own ideas and then set off towards an area fairly nearby.

Once on site, Parwati and Sarita began by working together, raking leaves from the ground with their fingers while shuffling backwards downhill. The two girls then concentrated on filling their own baskets. Parwati skilfully stuffed her basket with leaves, cut branches, threaded them through the basket and twisted them together. It was not long before Parwati had collected dense packs of leaves, placed these bundles carefully on top of the basket and used her twisted branches to secure the load. Nowhere near finished, Sarita stopped briefly to marvel at Parwati's basket. In envious and admiring tones, she pointed out how high above the basket the leaves were stacked and how neatly and securely tied it was.

While Parwati had been working, Sarita had managed to collect dense bundles of leaves and secure branches on her basket. But, when she came to tie the branches together at the top of her basket, they snapped, and leaves tumbled across the forest floor. Sarita hid her face, giggling with embarrassment. Parwati was quick to help her friend. The two girls gathered up the leaves and Parwati watched Sarita knotting together the broken pieces of branches, offering advice when necessary and interceding a few times to steady the basket and check that the branches would hold. Sarita eventually tied and secured her own load. Although Sarita's basket had involved several false starts, when finally ready it looked almost identical to Parwati's. The two girls could return to their homes confident that villagers would look approvingly on their work.

The example of Parwati and Sarita's September trip underlines the importance of camaraderie in exchanging information about where to collect leaves. The vignette also illustrates how the making of impressively large baskets often rests on close friendships. During conversations with Sarita a few days after the trip in late September it was clear that she was acutely aware of what was socially expected of her as a fifteen-year-old girl, not far from marriageable age. She had a clear idea of the size of basket she should carry and of the skill with which it should be secured. She admired girls who were stronger and aspired to master the skills they possessed. Sarita's trips to the forest were thus displays of pride and perseverance. In the privacy of the forest she could laugh at her failed attempts, but she never entered the more public arena of the village with an imperfect basket. It was Parwati's friendship and help that enabled her to do so. Close friendship was the medium through which village norms concerning levels of competence were realised and reproduced. Since most girls were able to form friendship groups that provided a sense of security and achievement, the majority view among girls in Bemni was that leaf collection was not too onerous, and could even be associated with 'fun' (*mazaa*). Many girls told me that their collecting leaves was something that they 'put their heart to' (*man laga*), and they sometimes said that they went to the forests on the basis of 'enthusiasm' (*shauq se*).

The type of assistance offered by Parwati to Sarita was not purely altruistic. Parwati knew that if Sarita returned to the village with a poor basket it would reflect badly on both of them. Villagers often assessed the work of the teams of girls who returned from the forest as well as assessing individual girls. Yet these pragmatic considerations cannot fully explain Parwati's actions. Parwati helped Sarita because she considered her a 'friend': someone whom she trusted and who might be able to provide her with some form of assistance in the future. Moreover, the process of leaf collection constantly consolidated the bonds of mutual trust and appreciation that existed between the two girls. What was especially striking about their working relationship was how both girls could anticipate the needs and abilities of the other. This intuition was expressed most clearly through the body, for example in the instinctive way in which Parwati and Sarita choreographed the raking of leaves and in the manner in which Parwati leant against Sarita's basket to prevent it from toppling.

The example of Parwati and Sarita's collaboration in the forest building baskets of leaves shows, too, that certain types of inequality are often inherent in friendships. Recent anthropological research has shown that friendship frequently occurs between people unequally placed within local and broader hierarchies. For example, friendship may develop between patrons and clients within clientelistic networks (Bell and Coleman 1999), unequally positioned trading partners (Santos-Granero 2007) or youth from different social backgrounds (Osella and Osella 1998; Nisbett 2007). The Bemni case shows how friendships could occur between girls of different ages or abilities as long as they shared a belief in the moral importance of meeting village expectations.

Girls largely reproduced wider societal expectations of how girls and young women should behave and relate to others. I did not observe girls challenging the notion that they should collect leaves, question why girls rather than boys should shoulder this responsibility or refuse to meet village norms. A good friend was one who worked diligently (*mehnat*), believed in the importance of meeting gendered expectations and was open to mutual assistance. In the forest, girls performed types of reciprocity that would make them attractive as brides on the local marriage market and as future wives and mothers. Girls closely monitored each other's labour, attitudes to work and skill level. In addition, GC girls' practices reinforced caste distinctions in the village. Girls argued that they could be friends only with other GCs, and that SC girls would not make good forest companions. The embodied character of the mutual assistance girls offered one another in the forest – the frequency with which shared work required touching, gripping and holding a work peer – further militated against inter-caste female friendships. Moreover, the routine interaction of GC girls in the forest collecting leaves had the effect of shoring up intra-caste solidarities and separating higher-caste and lower-caste girls.

It is interesting to note that girls' leaf collection practices offer a counter to the idea that kinship and caste relations predominate over friendship in many parts of south Asia (see Mandelbaum 1970) and elsewhere (Bell and Coleman 1999). An early strand of anthropological writing tended to dismiss possibilities for significant friendships in societies in which kinship structures are strong (see Santos-Granero 2007 for a review). Other work acknowledges friendship but tends to imagine this relationship as subordinate to kinship (see Cohen 1961; Paine 1969). My account dovetails with a more recent body of research (see Reed-Danahay 1999), which emphasises that friendship may be an important medium through which people relate to siblings, cousins and more distant relations. To make this point is also to invert the relationship between friendship and kinship discussed by Lloyd and Susanne Rudolph (1967) in their analysis of 'fictive kinship' in India. Rudolph and Rudolph describe a tendency in rural north India for people to apply kinship terms to friendships as a means of valorising social ties. This indeed is how my key informants related to me, as 'elder sister' (*didi*). But the attribution of terms of endearment also flowed in the other direction; girls in Bemni often came to refer to particularly trusted cousins as their 'friends', and when the relationship was broken they returned to simply being 'cousins'.

Read together, the stories of Bina and Gita and Parwati and Sarita also demonstrate the practice-based nature of friendship and the close relationship between friendship and the environment. In the forests surrounding Bemni, friendships were formed and strengthened through young people's tactile interaction with the local environment. Girls learnt to trust each other through sharing their knowledge about the qualities of different parts of the forest. More importantly, they built a sense of reciprocity and shared endeavour by embarking on shared physical tasks, literally 'working the environment': tying leaves together, whittling sticks and checking the density of a basket of leaves, for example. Things sometimes went wrong, and girls could laugh about their failures and encourage each other to persist. And, when a task was accomplished, girls could share in a sense of pride and achievement, which has its material manifestation in a large basket of leaves. Reflecting these points, girls in Bemni imagined close friendship not primarily as an affective relationship borne out of shared leisure interests or mutual appreciation of each other's personality (Montaigne 1972 [1603]; compare Allan 1996). Rather, close friendship related mainly to instrumental issues related to the local environment: who would be able to help you in the forest or who, at the least, demonstrated a basic commitment to meeting village norms for the construction of baskets.

Firm friends and cultural production

If friendship enabled girls to conduct difficult work in a relatively efficient and cooperative manner, it also offered them opportunities to try out social identities. It was via the social institution of firm friendship that girls came to engage in forms of cultural production and locate themselves within hierarchies of social maturation.

Sociologists analysing child friendship sometimes make a distinction between 'short-term contracts', wherein friends are imagined to be fairly short-lived, and 'long-term contracts', wherein children imagine that their link will endure over time, possibly for their whole lives (Hey 1996). Young female friendships in Bemni were of a relatively short-term nature for the obvious reason that girls married and moved away. In a patrilocal marriage system it is typically difficult for young women to sustain close childhood friendships after marriage. Adult women continued to offer moral support in the process of leaf collection and they sometimes provided assistance to young people who had not reached adult standards. But women were no longer able to depend on reciprocal relations. Instead, young women needed to be capable of independently filling their own basket of leaves.

I witnessed a great deal of short-term volatility in girls' friendships. Over a fifteen-month period I saw friendships bloom and others break up. In a few cases, the demise of a friendship followed a quarrel between girls or a family crisis that made it impossible for a girl to continue working in a leaf collection team. More commonly, however, the disintegration of friendships reflected the manner in which girls' ties formed in the forest articulated with broader kin and non-kin friendships between families in the village. In particular, girls' forest friendships often disintegrated in the wake of more general family feuds. For example, in April 2004 Sarita and Parwati ended their friendship and abandoned trips to the forest together after their parents argued. In certain instances girls could re-establish friendships at a later date, but family quarrels often had long-term effects on young people's sociality.

Reflecting the manner in which leaf collection changed over the course of a year, there was also a strong seasonal element to friendship. In particular, young people's social ties changed throughout the year depending on the settlement in which they lived. Some people lived in the same neighbourhood groups in different settlements; kinship groups, for example, were closely clustered in the highest and lowest settlements comprising Bemni village, so forest friendships continued as kinship groups moved between the villages. But often neighbours were different in each settlement, and friendship groups re-formed in different seasons. For example, while, in September, Bina went regularly to collect leaves with Gita, in June she usually collected leaves with another girl. There was a sense in which Bina's friendship with Gita, and the embodied understandings upon which the relationship rested, were 'latent' during the summer months.

In the context of such fluidity, many girls spoke of the need to be adaptable about friends. In particular, many of my informants said that it is important to maintain relationships with a number of people simultaneously rather than developing just one special friend. In the type of statement I heard several times, Saka (sixteen) explained:

> I shouldn't have just one special girl friend. If I always go with one friend, then tomorrow she might not go, and then who will I go with? Then, if I go with other people, they will ask me: 'Where is your friend?' So I have to go with everyone, so that I always have people to go with. We just need to go to do the work.

Other girls made similar comments, and sometimes also stressed the difficulties that girls encounter if their forest activity has become too closely attuned to the needs and proclivities of a few 'firm friends'. These observations stand in contrast to Gratz's (2004) work on friendship among gold miners in west Africa, where workers stressed the importance of maintaining 'just one or two friends'. A mine-worker told Gratz (2004: 111): 'Too many friends mean too many opinions to adjust to, too many people knowing too much about you.' The differences between these two contexts perhaps reflect the greater uncertainty of precisely who will be available to work with in Bemni, where the vicissitudes of family quarrels, seasonal shifts and the competing demands of schoolwork had elevated the process of making friends into a delicate and difficult art.

This observation about the fluidity of friendships helps to explain the general atmosphere of camaraderie that I observed when ascending the mountain with large sets of girls and women on leaf collection trips. In addition to being able to call on a few 'good friends' during any particular season, it was important for girls to get along fairly well with their peers more generally, because it was from this larger pool that future friends would be drawn.

For all this emphasis on fluidity, however, there was a certain degree of durability in the particular sets of close friends who worked together collecting leaves in Bemni, and this relative stability was crucial in the manufacture of youthful cultural practices in the forest. Within any particular season (roughly three months), the same group of girls often visited the forest many times to collect leaves, and, among these girls, the repetition of forms of mutual help created a fairly stable sense of belonging. Once among a trusted group of peers, girls attained a sense of social freedom; for example, they could periodically ease off and experiment with identities. Groups of relatively stable 'firm friends' therefore provided a crucial social context for the emergence of youthful cultural production. The example of Kamla (sixteen) and her cousin Prema (thirteen) brings out this point.

In October 2003 I accompanied three friends – Kamla, Prema and Archana (nine) – to collect leaves. It was ear-achingly cold as we set off, just before 6 a.m. After an hour's climb we arrived at the site of one of the village's cremation stacks. Prema and Archana were afraid, fearing the presence of ghosts, and nervously stayed close to Kamla. They marvelled at Kamla's bravery as she strode on, unafraid of the forest. We continued to a patch of forest that was deeply carpeted with leaves. The sun had not yet reached the forest; the dew-soaked leaves were icy cold, and our hands were instantly numbed by touching them. Kamla said, 'It's like dunking our hands into cold water,' and she demonstrated by plunging her hands into a large pile of leaves before beginning to rake the ground. Meanwhile, Prema and Archana were darting about, apparently unable to choose a single area, instead inefficiently creating scattered tiny piles of leaves. They mumbled about the cold and shook their hands vigorously before standing stubbornly, arms crossed and hands tucked into the warmth of their armpits.

When Kamla had raked up a large pile, she went to help Prema, scooping leaves into her basket and standing inside it to squash the leaves down. Then, with words of encouragement, she took Prema's hands between hers, blew hot air onto them and rubbed them warm. Kamla repeated this sequence several times over the next hour, and each time Prema looked briefly cheered and continued where her sister had left off.

When Kamla had finished securing her huge basket-load of leaves, she turned again to help both Prema and Archana. She sent them to fetch flexible branches and hold them in place as she skilfully loaded their child-sized baskets. Kamla said that Prema was learning how to tie on extra loads of leaves above her basket, but that she usually needed help. Soon, they too had compact and top-heavy baskets, and sometime after 9 a.m. we set off slowly down the hill, back into the sunshine.

A few weeks later, in November 2003, Prema's family needed more leaves for their livestock. The conditions had worsened in the interim; the nights were longer, and the temperature had plunged. Kamla was busy cutting winter hay, and Prema set off to the forest with another friend, Manju (twelve), as well as Archana. Just after 6 a.m. we tramped up the hill in the darkness, heads bent against a bitter wind. Again we were in a small group, and we did not see any other leaf collection teams. In marked contrast to a few weeks earlier, Prema was excited, chatting and joking from the start, in spite of the inhospitable conditions. As we approached an area of the forest thought to be inhabited by ghosts, Prema told me not to be scared. She said she was not afraid of the ghosts even though her own mother had been cremated nearby. Minutes later Prema was scampering over some rocks to enter a large cavern set into the mountainside. Prema laughed that she could die in there and nobody would find her. It seemed a surprising joke, given both Prema's personal experience of death and her fear of the ghosts in another area of the forest just two weeks earlier.

Once in the forest, Prema blithely assumed responsibility for deciding where to look for leaves. Settled on a location, she raked the leaves energetically, apparently not noticing the cold. Archana stood around, looking cold and fed up. She slowly filled her tiny basket, gathering small bundles of leaves to squash down the sides of the basket. After each bundle, Archana stood holding her hands silently before attempting another. She did not use extra branches to fill it over the top, although she could, and had done, on other occasions. Meanwhile, Prema was eagerly stuffing her basket with leaves. At the sides of her basket, Prema tied branches that she had brought from home. She attempted to gather the armfuls of leaves, but they repeatedly collapsed. Each time, Prema laughed and brightly tried again. Finally, with Archana holding the branches ready, Prema loaded and tied the leaves in place. Now, with her basket finished, Prema went to help Manju, who was working slowly and complaining about the cold. Prema piled more leaves into her basket and sought the branches that Manju had brought. But the branches were brittle and broke as she tied them, allowing the stack of leaves to slither to the ground. Prema, who had kept up a running commentary since arriving in the forest, gently and jokingly chided Manju for filling her basket badly, and for cutting brittle branches. Manju glumly replied, 'But I'm cold.' Prema ran off with a sickle to cut more branches, replaced them and began filling the basket again. All the while her chat continued, now encouraging Manju to help her: 'It's okay . . . that'll work . . . the leaves will stay . . . You hold that and we'll make a good basket now.' Together, Prema and Manju finished the basket, and by 9 a.m. were ready to return to the village.

These stories cast further light on the production of friendship in forest spaces. The institution of friendship afforded girls a certain freedom regarding how they acted while collecting leaves. Among a set of trusted intimates, girls could experiment with particular identities. On many occasions I watched girls imitating the behaviour of other villagers, especially older women or younger girls, as part of their social performances while collecting leaves. There was a measure of self-consciousness about these embodied cultural practices. In the examples above, Prema appeared to make a deliberate decision to 'play the little girl' or 'play the adult' and she felt her way into the roles, trying out specific gestures and movements. These cultural practices also required considerable improvisation. Girls decided how they should act within any particular situation on the basis of who happened to be in their team on that specific day. There was a mischievous quality to such spontaneity. In some instances I watched girls slyly assessing whether, in the context of a particular friendship group, they could be allowed to 'play the child'. In other instances this sense of mischief arose out of the rather mannered way in which girls signalled their movement from one role to another. For example, Prema could sense my confusion when she took on the role of leader on the November trip, and this seemed to spur her to new heights in how she sought to embody the character of the responsible adult, supervising the other students and encouraging them in their work.

It is crucial to locate girls' role playing within the space of the forest, for two reasons. First, the forest was a space figuratively and physically remote from the adult domain of the village. Girls could experiment with identities and engage in forms of play without the imperative to immediately conform to adult expectations. Second, the forest and surrounding mountainside provided a type of living stage upon which girls could perform specific roles. Thus, for example, Kamla could mark her position as team leader on the October trip to the forest by burying her hands in a near-frozen pile of leaves. Similarly, for Prema, the existence of a cave close to a cremation ground offered an opportunity to advertise her confidence and leadership in a striking manner. The forest was never a static container or backdrop for girls' work, but was actively embroiled in the social drama (see also Linkenbach 1998; Gururani 2002; compare Massey 2005). At a micro-level, girls took advantage of local materials and symbols – everything from a forest's association with ghosts to the flexibility of particular branches – in order to perform the role they had assigned for themselves.

For all this emphasis on inventiveness, however, girls' social performances in the forest borrowed from the cultural repertoire of adults in the village. As Bourdieu (1984 [1979]) has argued, intimate relationships are often highly effective vehicles for the consolidation of 'arbitrary' social norms, such as those based on age or gender. The roles of adult-like leader or childlike dependent played by Kamla and Prema and many other girls whom I accompanied on leaf collection trips reflected locally salient gendered ideas of responsibility, competence and maturity, thus contributing to the further institutionalisation of these ideas in the minds of other youth. Girls did not very often use these dominant norms as a basis for taunting their peers while collecting leaves. My informants did not engage in the type of aggressive policing of each other's behaviour that Marjorie Goodwin (2006) found to be a feature of girls' practices in her work in a US playground, or that Mary Thomas (2009) discusses as a characteristic of friendship groups in a Los Angeles high school. This perhaps reflects the relative importance in the Bemni setting of finding solutions to practical difficulties; in the forest setting, friendship was important as a basis for problem solving rather than being imagined as a context for staging conflict. But girls in Bemni did constantly monitor each other's leaf collection practices, checking for instances in which girls had failed to meet village standards and admonishing those who made mistakes. Moreover, there were moments in the forest when girls abandoned a commitment to assist a friend in favour of 'teaching a friend a lesson'. For example, I once observed a girl with a full load of leaves fall as she returned through the forest. The girl had cut her arm in the fall, and she lay on the ground for several minutes weeping. As I moved to help her, several other girls told me to stay back: 'Let her get on with it,' I was told. In this instance, girls saw little reason to extend sympathy to a member of their team whose behaviour contravened norms of assiduity and carefulness, even while they typically worked to assist each other in the forest and prevent such slips. The wider point is that, as Willis's (1982) work primes us to expect, the collective cultural practices of children simultaneously exhibit imaginative and conservative elements.

Conclusions

Collecting leaves was gruelling, painstaking work that girls often undertook somewhat reluctantly and that, on the face of it, offered little scope for self-expression or 'agency'. In Chapter 4 I stressed the opportunistic ways in which children dodged their herding work to play games, forage or hang out. In this chapter I have placed more emphasis on the constraints operating on young people's 'bricolage'. I have nevertheless shown in this chapter that girls were often able to imbue leaf collection work with meaning (compare Joyce 1987; Hodson 2001). They measured their growing strength and skill against standards produced by the village. They did not remonstrate with their parents about the need to collect leaves, but actually went beyond their parents' demands by rigorously seeking to meet and exceed villagers' expectations with regard to leaf baskets. Leaf collection work became, for these girls, a way of establishing reputations as hardworking young women and suitable future wives.

In this process, girls built, enjoyed and broke various friendships. There is a gathering sense within anthropology, sociology and related disciplines that friendship is becoming more important as a basis for social action among children and young people as well as older segments of the population (Dyson 2010). As families restructure in different contexts, kin relations are becoming increasingly 'optative', and friendship may be crucial in breathing life into family structures (see Reed-Danahay 1999). In Bemni in 2003/4, growing enrolment in formal education and a related increase in the age of marriage had created a phase of life in which girls could experiment with social relationships and establish homosocial intimate ties. Friendship had been institutionalised within this social space of youth, intersecting and overlapping with kinship relations in complex ways.

Friendship as a form of 'positive sociality' is a theme of wider studies (for example Featherstone 2008). Indeed, many scholars working with young people have referred to the empowering potential of friendship. Childhood and youth are often periods in which the need to establish and maintain friendships becomes an overriding concern (for example Griffiths 1995; Hey 1996; Conradson and Latham 2005). Indeed, friendship may be becoming more important to young people in the 1990s and 2000s, in the context of the decline in state support for social reproduction in many parts of the world (Jeffrey and Dyson 2008). In Bemni, friendship is a crucial 'resource' for girls, allowing them to meet gendered expectations, construct affirming identities and foster ties of mutuality.

Yet friendship is also a practice through which dominant ideas are played out. This is a theme of the work of Bourdieu (1984 [1979]) on class relations. It is also a theme that emerges in much youth research. For example, Goodwin's (2006) work with pre-adolescent girls in the United States has exposed the intensive and often cruel manner in which children monitor each other's behaviour. Similarly, Thomas (2009) shows in her study of teenage African American young women in a Los Angeles school that young women often entrench ethnic/racial differences in people's minds through the judgements they made about those inside and outside their friendship groups. In Bemni, girls learnt through intimate interactions with each other in the forest how to imagine and perform some of the gendered roles assigned to them by older villagers. Moreover, friendships among girls did not cross gender or caste boundaries and tended to reinforce assumptions about what constitutes 'good' and 'mature' behaviour. This did not amount to a passive process of 'socialization' (compare Aries 1962; Kakar 1978); girls actively appropriated rather than passively imbibed patriarchal norms around work, gender and sociality (see also Mahmood 2005). Indeed, a spirit of mischief and self-conscious imitation infused girls' practices. But it is equally evident that children's 'friendship work' (Hey 1996) in Bemni occurred largely within the terms set by older villagers and society at large.

In the discussion of herding in Chapter 4 I provided numerous examples of young people engaging with the environment and, in the process, finding ways to achieve their goals, whether to have fun or honour a local spirit. Consideration of girls' leaf collection practices foregrounds the micro-processes through which children enrolled the environment in their projects of self-making. Girls often said rather little while conducting forest chores. Their commitment to each other and desire to work collaboratively was communicated more often and more immediately through the manner in which they threw their bodies into working the environment, and in how they anticipated and counterbalanced their friends' movements – recall, for example, how Parwati helped Sarita with her leaf basket. As Michel Foucault's (2005) work might lead us to imagine, being an effective friend in Bemni entailed 'mastering' in some sense local 'technologies', and literally 'lending one's weight' to a common cause. The forest was deeply implicated in this process of cultural production, as the setting for practices and as a source of physical 'props'. It was also an imagined place. On the one hand, it was seen as a place where ghosts and dangerous animals lived, while being, simultaneously, a socially 'safe' site, far removed from the prying and judging eyes of village adults. Here, girls had the privacy to rework and master the skills that would establish them as competent young women.

The manner in which the forest became enfolded in young people's projects while working was even more evident in the participant observation I conducted among girls and boys collecting lichen (*mukku*). *Mukku* gathering also offers a lens through which to further understand the spirited social agency of young people in the high Himalayas.

6 Harvesting identities: *mukku*, gender and development

On a still winter afternoon in early January 2004 Anita and I were high in the forests surrounding Bemni. We were in the midst of a rather fierce snowball fight with girls from the village. We had come to the forests to collect lichen (*mukku*). But their baskets were empty, and they were thoroughly absorbed in their boisterous play. Our rough and tumble in the snow presented a vivid contrast to the boys, who were scattered around the surrounding forest working diligently, alone or in pairs, to collect large baskets of lichen. There was hardly time for me to take note of what was going on; soon I was being dragged to the ground by my unruly friends. 'Eat snow!' they shouted, stuffing it into my face (Figure 6.1).

Rather than gathering lichen in a begrudging manner, children found means to invest the collection of *mukku* with meaning, just as they did for herding (Chapter 4) and leaf collection (Chapter 5). For girls, *mukku* collection was an opportunity to have fun, and also partially to escape the standards of femininity that constrain their actions within the village. But in self-consciously contravening norms of femininity the girls also reinforced established ideas about what constitutes young female propriety.

Mikhail Bakhtin's (1984) work on carnivals and the carnivalesque is useful in theorising girls' practices while collecting lichen. Drawing on his study of peasant society in Russia, Bakhtin imagines the carnival as a moment in which notions of what is 'normal' are inverted. During carnivals, people commonly value forms of behaviour that are ordinarily prohibited. Moreover, patterns of hierarchy and behaviour are ignored and boundaries are systematically transgressed. Bakhtin emphasises the exuberance of carnivalesque practice and the location of carnivalesque acts in pockets of time and space peripheral to or outside those in which the powerful reside.

South Asian scholars have used Bakhtin's ideas to analyse attitudes towards street food (Mukhopadhyay 2004) as well as the Holi festival in rural north India. At Holi, specific ideas around hierarchy and proper conduct are often temporarily inverted and problematised (see Marriott 1966; Cohen 1995). As McKim Marriott (1966: 211) puts it, 'The servile wife acts the domineering husband, and vice versa; the ravisher acts the ravished; the menial acts the master; the enemy acts the friend; the strictured youths act the rulers of the republic.' I

Figure 6.1 Girls bombard author (second right) with snow while collecting *mukku* in the forest (note their empty baskets)

build on Bakhtin's ideas and the more specific Holi literature to examine girls' practices while in the forest collecting *mukku*. Girls' actions entailed the valuing of behaviour normally imagined as inappropriate, the transgression of boundaries and a type of mischievous exuberance. But the limits of girls' boundary crossing were also evident. Their practices occurred only in small groups of GCs of similar age, and girls did not question caste- or age-based hierarchies. Moreover, girls' practices reinforced notions of femininity prevalent in the village.

This chapter describes how young people used *mukku* collection to develop particular subjectivities. While GC girls perceived lichen collection to be an opportunity to have fun and subvert norms of femininity, boys eagerly sought to collect large baskets full of *mukku* in order to make money and project an image of themselves as competent breadwinners. In the case of both boys and girls, then, an activity apparently peripheral to the household economy was crucially significant in their developing identities. As in the case of herding and leaf gathering, the local environment was constantly enrolled in these projects of self-making, as a hidden space for particularly gendered performances, as supplier of materials and as a subject of children's conversations.

Mukku in Bemni

In Uttarakhand, rural people have begun to capitalise on the expansion of the road network to sell non-timber forest products (for example Nautiyal 2000;

Dhar *et al.* 2003). Lichen collection, in particular, emerged as an important source of income in high-altitude areas from the late 1990s onwards. Since 1999, when a dirt road was cut to within 8 kilometres of Bemni, villagers had been selling lichen in the nearby market 16 kilometres away. From there, it was sold on the Gangetic plains for the production of spices, paint and dyes. Lichen sale prices were low during the 1990s (Rs. 3 to 5 per kilogram), but by 2003/4 villagers were receiving Rs. 35 to 40 per kilogram. In 2003 one of the two main buyers in the region estimated that each year he sent around forty trucks of lichen for sale in the plains, each holding about 30 quintals (3,000 kilograms).

In order to collect *mukku* it is typically necessary to obtain a permit from the Forest Department. In many parts of Chamoli district a class of contractors had emerged who specialised in acquiring permits and then brought in wage labourers to collect *mukku* on a fairly large scale. By contrast, the forest guard in the Nandakini Valley wanted to restrict opportunities for *mukku* collection to local villagers, and he therefore allowed local people to collect *mukku* without obtaining permits. The sarpanch, the head of the village forest committee in Bemni, was somewhat concerned about this situation. He said that *mukku* collectors were damaging the forest by ripping lichen-rich branches from the trees. Indeed, the sarpanch was contemplating lobbying the FD to ban the collection of *mukku*. But he did not succeed, and so lichen was an open-access resource for Bemni villagers: There were no restrictions on who could collect it and how much they could gather. For the poorest households in the village, lichen sale represented a key means of raising cash.

While lichen was available throughout the year, growing on the branches of mature oak trees, its collection was largely restricted to the winter months. The lull in field work during winter provided time for some villagers to engage in other tasks. Among GC villagers, however, it remained predominantly the work of children and young people. *Mukku* collection entailed travelling to the forest for long periods, and work in the home or fields prevented adults from spending the entire day away from the home. This was particularly true for mothers with young children. Other older adults also said that they could no longer cope with the harsh conditions or climb the trees for *mukku*. Only a small handful of the poorer GC adult women collected *mukku*, and even these women went irregularly.

For GC households, *mukku* collection was therefore predominantly the work of children and young people. Most GC girls started collecting *mukku* from the age of eleven or twelve, and GC and SC boys started at thirteen or fourteen years. On a typical day of *mukku* collection large groups of children would leave their homes in Gwar around 7 a.m., with their baskets on their backs and a packed lunch of dense *manduwa roti*. They gathered at the foot of the forest, waiting for their friends, before heading off in single-sex groups, braving the bitter winds and snow to climb some 1,000 metres up to the forest peaks. In clusters of mixed ages, the older children made decisions about which parts of the forest to visit. Up above Chapra, towards the highest peak at Nilari, the children and young people collected *mukku* throughout the day. They returned home after 7 p.m., long past nightfall, to eat and sleep before starting again the following day.

With typically less land and a greater need to obtain cash, lichen collection was a major winter season occupation of SC adults and children. As well as making the daily trips to the lichen forest, many SC collectors also visited more distant jungles, where they stayed for between four and ten days at a time. Roughly six hours' trek from the village, these remote forests were thicker and the lichen more abundant. The parents of SC boys generally forbade their sons from making these long trips to collect *mukku*, citing the extreme cold and harsh conditions as being too dangerous for young men. As a result, SC boys, like their GC peers, made day trips to collect *mukku* from forests closer to the village, and it was SC parents and girls who undertook the long work trips to distant forests. SC women and their daughters travelled in groups of up to twenty people, carrying cooking pots and blankets. They slept in caves or the temporary rainy season cattle shelters belonging to other villages. In late 2003 and early 2004 separate SC groups made ten such trips to collect *mukku*.

Gathering lichen was skilled work. The best lichen grew on the uppermost branches of tall trees, and climbing them was difficult. The trunks of the oak trees were wide, making it difficult to gain a good grip, and, in the lower sections of the trunk, there were few radial branches to act as handholds and footholds. There was also considerable skill associated with stripping a tree of *mukku*. Once adept at the task, children often cut long straight branches, fashioning a V at one end, with which they hooked outlying branches to draw them within easier reach. Others pulled at branches until they snapped and fell to the ground for later use. Children who had not yet learnt to climb trees were left to rummage for *mukku*-covered twigs on the ground, which was tiring and unrewarding work, as I found during my own trips. *Mukku* collection thus created incentives for children to become good tree climbers, and many children told me that they were learning to climb in order to improve their efficiency. This learning took place through forms of informal apprenticeship of what Lave and Wenger (1991) term 'legitimate peripheral participation'. Children began by participating around the edges of work groups and then gradually assumed more central roles. They learnt to climb and gather lichen while off the ground, copying older friends and siblings and learning from their own and others' mistakes. In some cases, there were fairly efficient 'teams' of children with mixed abilities who coordinated their *mukku* collection work, especially when the children were siblings. An older child ascended the tree, and felled *mukku*-covered branches for a younger child on the ground to strip. But such coordinated work was not as prevalent as among girls collecting leaf litter.

The greater availability of *mukku* during the winter and agricultural cycle meant that *mukku* collection was principally confined to the period between December and March, especially the month-long winter school holidays, Sundays and public holidays. Young people who did not go to school collected *mukku* almost every day between mid-December and mid-March, or until the agricultural work picked up again.

I was unable to accompany SC households on their extended *mukku* trips, because of time restrictions and caste-based norms that prevented my research assistant from sharing food and limited sleeping space with SC villagers. I therefore rely on SCs' reflections on their *mukku* practices obtained during ethnographic interviews in the following discussion of their ten-day or two-week-long *mukku* trips. I was able to accompany GC and SC children on their day-long trips to collect *mukku*, however. Between January 2003 and March 2004 I accompanied children on fifteen trips to gather lichen, often conducting short interviews or informal focus groups while participating in their work and other activities.

Saka

Saka was the person I came to know best while working in Bemni, and I accompanied her on numerous trips to collect lichen and conduct other tasks. I first met her on a cold evening in 2003 inside her family's one-roomed house. The room was dark; Saka's face was only occasionally visible by the light of the flickering cooking fire. Behind her, I could hear, but not see, the livestock that also shared the room: the two cows, two bulls and a buffalo that quietly shuffled and snorted as they chewed on their night-time hay.

I had just arrived in Bemni village for my first time. I had made the long trek up to the village with Saka's paternal uncle, and had subsequently been invited to stay the night with Saka's family. My arrival that night had brought the key male figures of the village to Saka's house. The sarpanch, the head of the village forest committee, and the de facto leader of the village, had entered the room. Despite explaining that I wanted to work with the young people in the village, he sought to lay claim over me immediately, and loudly discussed my schedule for the next day with the assembled group of men. Sixteen-year-old Saka had no place in these discussions. She quietly continued making bread for our supper, slapping the bread from hand to hand before placing it by the fire to cook. As the men talked, though, we stole smiles and glances.

Early the next morning, before the men had even emerged from their houses, Saka announced that I would accompany her and her friends for a day's work in the forest. We made no mention of the sarpanch's instructions the night beforehand. In the growing light of that chill January day, we set off to the high reaches of the forest. It was there that I discovered a very different Saka.

Saka was from a Rajput family. She was the youngest of four children, and the only one remaining in the natal home. Her oldest brother, Vinod, had left Bemni in 1999 in search of salaried work, and in 2003 he lived in Delhi. Saka's sister was married into a nearby village, and, in 2003, her younger brother stayed temporarily with his uncle while he sought a position in the army. Saka had previously studied at the middle school in the neighbouring village, but had dropped out in 2002 having passed her class eight exams. Now she joined her parents working their 0.8 hectares of land, a relatively large holding by Bemni standards.

Like many other girls in Bemni, Saka had been contributing to this work since the age of five. By 2003 she was the household's main labourer. While her father enjoyed ploughing, he strenuously tried to avoid other types of work. Her mother increasingly suffered from ill health; her back and knees were continually aching and her blood pressure was high. She looked forward to the marriage of one of her sons, when she expected that a daughter-in-law would take over her toil. But, until then, Saka was responsible for the majority of the agricultural work, and particularly for the heavy labour.

Saka's days were thus structured around the particular agricultural needs of the season. In March and April she sowed millet, rice and potatoes, then harvested wheat, barley and pulses. Between May and June she weeded millet, rice and potatoes, cut grass for fodder and collected dry leaves from the forest. In July and August she collected firewood and weeded and fertilised the fields. In September and October she harvested the millet, rice and potatoes and sowed wheat and barley. A little later in the year she cut hay, collected fresh leaves for fodder and gathered more dry leaves – an activity that continued through the dark days of winter, along with more firewood collection.

Saka had shown little interest or promise in her schoolwork, but she had established a reputation as a diligent and skilful worker. I remember Saka during the summer evenings returning home long after dark, climbing the steep 2 kilometres carrying a basket of green grass that she had cut in the moonlight, having spent a lonely fourteen hours weeding the millet fields. With barely enough energy to eat, she would fall into bed at 11 p.m., only to be woken again before 5 a.m. Another abiding memory is of worrying about where Saka was during an early snow storm in November, only to see her returning from the fields having cut a huge load of winter hay, wearing just a thin cotton *salwar kameez* and laughing when she showed me how her hands were still warm.

Although Saka was proud of her contribution to her household's livelihood, she regretted that she had little time for socialising or meeting her friends. She often referred to the loneliness of agricultural work and talked wistfully of her younger days. She remembered the best and most carefree period of her life being when she was eleven or twelve years old. At that time she had spent long summer days herding cattle with a group of particularly close girls and boys.

But Saka was not entirely constrained in her ability to seek space for her own fun or to escape the social norms that dictated her behaviour in the public spaces of the village. Winter was a relatively quiet period in terms of agricultural work, and Saka seized upon her forest-related work as an opportunity to spend time with friends away from adult view. Saka created spaces of fun (*mazaa*) through her daily trips to collect lichen in high-altitude forests.

Saka had been collecting lichen since 1999. In 2003 she regularly played the role of a leader, making decisions about which part of the forest to visit and directing the work rhythms of the group. When I first started accompanying Saka and her friends on their lichen collection trips in March 2003, however, I was somewhat alarmed when, on arriving at a distant part of the lichen-abundant jungle, Saka sat down and started chatting. I thought I was perhaps disturbing their work, but Saka gaily insisted, 'No, no, we only come to the jungle to play and chat.' She said, 'We'll do some work later, but this is really why we come.' She beckoned me to join her.

During this and the many trips I made during the winters of 2003 and 2004, Saka and her friends' discussions were often extremely personal. They talked of their changing bodies, asking about menstruation and whether they should be wearing a bra. Saka often initiated discussions that reflected her own emerging sexual desires; they focused on the subjects of men and pre-marital affairs – subjects that I never heard discussed by unmarried girls elsewhere in the village. They told stories about lovers who had fallen pregnant, and the details of their 'affairs'.

The young women's conversations also focused on their futures. While Saka had been too shy to talk of marriage partners in the winter of 2002/3, the following year she began to speak of her eagerness to be married. In the relatively 'private' space of the forest, Saka said that the promise of a man, with its implication of sexual pleasure, tempted her towards a situation – marriage – that was otherwise publicly feared. As Saka began to articulate her criteria for a suitable husband, her friends teased her about possible families into which she could be married: perhaps in a family with little land, or to a husband in a village on a north-facing slope where the sun never melted the winter snow. Saka appreciated the privacy that the forest offered for such discussions, and said that she and her friends could talk more openly in these spaces than anywhere else: 'At home, we can't talk in front of our mothers, aunts and brothers' wives.' These conversations often dominated our mornings in the forest, and continued into lunch. Midday meals in the forest followed a standard pattern: Saka would gather together everyone's packed *roti* and vegetables and distribute them in equal portions (see Figure 6.2), while others mixed freshly ground chilli and coriander into handfuls of snow to make 'mountain ice cream'.

Saka and her peers also spent much of their time on *mukku* collection trips engaged in what they called 'dirty games' (*gundee khel*). The girls teased each

Figure 6.2 Saka shares out *roti* for the girls' picnic in the forest

other about their small lichen harvests, pretending to steal their sacks and provoking chasing games. Launching tackles between the trees, they dragged each other by the legs down the slippery mountainsides. They threw armfuls of damp leaves or snow inside their friends' clothes (see Figure 6.1 earlier) and used their sharpened sickles (*daranti*) in mock battles. At other times the games were more personal, ridiculing the smaller girls for their unformed breasts, pulling down their blouses to reveal and twist their nipples. Saka laughingly recounted how her older sister had once called to her from a tree canopy in the guise of needing help only to urinate from above.

During my first trips with Saka and her friends, they would occasionally break off from boisterous games to ask if I was shocked by their behaviour and found them to be 'childlike' (*jaise bachchhe*) or 'dirty girls' (*gundee larkiyan/lauri*). Having reassured them that I would neither make such judgements nor inform their parents of their conduct, they relaxed and continued their games. Similarly, other groups of GC girls who engaged in the same range of games and horseplay during lichen collection asked whether I had seen other girls play around in the same manner, and whether I disapproved of their activity. Once I had reassured Saka and her peers, I was often enrolled in young women's games and joking. After a few months living in the village, young women regarded me as a 'big sister' (*didi*) but not one who would criticise their behaviour or report their activities to their parents.

By 3 p.m. or 4 p.m. Saka typically called in mock panic for the group to start collecting lichen to take home. They would spread out, and the more skilled young women climbed nimbly up the trees. Those young women who had not yet learnt to climb scampered around beneath the more able climbers, gathering the lichen that had fallen from the tree canopy. The chat and games would continue. Young women would sing witty 'question and answer' songs to each other. Known as *bera*, these songs were partly a way of staying in touch with the group as it dispersed. On my trips, the young women often directed teasing rhymes at me, with even the youngest, shyest girls joining in:

> *Ek jelabi, do samosa,*
> *Janey-Didi ka kya barosa?*
>
> A sticky sweet and two salty snacks,
> When Janey's around, watch your back![1]

Sometimes we heard groups of young men who were also collecting lichen but had come from different villages. The young women would provoke shouting matches: 'Eh grandson!' started the girls. 'Eh girl, come here,' would be the reply. 'No, you come here – but what are you doing in my jungle?' the young women responded. I once expressed surprise that the young women shouted in such uncharacteristic ways to unknown boys. But Saka explained coolly, 'That's how people talk in this jungle.'

Saka greatly valued the opportunities for fun that lichen collection provided. Saka reflected on how trips to collect lichen were different from visits to the forest to collect other products. She said:

> When we go for green leaves or dry wood we are always with young married women, and they are afraid of being late because their mothers-in-law will punish them. So we have to collect the fodder quickly and can't sit and chat. But when we go for lichen we are just girls. We only have our parents and we are not afraid of them. We don't have mothers-in-law to be afraid of, so we can do as we like.

Saka demonstrated how the social norms that shaped her practices as an unmarried girl contrasted with those of a married woman. While Saka did the work of an adult woman for most of the year, she was free to join her younger peers for the winter lichen-collecting season.

Saka's ability to engage in fun (*mazaa*) on *mukku* collection trips was founded on an implicit understanding with her mother that lichen collection offered Saka a chance to take time off, to escape from the demands she faced at home. Saka would soon be married, and her mother empathised with her desire to be with

[1] The second line is translated more literally as 'Who can trust sister Janey?'.

friends and free of the social norms that dictated how she should behave in the village.

But for Saka these trips came with conditions. Saka had to convince her parents that she would make money for her family from her trips. Saka understood that she needed to alternate days when she returned with very little lichen with higher-yield days. Like other young women, she had a sharp memory for how much she had collected on each trip, and so she kept careful track of her negotiating position. Saka often laughed about the tactics she employed to explain particularly unproductive days. She said:

> If we don't want to, we do nothing all day and collect a little later. If we come back with very little lichen, we make up a story for everyone to tell her parents. We say we met a bear and we had to run away quickly. When we all have the same story, nobody will know what really happened. Our mothers don't go for lichen, so they don't know what we do.

On my first trip to collect lichen with Saka and her friends, they co-opted me into making similar excuses to account for their small harvests. They encouraged me to exaggerate the extent and depth of snow in the high-altitude forests and explain how it had hindered our access to the areas of most prolific lichen. On another occasion, I overheard two young women fictitiously tell their parents how they had come across a strange man in the forest, and, having run away in fear, had collected very little lichen.

Saka and her friends had also developed means of boosting the perceived quantity of their lichen harvest to fool their parents and the lichen trader. Rather than tearing the flowery lichen away from the branches on which it grew, they broke off small pieces of woody material with each lichen clump, making their bags heavier and more bulky. On other occasions they dropped lumps of snow into their bags to dampen and swell the absorbent lichen, or poured water into the lichen sacks before taking it to the market.

At the most basic level, mischief and humour provided a distraction from the burden and tedium of many tasks, and a means of releasing tensions attached to meeting older people's demands. But humour was also used to create what Michael Herzfeld (2005) has termed an 'intimate culture': a shared repertoire of jokes and tacit knowledge that provides groups with a sense of inner strength but that often provokes embarrassment when exposed to outsiders. For example, Saka and her friends spent the walk up the mountains to collect *mukku* exchanging furtive glances, warm in the knowledge that their trip was actually about games and having a picnic. But they were somewhat embarrassed by my presence in the forest, at least at first, and needed to check that I did not disapprove.

It is difficult to characterise young women's activities in the forest as 'resistance' in Scott's (1985) celebrated sense. Young women such as Saka did not seek to use their activities in the forest to challenge dominant notions of femininity, and parents were broadly tolerant of young women's efforts to 'have fun' in the forest. Rather, the practices of Saka and her peers accord with Bakhtin's (1984) notion of carnivalesque 'transgression'. Although obvious differences between the two cases prevent close comparison, the broad features of Bakhtin's notion of the carnivalesque were evident in the case of young women's activities on *mukku* collection trips. GC girls inverted moral codes concerning physical demeanour, engaged in high-spirited games and performed these versions of femininity at a physical and symbolic distance from older kin. As Bakhtin's work also leads us to expect, girls were preoccupied with their bodies and bodily products while performing transgression.

Unlike concepts of resistance, which typically seek to uncover a sense of real political change effected through everyday practice, notions of transgression do not necessarily imply any form of emancipation (Ortner 1995; Butz 2002). Just as Bakhtin's carnivals were 'permissible' episodes in particular spaces and times, Saka's moments of transgression were socially sanctioned: the implicit understanding between young women and their mothers allowed youths to engage in forms of 'fun' in the forest. Moreover, as other Indian work on subaltern practice suggests, carnivalesque transgressive actions frequently served to reproduce social norms by legitimising 'acceptable' behaviour (Mukhopadhyay 2004). By acknowledging the 'dirtiness' of her behaviour, Saka reinforced dominant ideas of how a 'proper' (*theek*), 'good' (*achhchee*) and 'straight' (*seedha*) young woman should behave. Marriott makes a parallel point in his classic work on Holi. The festival of Holi involved numerous transgressions, but its effect was that each person 'learnt to play his own routine roles afresh' (Marriott 1966: 259). Saka's winter season lichen collection provided a setting in which GC girls simultaneously subverted and reproduced notions of what it meant to be a dignified young woman, such that their actions are best characterised as forms of mischievous accommodation.

Perhaps more than did Bakhtin, it is necessary to emphasise how young women's efforts to engage in carnivalesque practice reinforced the symbolic distance between spaces of transgression and dominant relations. Saka and her peers spoke of the areas of the forest in which they collected *mukku* as 'their spaces' (*hamaari jungal*), where they were far from the judgemental gaze of village adults. These places were considered to be socially 'safe', and they often returned to the same areas, frequently large clearings, to engage in spirited mischief. In this context, Johan Huizinga's (1955) argument that 'play' is always associated with a distinct type of 'gaming space' appears important.

Here, the forest was not an abstract 'space' but a meaning-filled environment, full of social opportunities that were not available in the public space of the village. But young women also appreciated their environment at a more aesthetic level, and imbued lichen forests with valued attributes of intimacy and beauty. On many occasions, individual girls led me to their favourite clearings in the forest, some orientated towards the high peaks where the gods dwelt, others with bird's-eye views down onto the village, which they spoke about in loving terms. Young women's 'play' in Bemni was intimately connected to their visceral experience of the forest, and their youth cultures served to politicise and aestheticise everyday spaces surrounding the village, as well as lending a strong moral quality to them (compare Aitken 2001).

Contextualising girls' transgressions

Saka's capacity to enjoy *mukku* work partly reflects her age and experience. Younger girls often found *mukku* work burdensome and frightening. For example, when Bina, then twelve years old, began collecting *mukku* in 2003 she described it as an arduous and painful experience. Bina was small, and the long steep climbs to the forest peaks, the bitter wind and the occasional snowfall all tired her. On more than one occasion, Bina complained, 'I shouldn't have come today – it's too cold.' Bina had not yet learnt to climb trees and therefore had to pluck *mukku* from twigs on the ground. It was rather fruitless work, collecting but a few hundred grams by the end of the day. Bina was also afraid of the forest, particularly the possibility of encountering leopards, and she depended heavily on the company of her friends to counter her fears. Bina's frequent concerns about the conditions and wild animals prevented her from engaging fully and freely with the type of spirited, carnivalesque play that characterised Saka's trips to collect *mukku*.

As Bina went on *mukku* trips day after day, she grew in confidence. She learnt to stay close to the other girls, and, as she travelled to different areas of the forest, her fear slowly diminished. Bina learnt, like Saka and her older GC friends, that it was also a place for fun. The financial contribution from her *mukku* trips was not essential to her family, and Bina could capitalise on her family's relaxed attitude to her unproductive trips by taking time off to have fun. She no longer worried about coming home with lots of *mukku*, laughing if she brought back a single bag. At home, she learnt to make excuses for her small harvest, asking: 'If I don't find it, how can I bring it home?'

Caste and class inequalities also shaped girls' attitudes to *mukku* collection and their practices in the forest. I came to know five poor GC girls who were not able to participate as actively in the type of 'fun' activities in which Saka engaged. Fifteen-year-old Kabita's experiences illustrate the experiences and practices of these girls. Kabita came from a very poor GC family and had lived with her bachelor uncle for several years. Her family's poverty and their need for her labour had prevented her from ever having attended school. Like Saka, Kabita spent most of the year toiling in the fields, and she relished the winter with its more sociable work of *mukku* collection. Kabita's poor economic position, however, meant that she was under considerably more pressure to return from the forest with large quantities of *mukku*. She rarely stopped to sit and gossip, and, while she enjoyed the rough games at lunchtime – and was usually the strongest and most boisterous – Kabita would curtail her play before the other girls and quietly slip off to resume collecting *mukku*. On their way home, when the other girls had given up collecting and chatted as they walked, Kabita continued to dart around, picking *mukku* off fallen branches and running to catch up with the group. By the end of the 2003/4 season Kabita's efforts had paid off, as she had made Rs. 4,200 from her *mukku* trips. Kabita passed this money on to her uncle; 'It's my duty,' she said.

The practices of SC girls also differed markedly from those of Saka. I interviewed six SC girls aged between ten and seventeen about their experiences of collecting *mukku*, and the example of Papita is broadly indicative. Papita was ten years old in 2003 and came from a very poor SC family. As the oldest of three daughters remaining in the natal home, Papita was the household's main labourer besides her mother, and juggled her work with studies in class four at BPS. The family had large debts from weddings expenses and loans incurred for Papita's older sisters and brother. With land that did not cover their subsistence needs, and with no other sources of cash to pay off their debts, Papita's mother told her that she had to help raise some money through winter-season *mukku* collection.

Papita had started collecting *mukku* in the winter of 2002/3 through making day trips to the forests close to her home. The most efficient way to realise their family's economic goals, however, was through spending five to ten days at a time in distant forests. By the winter of 2003/4 Papita's mother considered Papita strong enough and sufficiently experienced to accompany her on longer *mukku* trips. But Papita hated these trips. She suffered from the extreme hardship; she was physically very small, and the long walks and freezing conditions exhausted her. These remote areas were snow-clad for most of the winter, and the living conditions were hazardous even for adults. She was reminded how, in 2003, a strong nineteen-year-old woman from Sunti had died from pneumonia after a prolonged period of *mukku* collection.

Papita was also afraid of the *mukku* forests. She said that *mukku* collection was markedly different from going to the forest to collect dry leaves. Even in September, when she went for leaves at 3 or 4 a.m., she was part of a large group, worked closely alongside others and felt safe. By contrast, on long trips for *mukku*, everyone quickly spread out and collected separately. It was difficult to see those collectors who had climbed up the trees, and Papita constantly had to check that she had not been left alone. Papita said she felt relentlessly scared. She claimed that these faraway forests were places filled with ghosts, and in which leopards, bears and wild pigs roamed. Although she never saw any of these animals, she heard the call of leopards every night and feared their daytime presence.

Papita's mother sympathised with her daughter. She said that, when she was a child, she also thought that even the nearby forests were 'bad', but that she slowly became accustomed to working in the forest. She told me: 'It's just like when you first came here [to our village]; it would not have been good for you, but now it's okay.' Although she suspected that Papita did not like the forest, she said, 'I don't know what she really thinks, but she has to go anyway.'

Although this was Papita's first season of sustained *mukku* collection, her mother took her on four long trips to remote forests. By March 2004 they had collectively earned Rs. 2,300 from their *mukku*. The *mukku* buyer, at whose shop Papita's brother has bought goods on credit, retained at least Rs. 1,000 of this money, while the remainder was spent on food. Papita received no gift or financial reward for her labour. Moreover, while the first two trips had been during her school holidays, Papita was forced to miss several days of school for the second two trips. Papita enjoyed and did well at school and hated missing classes. Papita's mother looked forward to the following year, however. She expected to withdraw Papita from school when she had passed class five, and she eagerly anticipated making regular trips for *mukku* with her daughter. Papita's mother said that her daughter would then make a greater contribution to the household's livelihood.

As a relatively young SC girl, Papita was more susceptible to fears about ghosts and wild animals than were older girls. For example, I also got to know a SC girl named Basanti, who came from an SC family as poor as Papita's. Like Papita, Basanti collected *mukku* out of economic necessity. Her family had been left with large debts after their major source of income had been curtailed with the deaths of their three mules. Basanti thus also made the more profitable, but significantly more demanding, long trips to the forest, staying for five or six days at a time in the company of her mother and other adult women. Like Papita, the continuous adult supervision under which Basanti's collecting took place precluded any opportunities for her to play and take time out like her GC contemporaries. But Basanti had had more experience of the forest, and did not suffer the same perpetual fear. Moreover, Basanti was bigger, more physically able and less challenged by the severe conditions.

SC girls may, in practice, have been capable of certain forms of spirited 'improvisation' such that they were able to imbue their work in the high forests distant from the village with a measure of worth, and even enjoyment. My inability to accompany SC girls on their trips prevents my being able to comment on this possibility. The point remains, however, that SC girls generally appeared to lack the capacity to use *mukku* collection as an opportunity to have fun (*mazaa karna*) and tended to suffer multiple hardships on long trips to collect lichen. They had to prioritise earning money from lichen collection, worked under the supervision of parents, endured a painful apprenticeship when they worried about the work and were also exposed to real dangers: three young women from the region had died collecting *mukku* in the five years preceding my stay in Bemni, one from hypothermia, one from pneumonia and one after being attacked by a leopard.

Social inequalities based on age, caste and class therefore influenced how girls engaged with the collection of *mukku*. Two further points emerge from this section. First, analysis of girls' *mukku* collection highlights the importance of attending to the diverse representations of the forest in Bemni. Just as young GC women were actively engaged in imagining the forest as a space of freedom and beauty, young SC women described the distant forests in which they worked as malevolent, dark and terrifying. Age and caste therefore intersected to create particular clusters of environmental subjectivity – a point that is at odds with Arun Agrawal's (2005) work. Second, the discussion of girls' work collecting lichen provides further evidence of children's capacity for 'shrewd improvisation', a type of bricolage in which children are attentive to opportunities for play, sociality and identity formation.

Rakesh

The *mukku*-collecting tactics of Saka and her GC girl friends contrast not only with those of their SC contemporaries but also with those of GC and SC boys. Like their GC contemporaries, SC boys conducted only day trips for *mukku*. The parents of SC boys generally forbade their sons from making the four- to seven-day trips undertaken by SC girls, citing the extreme cold and harsh conditions as being too dangerous. I therefore discuss GC boys and SC boys together.

There were some differences in the manner in which SC boys and GC boys collected *mukku*, however. SC boys tended to come from poorer households and were under more pressure to be productive than were GCs. As a result, SC boys favoured collecting *mukku* from high-altitude and particularly mature parts of the forest, such as Nilari. Here, the especially tall trees had large canopy branches holding more prolific supplies of lichen. To reach these greater rewards, however, SC boys had to climb dangerously high, often double the height that most GC boys were prepared to climb (see Figure 6.3). To gain maximum productivity, SC boys also practised rather unsustainable *mukku* collection, by knocking to the ground large canopy branches, from which they later stripped the *mukku*. In a single day these boys succeeded in decimating the mature canopy of one area. The difficulty of reaching these areas, involving either a very long circuitous route or a very steep and rather dangerous scramble, meant that the van panchayat *chowkidar* was unlikely to witness this destruction, and the boys felt free to fell the branches illegally.

Figure 6.3 An SC boy climbs high into the tree canopy to collect *mukku*

We regularly accompanied groups of both SC and GC boys on their day trips to collect *mukku*. In contrast to the girls, we found that the boys' incentives for collecting *mukku* lay not in the search for a space of fun but in their quest for money. The following case study of Rakesh exemplifies the attitudes of GC and SC boys.

Rakesh was sixteen in 2004 and came from a GC family owning a small amount of land. He was orphaned when he was young and lived with his older brother and grandmother. Rakesh's older brother was married in 2003, but his wife still studied at school and did not yet live permanently with her husband. Rakesh had dropped out of school in 2003 and worked alongside his brother at home, in the fields and in the forest. Despite his young age, Rakesh was keenly aware of his responsibilities to his family and the need to supplement his farming work with a cash income.

Lichen collection was the most important source of cash for Rakesh, and he spent his first full winter out of school (2003/4) harvesting lichen on a daily basis. Rakesh had started collecting *mukku* at the age of twelve and was widely admired for his tree-climbing ability. Rakesh talked about his lichen collection as his salaried job (*naukri*). In 2004 Rakesh made between Rs. 140 and 175 a day from *mukku* collection, considerably more than the standard Rs. 80 per day available for manual labour (*mazdoori*) in the village.

I accompanied Rakesh on four of his lichen collection trips in early 2004. Like young women, Rakesh and his male peers regarded me as an older sister. But the young men whom I accompanied to collect lichen, unlike the young women, did not expect me to participate in their work and 'play'. Rather, they regarded me as someone who would provide a good 'audience' for their lichen collection practices and whom they could teach about the forest. Knowing that I often accompanied girls to collect lichen, many young men emphasised that it was only with *boys* that I would learn to appreciate how to harvest *mukku* effectively. But boys sometimes excluded me from conversations about their *mukku* harvesting, particularly from their jokes about girl's lichen collection practices.

Rakesh and his friends typically began their day in the open, grassy plains above the uppermost village but beneath the forest edge. Here they would start an impromptu game of cricket, using a piece of wood as a bat. On other occasions Rakesh would play in the small stream, smashing the large slabs of ice 5 centimetres thick and distributing chunks of 'mountain biscuits' for his friends to suck on. They dawdled there for nearly an hour, savouring the morning sun before entering the darker, cooler forest.

Once in the forest, Rakesh worked diligently. The boys usually wandered off either on their own or in pairs to climb trees. They filled the cloth bags slung around their shoulders and regularly emptied them into large plastic sacks. Despite gathering lichen at a feverish pace, Rakesh and his peers found many opportunities to 'joke around' (*mazaak karna*) while working. Rakesh was a renowned comedian, and his jokes often centred on the 'inferior' lichen-collecting or tree-climbing skills of other young people. For example, Rakesh used a range of high-pitched comic voices to impersonate young women climbing trees, to the uproarious delight of his friends. Later, he demonstrated his own relative prowess by rocking dangerously from the tops of trees or swinging from the canopy of one tree directly into another.

Despite his comic performances, Rakesh rarely took breaks from lichen collection, even for lunch. Rakesh compared his lichen collection with that of the girls who he had seen as he passed through the forest. He told me: 'Girls hang around beneath our trees and steal the lichen that falls. Anyway, they just go for fun, for passing time [timepass]. But the boys are serious and go just for lichen.'

Rakesh had not sold his lichen harvest by the time I left the village, but he had made around Rs. 6,000 the previous year. This sum represented a major contribution to his family's income. In 2004 he planned to buy large supplies of flour and rice for his household. Rakesh also proudly explained how his financial contribution had helped to pay for his brother's wedding in 2003 (see

Figure 6.4 Rakesh on his brother's wedding day (the wedding was paid for largely through the sale of Rakesh's *mukku* harvest)

Figure 6.4). He expected that his lichen collection would also help provide for his own wedding in the next few years.

As Rakesh's case suggests, young men usually spent less time engaged in non-work activities than did young women. Although boys often took some time off to play cricket or mess around in the sun before entering the *mukku* forest, once the boys had decided to start collecting *mukku* they went about it in a determined manner. They collected continuously, climbing one tree after another without stopping to chat. The boys also tended to work independently, often running off for long periods to collect *mukku* alone before rejoining the other boys. The boys claimed that, by working independently, they avoided unnecessary competition for *mukku*. Moreover, the boys did not often group together for lunch. When they did meet for lunch, they did not, in the manner of the girls, amalgamate and share the bundles of food that they had brought with them. Having eaten their individual picnics, the boys tended to run off quickly to resume their *mukku* work, often claiming that it was too cold to sit around chatting.

Aware of the gender differences in lichen-collecting strategies, young GC women often sought to justify their engagement in 'having fun'. The girls claimed that they were, for most of the year, under more pressure than were boys to work and conform to demure and modest behavioural norms in the village. They could not be 'open' (*khulha*) or 'free' in public spaces. The girls argued that the *mukku* forest afforded them a rare opportunity for private activity. The girls also claimed that the boys had no need to use their *mukku*-collecting days to take time off, for they were regularly granted free time. Girls argued that boys were always playing cricket, and could behave as they liked in the village. Boys tended to concede this line of argument. As Rakesh put it, 'Young women need this time in the forest to mess around.'

There was also an important difference in the social organisation of *mukku* collection among boys as compared to girls. The boys policed themselves and their progress individually, while girls viewed their activities collecting *mukku* as a collective endeavour. While the girls saw it as a moral obligation to assist the *mukku* collection of lesser-skilled girls who could not climb trees, by throwing *mukku* to them on the ground, boys perceived such strategies to be 'stealing'. The boys' independent working styles further contrasted with the girls', who, for fear of being left alone, emphasised the need to stay in touch with the group. When I accompanied the girls, particularly on the first few occasions before Anita came with me, the girls were careful never to let me out of their sight, and, when they had climbed high into the trees, they called to me constantly so that I did not feel alone. By contrast, we often found it difficult to keep up with the boys during their *mukku* trips, as they quickly spread out and worked separately.

The example of Rakesh also highlights the central role of money in boys' lichen collection. Boys frequently spoke proudly of the money they had earned from *mukku* harvesting and argued that these financial incentives were far more important than were opportunities to have fun. When I asked Rakesh if he derived any enjoyment from lichen collection, he instantly exclaimed, 'Bah! We just tear our clothes climbing trees for lichen. There is no fun, but we get money from it so that's why we go.' Other boys similarly stressed the importance of gaining an income from their *mukku* harvest, and cited cash as their incentive to work.

The amount of cash that these boys made from their *mukku* collection was often rather small. While Rakesh had derived a large amount of cash from his *mukku* collection, younger boys earned much less money, partly due to their relative inexperience and partly because their school timetable restricted their collection. Three other boys I came to know well, Mehendre, Ashish and Sanjay, had made almost Rs. 900, just over Rs. 500 and Rs. 700, respectively, by mid-March of the 2004 winter *mukku* season, having collected between 2.5 and 3 kilograms each day (opposed to Rakesh's 4 to 5 kilogram average). These boys said that they were still learning the skills required for prolific *mukku* collection, and that they would slowly improve and become more productive.

In spite of the meagre returns, however, boys were frequently able to use money made from *mukku* collection to develop a sense of themselves as accomplished young men. When boys had control over the money they earned through *mukku* collection, they sometimes spent it on themselves. For example, after receiving money for a large contingent of *mukku* in Ghat, boys often went for a shopping spree in the bazaar. On these trips, boys also often had their photographs taken and ate at tea stalls, and bought second-hand clothing. As in other parts of India (Osella and Osella 2006), acts of conspicuous consumption were an attractive means through which young men could project a sense of themselves as competent and successful.

Such conspicuous consumption occasionally brought boys into conflict with their parents or guardians. For example, one young SC man whom I came to know well, Manoj, angered his parents by spending most of his *mukku* money on clothes and sweets for himself. Manoj told his parents that, since it was his salaried work (*naukri*), he should spend the fruits of his labour as he liked. Manoj's mother became frustrated and told Manoj, 'I also do *naukri*; I cook the food and wash up and look after the livestock, but nobody pays me.' She complained that, in 2003, Manoj had also kept all the *mukku* money for himself. Manoj's oldest brother added, 'We even gave him an extra Rs. 100 for the transport to Ghat, but he still brought nothing back!'

But, in most cases, boys gave the money they earned from *mukku* collection to their parents. Either they simply handed over the money to their elders, as in the case of girls, or they used their earnings to purchase gifts for family members, often non-essential items. For example, on one trip to Ghat in February 2004 a young GC man named Sanjay brought presents of clothes for his brothers, a headscarf for his mother and a pocketful of cash for his father. Sanjay's friend, Mehendre, had similarly bought nothing for himself on his trip to Ghat, but happily exhibited his purchases for the rest of his family: plastic shoes for each of his three siblings and bags of pulses and spices as requested by his mother. The boys' acquisitions, or their contributions towards expenses such as weddings, became visible symbols of their toil and their effectiveness as male providers (see Figure 6.4 above).

Proud of their financial contributions, and the associated image of themselves as successful young men, boys tended to talk about their *mukku* collection as their *naukri*, or job. Their use of the term *naukri*, as distinct from the term *mazdoori* (manual labour), was revealing. *Mazdoori* usually referred to the low-waged and temporary manual labour that was the only form of externally paid, organised employment available in the village. It was a term used negatively, suggesting the least prestigious and most insecure form of labour conducted under the supervision of an employer or supervisor (compare Jeffery and Jeffery

1996). By contrast, *naukri* connoted work with a regular salary, a degree of job security and, often, a lack of dependence on a 'boss' (*maalik*). Although *mukku* collection was both manual and temporary, the boys' choice of the word *naukri* over *mazdoori* was perhaps indicative of their perceived control over their work. In *mukku* collection, the boys themselves set the parameters and conditions of their labour in the absence of an employer. It also hints at the boys' pride in their skills. Villagers tended to argue that 'anyone' (*koi bhi*) could do *mazdoori*, but they argued that particular skills were necessary for *naukri*. Thus, by labelling their work *naukri*, the boys also sought to emphasise the dexterity, strength and more general 'experience' required to be a competent *mukku* collector. In linking *mukku* collection to *naukri*, the boys also tried to create an imaginative connection between their forest work to the occupations of their older peers who had migrated to work in urban areas or outside the hills.

Finally, the Rakesh case study points to how boys derived symbolic value from their prowess in physically engaging in lichen work. It was partly the difficulty of their *mukku* work and the skills required for its successful accomplishment that gave lichen collection meaning. I encountered numerous examples of boys using taunts and jokes to stress their own toughness and others' incompetence in the sphere of *mukku* collection. While the boys claimed not to compete with each other over their respective lichen harvests, at the end of each day many GC boys enjoyed the public act of weighing their lichen sacks on a shopkeeper's scales. I became an important audience for their growing achievements; as they passed my room on their way home, the boys happily told me how much *mukku* they had collected and how it compared to the previous day's harvest.

While for young GC women *mukku* collection offered a setting in which to mischievously invert notions of proper femininity (albeit in ways that reproduced gendered ideas), for young men it provided an opportunity to test, develop and display a culturally mediated version of what Raewyn Connell (1995) calls 'hegemonic masculinity'. Philippe Bourgois (1995) makes related observations working in the very different context of urban New York. He shows how teenage Latino and Latina crack dealers use their informal work as a means of expressing their developing sense of masculine adulthood and countering economic marginalisation. Similarly, Willis (1977) emphasises the crucial importance of the pay packet in young men's decision to enter factory employment in a west Midlands town in the 1970s; becoming a breadwinner was key to establishing oneself as an adult man. As in Bourgois's and Willis's cases, young men's masculinities in Bemni were produced socially and, once developed, served to bind small groups of young men together. And – again as in Bourgois's and Willis's work – young men in Bemni did not always or inevitably agree on what constitutes a successful masculinity. For example, some young men argued that it is the physical prowess demonstrated through *mukku* collection that provides them with a sense of accomplishment, while others stressed their financial gains. Still others seemed to derive a sense of their emerging masculinity from the jokes they made while working in the forest. In addition, a type of emotional attachment to the forest, also evident among young women, complicated young men's efforts to develop a hegemonic masculinity through *mukku* collection. On several occasions, young men left their work to identify particularly scenic areas of the forest or put aside their harvesting to sing romantic songs about the beauty of the hills, the coldness of the local water, the abundant and life-giving forest and the awe-inspiring nature of the high peaks. For all the inconsistencies and fissures in these local examples of masculinity, however, most young men in Bemni agreed that diligent *mukku* collection provided a good example of 'men's work' (*admi ka kaam*) and that their conscientiousness marked them out from allegedly wayward, restless and lazy younger boys.

Conclusions

An income-generating opportunity that was quite new, and not centrally part of the agro-pastoral regime in the village, was a highly significant part of young people's social and cultural worlds. For GC girls, *mukku* collection work presented an opportunity to subvert dominant gender norms, and, for boys, it was a means to establish themselves as independent male providers. It was important that *mukku* collection was a fairly new income-generating opportunity: parents had relatively little knowledge about the nature of the work, and this opened up opportunities for girls to carve out opportunities for fun.

This chapter offers a basis for reflecting further on gender inequalities in Bemni. Recent research on gender and youth in the West has raised the possibility that young women may be able to use the expansion of the market economy to contest established forms of gender privilege (Arnot, Maton and Millen 1996; see also Butler 1990; Jeffrey and McDowell 2004). Cole's (2004) work in Madagascar – where young women have used transactional sex with outsiders to position them as effective 'heads of household' – points to the possibility of such gender transformation in widely different settings. In the Uttarakhand case, though, girls and young women remained poorly placed to challenge patriarchal dominance in Bemni. While capable of transgressing local norms in distant forests, young women's efforts to 'have fun' ultimately reinforced, more than they unsettled, patterns of unequal gender relations. Meanwhile, for SC girls, even these spaces of fun were not available. Among boys, *mukku* served as a basis for cultivating a notion of adult masculinity based around physical prowess, income generation or both (compare Jackson and Palmer-Jones 1999). Just as girls used leaf collection as a means of establishing a sense of themselves as competent, diligent workers, young men discovered in the process of collecting *mukku* a basis for making claims about their own masculine strength and conscientiousness.

In his book on the strategies of the children and young people in Harlem, New York, Bourgois (1995) argues that the physical location – in an area marked by economic decline and poverty – influenced young people's practices. Young people discussed what it meant to grow up in Harlem, they used the physical landscape to express ideas and they came to associate particular spaces in the city with opportunities for fun and sociality, or as 'threatening'. Moreover, over time, young people's social practices politicised space in powerful ways, such as in the manner in which specific groups of young men came to understand particular locales as their 'territory' (compare Massey 2005). In a similar vein, the local environment was constantly enrolled in young people's practices while collecting *mukku* in Bemni. The forests in which *mukku* was collected were far from the village and could serve as relatively 'safe', hidden spaces for young people to experiment with gendered performances.

The environment was also crucial as a source of the raw materials for children's practices: for the snowball fights among the girls, for example, and, for the boys, the sheer quantities of lichen, which they so ostentatiously weighed as evidence of their prowess. As in the case of herding and leaf litter collection, young people also reflected constantly on the environment while collecting *mukku*. Among boys, these discussions were usually organised around the business of collecting the lichen: which trees might be most fruitful, and how to climb particularly difficult parts for example. For girls, their discussion centred more on the aesthetic quality of the forests: the abundant rhododendron flowers and the views of the distant high peaks. Over time, young people came to associate specific parts of the forest – individual trees, clearings, vistas – with specific events from the past, such as a particularly good *mukku* harvest or an especially fun picnic, such that the forests around Bemni became for these young men and young women a living repository of memories.

7 Conclusions

When I arrived in the Indian town of Gopeshwar in December 2002, I struck up a conversation with a local newspaper agent in his small tin office on the edge of the busy high street. Intrigued by the presence of a foreigner in the winter, when trekking is impossible and the roads to Hindu pilgrimage centres are closed, he asked why I had come to Gopeshwar. I explained that I was interested in studying children's work (*kaam*) in the Indian Himalayas. I tentatively suggested that a lot of academic and social activity had focused on women's labour but that there had been less attention to children. The man looked disdainful: 'The children in the villages only play cricket. They go to school, come back, hassle their parents, go to play cricket. So what have you got to study?' Rather defensively, I pointed to the large number of girls I had seen struggling up the slopes with huge baskets of leaves on my trip to Gopeshwar. The newspaper agent looked unimpressed: 'Maybe very occasionally they do some work. The girls do some work, I suppose. But the boys only laze around (*araam*).'

One response to the newspaper agent would be to detail children's 1,000 metre climbs to snowy forest peaks to gather lichen. One could recount the chilling touch of wet leaves on early autumn mornings, and of standing under dripping trees watching children watching cows. Another response would be more prosaic. One could recount simply the range of tasks in which children engaged. In Bemni, children as young as six years old helped their parents a great deal, and by ten they were tenaciously working across a bewildering array of fronts: in their homes, in livestock stalls, in the fields and in the forests overlooking the Nandakini Valley. Young people's diaries provided a humbling insight into the workload of young people in Bemni, the tasks virtually toppling over one another in quick succession. Many young people managed to juggle these competing commitments alongside the need to acquire important school-based skills and the 'cultural capital' (Bourdieu 1984 [1979]) that is attached locally to having a school qualification.

A key contribution of my work to wider understandings of young people has been to demonstrate the extraordinary importance of children and youth to the agrarian economy. I have done this not through trying to develop quantitative measures of their input but ethnographically, by literally clambering into the spaces in which young people work, talking to them about their effort, across the course of a full yearly cycle.

In the early 2000s Bemni was in a process of transformation from a situation of direct social reproduction, wherein resources are passed down intergenerationally via the transfer of property at inheritance, to mediated reproduction, in which power is simultaneously transferred through schooling (Bourdieu 1990 [1980]). In Berry's (1985) terms, a slow move was afoot from a situation in which young people work for parents to one in which parents work to keep their sons and daughters in school. But such processes of change, which are rarely unilinear, were not very well advanced in the high Himalayas. For the most part, young people remained integral to the economy of the household, plugging gaps in times of high labour demand, conducting some of the more tedious, burdensome tasks and sometimes – such as the SCs working for long periods collecting lichen – finding themselves exposed to considerable danger. They also carried out a great deal of care work in the household, such as assisting elderly or disabled relatives, or doing things as simple as cleaning younger siblings and keeping them out of fires. Young people in Bemni were therefore not 'becomings' but competent, important and influential 'beings'.

Moreover, young people found numerous ways of instilling meaning in their work (for example Willis 1977; Katz 2004). Girls charted their growing strength and skill through reference to their ability to build and haul leaf baskets. Boys could measure their own growth in terms of the trees they could climb for *mukku* and the amount they could earn from their crop. In addition, girls and boys chronicled their increasing maturity with reference to the tasks with which they were entrusted in the home: By ten you might be allowed to resurface the floor, for example, and by nine you might be left in sole charge of the livestock. Far from being simply 'work', everyday household labour within and outside the home was conducted flexibly and served as a basis for young people's subjectivities.

Young people were not passive 'cogs' in the wheel of the agro-pastoral regime. As others have also pointed out (such as Nieuwenhuys 1994), young people can often negotiate over the timing, sequencing and character of their labour. Young people in Bemni changed the rhythms, timing and spaces of work to suit their own needs, as in the case of *mukku* collection practices, when boys and girls combined their work with periods of fun. It was evident, too, in the efforts of children to juggle their domestic, agricultural and school-related work. In Chapter 3 I described how many children used the excuse of schoolwork to avoid performing other tasks, while others used household work as an excuse for not going to school. It is important to stress the limits to young people's agency. The agro-pastoral regime is oriented around rules, some of them set out by the van panchayat regarding, for example, where to graze, and some dictated by custom and precedent. The climate, and the passing of the seasons, dictate what can be done when in terms of crop cycles and livestock grazing. This system inevitably imposes a series of patterns on work, life and movement in Bemni. I have set out in the book the key features of Bemni's agriculture, forest use and pastoral 'cycle', explaining what people do at particular times (Chapter 2) and how young people fit into this regime (Chapter 3). The point remains, however, that parents and young people adapt flexibly to these circumstances, and the manner in which young people juggle schooling alongside the demands of the agro-pastoral regime is a case in point.

Improvisation also occurred at a finer scale, too. Young people could play different roles in work settings, according to the situation in which they found themselves. This was evident when boys were herding. They took advantage of the particular array of local resources – a burst water pipe, for example – to create opportunities for fun. Similarly, it probably would not have occurred to boys to build a temple for the herding *puja* if they had not happened to be standing around the broken-down cottage when discussing the event. Such improvisation was also conditioned by who happened to be present in specific work sites. Thus, for example, girls often assumed different roles according to who happened to be present when they were collecting leaves. A girl might be an adult-like leader one day and play the dependent child the next. Another advantage of the term 'improvisation' is that it hints at the performative nature of young people's practices.

Improvisation was also evident in terms of the mechanics of actually doing work. This was especially evident in the case of gathering lichen, which is a fairly new activity. If young people could not reach a branch or climb a tree to collect lichen, they would do some form of *jugaad*: knock a branch down with a stone, use a rope to hook a clump of lichen or stand on one another's shoulders. In much of north India, *jugaad* has precisely this connotation of working materials in a shrewd and opportunistic manner – 'craft', it might be called – in order to effect a desired outcome. In the case of this type of micro-scale improvisation, in particular, young people acted on the spur of the moment. Other accounts of young people's agency have also referred to *jugaad*-like improvisation. For example, Henrik Vigh (2006), in his study of youth militias in Guinea-Bissau, refers to the ubiquity of the idea of 'dubragiem', which means ingeniously finding solutions to problems of resource scarcity. Janet Roitman (2004) refers to how the notion of creatively searching for 'spoils' was important in the work of the young men involved in illegal trade in the Chad Basin. *Jugaad*-like behaviour is not a peculiar attribute of young people, but it is a theme that runs through work with children and youth – and it was a prominent feature of my conversations with young people in Bemni.

Active quiescence

Children and youth work hard, respect their elders and, for the most part, fulfil obligations in school and in the home. But this quiescence should not be taken to imply that children and youth are straightforwardly under the thumb of their seniors or that they reproduce in the same form ideas communicated by older members of society. Such a view, enunciated in much of the literature on young people's socialisation within and outside India (for example Kakar 1978; compare James, Jenks and Prout 1998), ignores several important points that have emerged from my fieldwork.

First, it is evident from my description of young people's lives in a high Himalayan village that children and youth fulfil work demands and seek to impress their seniors because they see that it is in their interest to do so, not because they are straightforwardly 'programmed' by their parents to act in a certain way. There are some parallels here with Mahmood's (2005) ethnography of the Da'wa religious movement in Egypt. Mahmood shows that many Egyptian women active in religious organisations are not seeking to challenge patriarchal norms. Mahmood argues that, instead, they abide by the precepts of established gendered hierarchies. They do so in large part in order to fulfil religious goals that, Mahmood observes, US-based feminists might find difficult to understand. In Bemni, young people also tended to abide by dominant norms. But their motivation is easier to understand from a Western perspective than the motivations of the women at the centre of Mahmood's study. Young people conformed to the demands of society for pragmatic reasons. They saw that fulfilling particular ideals, for example of femininity or masculinity, would lead to rewards, be they positions in the army or a 'good husband'. For example, there was a strong measure of self-interest in girls' efforts to develop their competence in the collection of leaf litter. Future in-laws from other villages asked about a girls' capacity to perform forest work before agreeing upon a marriage. In line with Reynolds (1991) and Nieuwenhuys (1994), my research suggests that girls' work may assist them in developing secure futures.

What also emerges powerfully from my account is the energy that young people put into building and strengthening social networks with a view to securing their own futures. Much of the literature on young people's agency works under the assumption not only that their action must be in some respect 'nonquiescent' in order to qualify as 'agency' but also that young people inevitably become more independent as they mature (see Mannheim 1956 [1923]). But in Bemni young people's agency emerges not through children and youth trying to escape the home and assert independence but through patient efforts to strengthen social networks. Earlier work by psychologists partly anticipated this. For example, Rudolph and Rudolph (1976: 146) show in their study of Rajput adulthood that becoming a mature adult meant creating individuality within an 'interdependent, corporate setting'. The literature on 'social capital' in the global South and some forms of formal network analysis has similarly emphasised positive sociality (Putnam 1993). But this has simultaneously distracted scholars from how social relations actually work: we learn about the shape and form of networks, but very little about the flows of materials, ideas, affection and trust through which networks are produced and through which they morph or dissolve through time.

It is therefore important to note that young people's 'active quiescence' emerges through their social practices. The ties that bind young people to each other and senior kin are usually ones of mutual dependence. In the language of 1970s sociology, the connections are 'multiplex': they operate along several lines at once. Two girls are friends, cousins, classmates and workmates. A boy is his mother's son, as well as her employee, carer, advisor and friend. Some of these ties can change over a very short time scale – a few days or weeks – because of quarrels or illness. A 'firm friend' established through collecting leaf litter can be shunned when the wider families of the two girls quarrel the following week. Connections also vary seasonally. For example, girls who are neighbours in Danda (the highest settlement) may live apart in Gwar (the lowest settlement). There is logic to their friendship in Danda that does not exist in Gwar. People's connections vary over long time scales, too. Young women pass out of the stage of 'youth', marry and move away, for example, thus disconnecting intimate ties. Of course, all these temporal processes have cyclical elements: ties may lie latent for weeks, months or years and be resuscitated at a later date. A key implication of this focus on time is that the interdependences that young people create through their work are ones that require regular reiteration in practice. A young person cannot say simply 'She is my friend'. This statement can be meaningful only if the young person works with the friend, plays with the friend and solves problems with the friend.

Other scholars have stressed the importance of social relationships in the process through which young people and others express their agency in the contemporary global South (for example Mains 2007; Desai and Killick 2010; Thieme 2010). For example, Mahmood has discussed how women in Egypt cultivate conservative kin-based relations to advance their interests. Similarly, in an Indian context there is a long line of anthropological literature on kinship and family as the routes through which people gain a sense of their own effectiveness and power (see Mandelbaum 1970; Uberoi 1994). A distinctive contribution of this study is to highlight the particular significance of friendship in the social production of agency. An early strand of anthropological writing tended to dismiss possibilities for significant friendships in societies in which kinship structures are strong. Other work acknowledged friendship but tended to imagine this relationship as subordinate to kinship (see Cohen 1961; Paine 1969). But friendship may be the medium through which people relate to sibling, cousins and more distant relations (for example Reed-Danahay 1999). There are interesting parallels between these conclusions and Western accounts of kin and friend relations. Many scholars argue that, in western Europe and North America, kinship relations are becoming increasingly 'optative' (Ortner 2004). People pick and choose between siblings, cousins and other kin to decide which relationships will take on the characteristic of a friendly relation.

In most places friendship is imagined as a relatively durable form of personal relationship, in which people seek out each other's company, cooperate with one another and articulate shared moral understandings. But the particular form that friendship takes, and the manner in which people discuss friendship, vary a great deal. Among girls in Bemni, friendship was primarily imagined as a relationship of trust reflected and produced through labour. Other ethnographic work has demonstrated that friendships may be based on self-interest as well as affection (Gratz 2004). But the link between friendship and the need to achieve social goals is perhaps especially striking in the Bemni case. Notions of friendship acted as the lubricant for working relationships between different girls and also allowed girls the time and opportunity to have fun in the forest, even while conducting the relatively laborious task of leaf litter collection. Yet friendship also served as a means of control, entrenching norms around work and femininity.

Social inequality

Gender, class and caste inequalities shaped young people's working lives in a way that is likely to be more powerful than in many other settings in which young people's lives have been chronicled in detail (for example Katz 1989, 1991; Swanson 2009). Work in the home, in the cultivated fields and with respect to leaf litter collection was associated, in adulthood, with women. As a result, parents expected girls to start work earlier than boys. Girls were also encouraged to acquire higher levels of physical and technical competence in household and agricultural tasks. In the case of leaf litter collection, for example, a ten-year-old girl was expected to carry the same amount as a twelve-year-old boy. It followed, too, that girls found it more difficult to negotiate with their parents over the nature, timing and extent of their work than did boys. Moreover, the one task that was quite closely associated with boys and young men – herding – was the one that required least effort. Added to this, girls often found that their ability to conduct relatively 'fun' work, such as herding, was curtailed after puberty.

Young people's work practices also tended to reflect and reinforce gendered expectations. Boys used lichen collection as a means to test and elaborate ideas of themselves as strong, daring breadwinners. In their urge to demonstrate their prowess as providers, boys reinforced corresponding notions of young masculinity, for example through ridiculing girls' lack of strength and skill in the forest (Chapter 6; compare Willis 1977).

Such gendered practices were not always straightforward. Girls' efforts to develop reputations of competence centred on paying almost forensic attention to the practice of leaf collection and the process of constructing tall, densely packed and securely tied baskets of dry leaves (Chapter 5). Girls constructed a vision of themselves as skilful forest workers and 'good girls' (*atchchhi larkiyan*) through repeated efforts to meet village expectations of what constituted good baskets (*atchchhe kandhe*). At the same time, girls could obtain for themselves a certain room for manoeuvre by sometimes presenting themselves as being at different positions in the age hierarchy. By playing the role of 'little girl', for example, a teenager could obtain some respite from the demands of leaf collection, at least in particular situations. In the case of *mukku* collection, girls toyed with gendered expectations more directly, using the high forests as a means to subvert, partially and temporally, dominant notions of gender and propriety. As Bakhtin's (1984) work primes us to expect, these transgressions had the effect of reinforcing girls' conception of what constitutes 'proper conduct' rather than leading to any type of shift in understandings of what it is to be a girl and young woman in Bemni.

At the same time, 'development' (*vikaas*) in its different guises was changing some aspects of young people's relationship to notions of gender and sexual difference. On the negative side, the shift from bride price to a system of dowry was reducing young women's capacity to negotiate over marriage partners. This was not an area that I investigated in detail, but it seems likely that the fuller development of a dowry system would also lead to the commodification of young women and perhaps render them vulnerable to the type of intimidation and physical harm that have been documented in plains India (Roulet 1996).

More positively, a rise in schooling for boys and girls, linked to shifts in marriage, was creating a life stage of 'youth' (*jawani*) for girls that did not exist in the past. Girls used to be married in their early teens and move to live with agnatic kin. In the early 2000s they were marrying much later, and spending their teens working for their households in Bemni. Girls such as Saka (Chapter 6) spent most of this period engaged in intensive household and agricultural labour. But the expansion of the road network and the growth of Ghat as a commercial centre had recently opened up new markets, in particular for the sale of lichen. The winter collection of *mukku* presented girls with new opportunities to escape to the forest, and provided both an economic and a social resource. That they had to climb 1,000 metres or so in the depths of winter to obtain these opportunities for unchaperoned 'fun' says much about the scale of gender inequality in Bemni. That this opportunity was open only to GCs, in turn, highlights how caste and gender can intersect to marginalise those at the bottom of the pile.

Caste difference, intersecting with class inequalities, was a major feature of social life in Bemni. This is notable because there is substantial evidence of increased cross-caste cooperation and understanding in contemporary India. For example, Arjun Appadurai (2002) has described middle-class activists and the poor working across caste and class lines to improve urban infrastructure in Mumbai. Sarah Pinto (2008) records numerous examples of cross-caste friendship and mutual understanding in her ethnography of birth practices in UP. Jeffrey (2010) has likewise described how young people in the north Indian city of Meerut often put aside religious and caste differences when hanging out in and around universities. In Jeffrey's case, young people's age and generational standing appear to override entrenched caste prejudices.

In Bemni, I sometimes saw different castes socialising in school. Moreover, overt forms of caste discrimination, such as GCs taunting and humiliating SCs, were uncommon. But there was, on the whole, no 'melting pot' effect in the case of young people's work in Bemni to parallel the observations of Appadurai, Pinto and Jeffrey. Different castes of children (GCs and SCs) tend to work apart. Whether it was cricket matches, *pujas*, leaf collection, or *mukku* gathering, SCs and GCs tended to occupy separate spaces. SCs and GCs herded cattle, collected leaf litter and gathered *mukku* in separate groups. In addition, caste often influenced the nature of children's work practices. For example, GC girls went on day trips in peer groups to collect lichen, while SC girls accompanied their mothers and other women on long trips to relatively distant forests. Such caste-based differences were largely a result of the greater pressure that SCs were under to contribute to work and income-generating practices. I did not find any close friendship across caste lines among girls or boys, nor any instance of inter-caste marriage.

The social construction of the environment

Aside from advancing ethnographic understandings of children and youth in India, the other main contribution of this book has been to an understanding of young people's relationship to the environment and the wider literature on the social construction of the environment. There has been considerable work in south Asia on the forest as a site of political struggle (for example Mawdsley 1997; Rangan 2001) and a site for the emergence of gendered identities (Linkenbach 1998; Gururani 2002). My book has tried to wrestle some of these broad understandings of people/forest relationships to the ground in order to investigate young people's lived and tactile engagement with the forest and forest products. Young people actively and imaginatively related to the environment around them, often in ways that older villagers could not anticipate.

Young people's working lives were thoroughly entangled in the 'stuff' of the fields and forests. This is true in the obvious sense that they needed to grow food to live, and feed cattle for manure and dairy products. Young people were connected to local fauna and flora via the system of agro-pastoralism in a way that was more immediate than for, say, young people in many parts of the United States or western Europe. They were also much more closely attuned to variations in the environment and the vagaries of the weather, seasonal change and freak events, in particular. Their relationship to nature was also evident, however, in a myriad of smaller micro-engagements with the things that surrounded them on the mountain. Groves were hiding places, bushes were sources of wild fruit, and stones and branches in the forest or on pastures could be crude cricket bats or balls. The ice on the stream could be collected to make 'mountain biscuits', and the leeches and insects, while annoying, were useful for practical jokes. Such examples of everyday intimate relationships with the environment could be multiplied almost endlessly: to be young in Bemni was to be wholly enmeshed in the fabric of nature.

I have stressed especially the degree to which young people encountered their environment while moving across it. I have found Ingold's (2007) notion of 'wayfaring' suggestive as a concept to work with, because it foregrounds how people experienced their surroundings as they moved through them, the spontaneous nature of this movement, and travel as a basis for learning, sociality and cultural production. At the same time, Ingold's idea of wayfaring, when viewed through a north Indian lens, needs to be problematised. There was no general 'wayfaring culture' in Bemni, and the capacity to meander slowly through the environment, picking up cues from surrounding nature, varied according to people's age, gender and caste. For example, young women found that they could 'wayfare' while herding until their early teens, but afterwards they were barred from doing so. Wayfaring cannot be described as some general aspect of being human; it reflects gender, class and other inequalities.

My analysis has also been taken up with what might be termed the social construction of the environment. The first and most obvious point is that young people instilled particular meanings in their local surroundings. The forest was sometimes a site of fear. Young people measured their maturity in terms of conquering anxiety, especially worries about malignant ghosts and wild animals. Others seemed plagued by fears over the security of their livestock in the face of leopard attack, or, in the case of SC girls, threats to their safety associated with long trips to distant forests. Many boys and girls expressed a love for their home area. One might imagine that villagers would be rather unconcerned about the beauty of their environment: would you really think about the view when you were trying to eke out an existence from the soil? But young people felt deeply attached to the Bemni environment, emotionally and aesthetically, and this was made evident both in their conversations and through song. They told of the cleanliness and purity of the natural environment: the relative superiority, for example, of 'their' water, air and forest. They contrasted the peaceful countryside with the rush and dirt of the town, and spoke of the serenity of the mountains and the rich array of flowers and wildlife around the village. It is striking that young people in Bemni often extracted from the environment opportunities for humour and fun. This mischievousness was most evident in GC girls' *mukku* collection, when 'fun' was associated with such things as snowball fights and pulling each other down the mountain. But humour and mischief were also important themes in young people's herding, leaf litter collection and daily tasks around the home.

Another aspect of the social construction of the environment was young people's judgements about the social risks and social opportunities associated with various spaces around the village. These judgements interrelated with, but were distinct from, their ideas about the environment's innate qualities, for example as scary or beautiful. Thus, young women perceived the spaces in which young people congregated to herd animals in mixed groups as 'dangerous' not because they feared attack from a leopard or ghost but because they were anxious about acquiring a bad reputation among older villagers. Conversely, young women imagined the relatively distant forests not only as beautiful in their own right but also as prized sites in which they could experiment with gendered identities, in the case of *mukku*, or collaborate to build large baskets of leaves, in the case of harvesting leaf litter, free from the eyes of prying parents. To make this point is to imbue the term 'social construction of the environment' with a double meaning. Young people drew from their experience of the physical environment a set of associations about its character – beautiful, rocky, wild, and so forth – and at the same time derived from their experience of specific places a set of judgements about the social possibilities of their locales: environments were 'safe', 'risky', 'dangerous' from a *social* perspective.

The term 'social construction of the environment' acquires yet another meaning when we consider that young people build up their sense of the environment as a set of physical characteristics and social risks and possibilities through distinctly social experiences: interacting with others during picnics, games and burdensome work sessions. Young people discover sites of particular interest together on work trips. They collaborate in testing and utilising a particular site, for example where they want to erect a swing or collect a large amount of leaf litter. And they share memories of the qualities of specific environments, such as a clearing in which they had an especially good game of cricket, or a spot where older villagers caught them chatting to members of the opposite sex.

Conclusions

My book has made two main contributions to the wider literature on young people, work, agency and the environment. First, I have demonstrated the strength of young people's agency, which, while not directed towards countering dominant norms, pointed to young people's active and creative engagement with broader structures. This creativity was evident in young people's capacity to inject humour into their work, improvise and engage imaginatively with the forest. Children and youth managed gruelling work practices and developed a sense of their own power through investing in local social networks. Mannheim's famous essay on generations is therefore partially useful: it highlights young people's creativity, but it also suggests that youth agency is likely to be expressed only through young people breaking from their families and finding themselves in the city. What is required in the Bemni case is a less romantic vision of agency that accepts that young people are always able to select only from a narrow range of symbolic resources, and do so in ways shaped by broader structures. This suggests the need for a culturally sensitive political economy approach to the study of young people's lives that allows simultaneously for invention and reproduction. Willis's notion of cultural production, in conjunction with the work of Durham on agency, together provide a useful starting point for such an approach. Improvisation, humour and the materiality of young people's cultural practices remain crucial areas for further research and reflection.

Second, I have demonstrated the importance of examining the materiality of young people's everyday work and lives and the environment as a site of social activity and cultural production. Young people are central to the reproduction of the agricultural and pastoral economy. They have vitally important knowledge about the properties of the forest. But still more important is the process through which young people interact on a daily basis with their natural surroundings collectively and imbue their natural environment with meanings. The social construction of the environment has a triple sense in this context: young people perceive particular spaces to have inherent qualities (such as 'rocky'), imagine these spaces as being associated with different social risks or possibilities, and do both these things in conversation one with another.

My book has not been about policy, but it does highlight two key points. First, it points to the dangers associated with taking a stand 'for' or 'against' most forms of child labour. There are, obviously, some types of child labour that are self-evidently pernicious, such as trafficking for sex and highly exploitative labour in manufacturing plants. But for the most part the answer to the question of whether children and young people should be working depends upon context: the meaning that work has for children, the skills they can acquire from it, the relationship between labour and school and how work might fit with young people's futures. None of these complex contextual factors can easily be summed across regions and nations, still less for the global South as a whole. It is here that ethnographic work remains vital. Second, I have also shown how the environment needs to be protected not only because of its utilitarian value to people but also because of its significance as a cultural and social resource. Young people have woven out of their everyday surroundings a living tapestry of meaning, effort and achievement; damage to Bemni's ecosystem would therefore be a social, as well as a natural, disaster.

Epilogue

In April 2004, after fifteen months in the village, our final morning in Bemni began with tears. With nervous stomachs, we could barely eat the special breakfast prepared for us before we emerged, blinking, from the gloom of the tiny house to find the whole village assembled. The small courtyard had been laid with *durris* and gifts of homespun woollen shawls laid out on a makeshift table decorated with rhododendron flowers. There were speeches and more tears. And then the drummers began their doleful beat, leading us down through the fields, with us stopping to grasp at friends, saying goodbye, as they peeled off from the procession. Only a small group of our closest friends accompanied us to the high cliff above a river, halfway down the mountain. There we collapsed, with sobs and wails and no words. I knew I would return to Bemni, but had no idea when. We also knew that each of us, and the village, would never be the same again; that time moves on and changes happen.

It's now 2013, ten years after I first arrived in Bemni. I'm sitting in a muggy office in Oxford having just returned from a few weeks in the village. I continue to work in Bemni, and, each time I return, there is always so much to catch up with. There are weddings to hear about or attend, babies to marvel at and students to encourage, anxious about passing their latest exams. As I make the final alterations to this book, I am once again struck by the changes that have occurred in that intervening decade, not least to the individuals themselves. The children I have written about are now all in their twenties, and two are parents of their own children. Half my key informants are married; indeed, after a teenage romance, two married each other in a so-called 'love marriage'.

Charting their circumstances reveals much about the huge changes that have occurred more broadly in Bemni. Take their education, for example. Four young women, now in their early to mid-twenties, are still studying, completing BA degrees from the university in the district town of Gopeshwar. Two of these are SC girls, of whom one is already married. In 2004 one of the GC girls had dropped out of school in class eight, and I assumed that had spelt the end of her education. But she had picked it up again, and now she is in her final BA year. It is a staggering achievement, particularly in a context in which almost all the mothers of these girls are illiterate.

Two of my key informants were among the first cohort of girls in the village to study up to class twelve at the nearest high school, three villages away along the valley and a ninety minute walk each way. They set a precedent, and have broken the fear of so many parents who were reluctant to allow their girls to stray so far from the village. Now, each year, more and more girls make the same trek. Two of my key informants who passed class twelve are now employed as assistant teachers in the Bemni Primary School, enjoying paid employment before they get married. Another is training to become a nurse even after her marriage and her shift to her husband's village.

Among the boys, two are currently completing their masters degrees from the college in Gopeshwar. One SC boy completed class twelve and then passed the difficult tests to enter the army, and one GC boy emigrated to work in Mumbai. Others have stayed in and around the village, farming, setting up shops, learning to build houses or running mules in the local transport trade. Many make the seasonal migration to find labouring work at the pilgrimage sites of Badrinath and Kedarnath. Since 2007 some have been climbing to the high-altitude meadows for the gruelling work of collecting caterpillar fungus, which they sell to local traders. In China the fungus is considered to be an aphrodisiac and fetches startlingly high prices.

There has been tragedy too. One young woman with whom I worked became ill and died suddenly soon after her wedding. Another has suffered the loss of her own child. Among the wider group of children with whom I came into contact there have been other fatal accidents and illness, even a suicide.

My own life, and position in the village, has also changed. Although I was married when I first arrived in Bemni, I spent most of the fieldwork period without my husband, and was never really considered a legitimate 'adult'. Perhaps this helped build my relationship with the children. Now, when I return, I am accompanied by my husband and two young children, and their presence transforms my relationships in the village. I am now seen as a mother, with all its associated responsibilities.

The last three years in particular have seen changes to the village infrastructure that were unimaginable in 2003/4. Perhaps the most astonishing is the new 'road'. After years of broken promises from the government, Bemni villagers had had enough of their isolation. In 2005 a group of men and women armed themselves with picks and shovels and began building the road alone. After ten days, and an effective media storm, the local state was shamed into action. By 2012 the government finally completed cutting a rutted dirt track leading right up to the village. It is still not a legal road, and is incredibly dangerous, as it skirts along the precipitous edge of the forest, but every day two private jeeps bump for two hours each way bringing passengers and goods to and from Ghat. It is transforming the village: the elderly and sick can reach hospitals, villagers can send crops to market, the handful of shops are growing in content and number and, with the transport of cement, the village is beginning to look different too. Villagers still gasp slightly when they talk about it: 'Can you believe that we really have our own road?'

In 2011, a year before the road, the village was also electrified. While the electricity is still very intermittent, and seems to falter every time it rains, it has changed everyday life in small but important ways. Children and young people now have light to study in the evening, no longer having to fight over a single paraffin lamp. Some of the wealthier households have bought televisions, and, now in 2013, one household has a computer.

In 2010, a year before electricity arrived, a telecommunications tower was erected. The arrival of mobile phones (initially powered by solar panels) has transformed the ways in which villagers interact with life outside Bemni. It is now a common sight to see young women wandering up the hill to collect leaves chatting in loving tones to their husbands, perhaps in the army in far-off Kashmir, or in private business in Delhi.

The implications of these infrastructural and educational changes are complex and manifold, affecting employment strategies and aspirations, upsetting labour availability and the agricultural cycle and bringing repercussions for intergenerational relations and even the ways in which marriages are arranged. Along with fresh opportunities come a new set of political questions, and it is this very generation of young adults, once the children of this book, who are forging their way through new – and uncertain – times.

But one should also not overemphasise the extent to which everyday life in the village has been transformed. The young men are finding it increasingly difficult to find secure, meaningful employment, and most resort to diversifying their strategies to make a meagre living in the village and surrounding areas. Meanwhile, the women continue with their work: 'Yes,' they say, 'we have a road and electricity, but the cows still need feeding, and the crops need weeding. We still have to go to the forest to collect leaves, and carry the cow dung to the fields. If we have to eat, we have to work.' Therefore, those women who are studying for their BA degrees do so by correspondence, living in the village, working the land and studying at night. Their blistered hands are still stained with *gobar* and they imagine marrying into the agrarian economy of the surrounding villages. It is what they know and what many continue to want for their own children.

Glossary of Hindi and Garhwali terms

'H' denotes a word that originates in Hindi but is also used in Garhwali.
'G' denotes a Garhwali word.

achchhee	H	good
Angrezi	H	English
araam	H	rest
badnaam	H	bad reputation
bahadoor	H	brave
bahana	H	excuse
bangla	H	bungalow
bera	G	teasing 'question and answer' songs, sung in the forest
boliya	H	labour-sharing arrangements
bugyal	H	high-altitude meadows used for summer grazing
carrom	H	Indian board game
chaadar	G	black cloth worn by women, tied rather like a sari
cheena	G	hog millet (*Panicum miliaceum*), grown as a crop
chipkali	H	lizard
chiuna	G	wild root vegetable
chowkidar	H	guard
chukki	G	watermill
chuwa	G	amaranth (*Amarenthus frumentaceus*), grown as a cash crop
daal	H	lentil dish
daranti	G	sickle
devtar	G	dancing religious festival
Diwali	H	Hindu Festival of Lights
dugri	G	friend (girl)
durri	H	handwoven rug
farz	H	duty
ganv	H	village/home
gareeb	H	poor
ghar	H	house/home or building

gobar	G	cattle bedding soiled with dung, used as organic compost
gosaala	G	cattle stall, often combined with living quarters
gram panchayat	H	village committee, lowest level of government
gunda	H	bad or dirty
halwa	H	sweet dish
jawaan	H	youth
jhangora	G	barnyard millet (*Echinochloa frumentácea*), grown as a crop
jugaad	H	improvisation
kaam	H	work
kabadi	H	children's team game
kareli	H	green pod vegetable
keer	H	sweet dish, made with rice and milk
khandhe	H	basket (carried on back like a rucksack)
laparwah	H	lazy
maalik	H	boss (or head, or landlord)
mainka	H	natal home
manduwa	G	amaranth (*Amaranthus oleracea*), grown as a crop
mazaa	H	fun
mazdoori	H	manual labour
mehnat	H	hard work, or hardworking
mela	H	festival
mukku	G	lichen
naukri	H	salaried employment
neeche	H	below, often meaning 'plains India'
parath	H	large plate used for kneading dough
parhe likhe	H	educated
parishanee	H	troublesome
peeche	H	behind
pradhan	H	elected village leader, head of gram panchayat
prasad	H	gift, often food, given to deity, and eaten by participants in the name of the deity
puja	H	religious ceremony
puri	H	deep-fried flatbread
puria	G	children's team game
roti	H	flatbread
salwar kameez	H	two-piece suit worn by girls (baggy trousers and long tunic)
sarkari	H	of the government (adjective)
sarpanch	H	leader of village forest committee

seedha	H	straight, trustworthy
shauq se	H	willingly, out of enthusiasm
shetaanee	H	naughtiness
sust	H	feeling disinclined to work
suttoor	G	leaf litter
taaqat	H	strong
tai-ji	H	aunt
tao-ji	H	uncle
tard	H	having little work to do (adjective)
tikki	H	mark on forehead given during religious ceremonies
van panchayat	H	village forest committee
videshi	H	foreigner
vikaas	H	development

Average exchange rate in 2003/4: US$1 = Rs. 40

Bibliography

Adebe, T. 2007. 'Changing livelihoods, changing childhoods: patterns of children's work in rural southern Ethiopia', *Children's Geographies* 5 (1), 77–93.

Agarwal, B. 1994. *A Field of One's Own: Gender and Land Rights in South Asia*. Cambridge University Press.

Agrawal, A. 2005. *Environmentality: Technologies of Government and the Making of Subjects*. Durham, NC: Duke University Press.

Agrawal, A., and Sivaramakrishnan, K. 2000. *Agrarian Environments: Resources, Representations, and Rule in India*. Durham, NC: Duke University Press.

Aitken, S. 2001. *Geographies of Young People: The Morally Contested Spaces of Identity*. London: Routledge.

Alanen, L. 2007. 'Theorizing children's welfare', in Wintersberger, H., Alanen, L., Olk, T., and Qvortrup, J. (eds.) *Childhood, Generational Order and the Welfare State: Exploring Children's Social and Economic Welfare*, 27–44. Odense: University Press of Southern Denmark.

Allan, G. 1989. *Friendship: Developing a Sociological Perspective*. Boulder, CO: Westview Press.

1996. *Kinship and Friendship in Modern Britain*. Oxford University Press.

Anagnost, A. 2008. 'Imagining global futures in China: the child as a sign of value', in Cole, J., and Durham, D. (eds.) *Figuring the Future: Globalization and the Temporalities of Children and Youth*, 49–72. Santa Fe: SAR Press.

Ansell, N. 2004. 'Secondary school and rural youth transitions in Lesotho and Zimbabwe', *Youth and Society* 36 (2), 183–202.

2008. 'Substituting for families? Schools and social reproduction in AIDS-affected Lesotho', *Antipode* 40 (5), 802–24.

Appadurai, A. 2002. 'Deep democracy: urban governmentality and the horizon of politics', *Public Culture* 14 (1), 21–47.

Aries, P. 1962. *Centuries of Childhood: A Social History of Family Life*. New York: Transaction Books.

Arnot, M., Maton, K., and Millen, D. 1996. *Current Innovative Practice in Education in the UK*. Strasbourg: Council of Europe.

Bakhtin, M. 1984 [1968]. *Rabelais and His World* (trans. H. Iswolsky). Bloomington: Indiana University Press.

Baviskar, A. 2003. 'States, communities and conservation: the practice of ecodevelopment in the Great Himalayan National Park', in Saberwal, V., and Rangarajan, M. (eds.) *Battles over Nature: Science and the Politics of Conservation*, 267–99. New Delhi: Permanent Black.

Bayart, J.-F. 2007. *Global Subjects: A Political Critique of Globalization*. Cambridge: Polity Press.
Behera, D. (ed.) 2007. *Childhoods in South Asia*. Oxford: Pearson Education.
Bell, S., and Coleman, S. 1999. *The Anthropology of Friendship*. Oxford: Berg.
Bénéï, V. 2008. *Schooling Passions: Nation, History and Language in Contemporary India*. Stanford University Press.
Berlastein, L. (ed.) 1993. *Rethinking Labour History: Essays on Discourse and Class Analysis*. Urbana-Champaign: University of Illinois Press.
Berreman, G. 1972. *Hindus of the Himalayas: Ethnography and Change*. Berkeley: University of California Press.
Berry, S. 1985. *Fathers Work for Their Sons: Accumulation, Mobility, and Class Formation in an Extended Yoruba Community*. San Francisco: University of California Press.
Bissell, S. 2003. 'The social construction of childhood: a perspective from Bangladesh', in Kabeer, N., Nambissan, G., and Subrahmanian, R. (eds.) *Child Labour and the Right to Education in South Asia: Needs versus Rights?*, 47–72. New Delhi: Sage.
Blanchet, T. 1996. *Lost Innocence, Stolen Childhoods*. Dhaka: University Press.
Bora, R. 1996. *Himalayan Migration: A Study of the Hill Regions of Uttar Pradesh*. New Delhi: Sage.
Bose, A. 2000. 'Demography of Himalayan villages: missing men and lonely women', *Economic and Political Weekly* 35 (27), 2361–3.
Bourdieu, P. 1977 [1972]. *Outline of a Theory of Practice* (trans. R. Nice). Cambridge University Press.
1984 [1979]. *Distinction: A Social Critique of the Judgement of Taste* (trans. R. Nice). London: Routledge.
1990 [1980]. *The Logic of Practice* (trans. R. Nice). Cambridge: Polity Press.
Bourgois, P. 1995. *In Search of Respect: Selling Crack in El Barrio*. Cambridge University Press.
Boyden, J., and Ennew, J. 1997. *Children in Focus: A Manual for Participatory Research with Children*. Stockholm: Radda Barnen.
Bruyn, S. 1966. *The Human Perspective in Sociology: The Methodology of Participant Observation*. Englewood Cliffs, NJ: Prentice Hall.
Bucholtz, M. 2002. 'Youth and cultural practice', *Annual Review of Anthropology* 31, 525–52.
Burchell, G. 1996. 'Liberal government and techniques of the self', in Barry, A., Osborne, T., and Rose, N. (eds.) *Foucault and Political Reason: Liberalism, Neo-Liberalism and Rationalities of Government*, 19–36. University College London Press.
Burra, N. 2003. 'Rights versus needs: is it in the "best interest of the child"?', in Kabeer, N., Nambissan, G., and Subrahmanian, R. (eds.) *Child Labour and the Right to Education in South Asia: Needs versus Rights?*, 73–94. New Delhi: Sage.
Burridge, A. 2010. 'Youth on the line and the no borders movement', *Children's Geographies* 8 (4), 401–11.
Butler, J. 1990. *Gender Trouble: Feminism and the Subversion of Identity*. London: Routledge.
Butz, D. 2002. 'Resistance, representation and third space in Shimshal village, northern Pakistan', *Acme* 1 (1), 15–34.

Carstairs, G. 1958. *The Twice-Born: A Study of a Community of High-Caste Hindus*. Bloomington: Indiana University Press.
Chambers, R. 1983. *Rural Development: Putting the Last First*. Harlow: Pearson Education.
Chari, S. 2004. *Fraternal Capital: Peasant-Workers, Self-Made Men, and Globalization in Provincial India*. Stanford University Press.
Chauhan, V., and Bhatt, J. 2000. 'Agriculture in Uttaranchal: from subsistence towards self-sufficiency', in Sati, M., and Sati, S. (eds.) *Uttarakhand Statehood: Dimensions of Development*, 168–80. New Delhi: Indus Publishing.
Chopra, R. 2005. 'Sisters and brothers: schooling, family and migration', in Chopra, R., and Jeffery, P. (eds.) *Educational Regimes in Contemporary India*, 299–315. London: Sage.
Chopra, R., and Ghosh, D. 2000. 'Work patterns of rural women in central Himalayas', *Economic and Political Weekly* 35 (52), 4701–5.
Chopra, R., Osella, C., and Osella, F. (eds.) 2004. *South Asian Masculinities: Context of Change, Sites of Continuity*. New Delhi: Kali for Women.
Cleaver, F. (ed.) 2003. *Making Men Matter: Men, Masculinities, and Gender Relations in Development*. London: Zed Books.
Cohen, L. 1995. 'Holi in Banaras and the *Mahaland* of modernity', *GLQ: A Journal of Lesbian and Gay Studies* 2 (4), 399–424.
Cohen, Y. 1961. 'Patterns of friendship', in Cohen, Y. (ed.) *Social Structure and Personality: A Casebook*, 351–86. New York: Holt, Rinehart and Winston.
Cole, J. 2004. 'Fresh contact in Tamatave, Madagascar: sex, money, and intergenerational transformation', *American Ethnologist* 31 (4), 573–88.
Cole, J., and Durham, D. (eds.) 2006. *Generations and Globalization: Youth, Age and Family in the New World Economy*. Bloomington: Indiana University Press.
Coleman, J. 1990. *Foundations of Social Theory*. Cambridge, MA: Belknap Press.
Comaroff, J., and Comaroff, J. 2005. 'Reflections on youth: from the past to the postcolony', in Honwana, A., and De Boeck, F. (eds.) *Makers and Breakers: Children and Youth in Postcolonial Africa*, 19–30. Oxford: James Currey.
Connell, R. 1995. *Masculinities*. Berkeley: University of California Press.
Conradson, D., and Latham, A. 2005. 'Friendship, networks and transnationality in a world city: antipodean transmigrants in London', *Journal of Ethnic and Migration Studies* 31 (2), 287–305.
Corbridge, S. 1993. *Debt and Development*. Oxford: Wiley-Blackwell.
Corrigan, P. 1979. *Schooling the Smash Street Kids*. London: Palgrave Macmillan.
Da Costa, D. 2010. *Development Dramas: Reimagining Rural Political Action in Eastern India*. Delhi: Routledge.
Das, J. 2000. 'Institutions and incentives in a Garhwal village – II: changing state–village interactions', *Economic and Political Weekly* 35 (50), 4445–53.
Davidson, E. 2008. 'Marketing the self: the politics of aspiration among middle-class Silicon Valley youth', *Environment and Planning A* 40 (12), 2814–30.
De Certeau, M. 1984. *The Practice of Everyday Life*. Berkeley: University of California Press.
De Mause, L. (ed.) 1976. *The History of Childhood*. London: Souvenir Press.
Desai, A., and Killick, E. (eds.) 2010. *The Ways of Friendship: Anthropological Explorations*. Oxford: Berghahn Books.

Descola, P., and Palsson, G. (eds.) 1996. *Nature and Society: Anthropological Perspectives*. London: Routledge.

Dhar, U., Rawal, R., Manjkhola, S., Joshi, M., Joshi, M., Bhatt, A., and Bisht, G. 2003. *Conservation, Propagation and Utilization of High Value Medicinal Plants of Himalaya*. Almora: G. B. Pant Institute of Himalayan Environment and Development.

Doron, A., and Jeffrey, R. 2012. *The Great Indian Phone Book: How the Cheap Cell Phone Changes Business, Politics and Everyday Life*. Harvard University Press.

Driskell, D., Fox, C., and Kudva, N. 2008. 'Growing up in the new New York: youth space, citizenship, and community change in a hyperglobal city', *Environment and Planning A* 40 (12), 2831–44.

Durham, D. 2008. 'Apathy and agency: the romance of agency and youth in Botswana', in Cole, J., and Durham, D. (eds.) *Figuring the Future: Children, Youth, and Globalization*, 151–78. Santa Fe: School of American Research Press.

Dwyer, R. 2000. *All You Want Is Money, All You Need Is Love: Sex and Romance in Modern India*. London: Cassell.

Dyson, J. 2007. 'Respite and rupees: the impact of a new market opportunity on the everyday lives of children and young people in the Indian Himalayas', in Behera, D. (ed.) *Childhoods in South Asia*, 1–42. Oxford: Pearson Education.

2008a. 'Saka: growing up in the Indian Himalayas', in Jeffrey, C., and Dyson, J. (eds.) *Telling Young Lives: Portraits of Global Youth*, 15–26. Philadelphia: Temple University Press.

2008b. 'Harvesting identities: youth, work, and gender in the Indian Himalayas', *Annals of the Association of American Geographers* 98 (1), 160–79.

2010. 'Friendship in practice: girls' work in the Indian Himalayas', *American Ethnologist* 37 (3), 472–98.

Elson, D. 1982. 'The differentiation of children's labour in a capitalist labour market', *Development and Change* 13 (4), 479–93.

Ennew, J. 1994. *Street and Working Children: A Guide to Planning*. London: Save the Children.

Fanger, A. 1987. 'Brideprice, dowry and diverted brideprice among the Rajputs of Kumaon', in Raha, M. (ed.) *The Himalayan Heritage*, 139–53. New Delhi: Gian Publishing.

Favero, P. 2005. 'India dreams: cultural identity among young middle class men in New Delhi', doctoral dissertation, Stockholm University.

Featherstone, D. 2008. *Resistance, Space and Political Identities: The Making of Counter-Global Networks*. Oxford: Wiley-Blackwell.

Ferguson, J. 1999. *Expectations of Modernity: Myths and Meanings of Urban Life on the Zambian Copperbelt*. Berkeley: University of California Press.

Folbre, N. 1986. 'Hearts and spades: paradigms of household economics', *World Development* 14 (2), 245–55.

Foucault, M. 2005. *The Hermeneutics of the Subject: Lectures at the Collège de France 1981–1982* (ed. F. Gros, trans. G. Burchell). New York: Palgrave Macmillan.

Freeman, C. 2000. *High Tech and High Heels in the Global Economy*. Durham, NC: Duke University Press.

Froerer, P. 2011. 'Education, aspiration and inequality in central India', *European Journal of Development Research* 23 (5), 695–711.

Fuller, C. 2011. 'Timepass and boredom in modern India', *Anthropology of This Century* 1, http://aotcpress.com/articles/timepass-boredom (last accessed 11 December 2012).

Fuller, C., and Narasimhan, H. 2007. 'Information technology professionals and the new-rich middle class in Chennai (Madras)', *Modern Asian Studies* 41 (1), 121–50.

Gagen, E. 2000. 'An example to us all: child development and identity construction in early 20th-century playgrounds', *Environment and Planning A* 32 (4), 599–616.

Garfinkel, H., and Sacks, H. 1986. 'On formal structures of practical actions', in Garfinkel, H. (ed.) *Ethnomethodological Studies of Work*, 160–93. London: Routledge.

Garvey, C. 1977. *Play*. London: Fontana.

Gibson, K. 2011. *Street Kids: Homeless Youth, Outreach, and Policing New York's Streets*. New York University Press.

Gidwani, V. 2001. 'The cultural logic of work: explaining labour deployment and piece-rate contracts in Matar Taluka, Gujarat – parts I and II', *Journal of Development Studies* 38 (2), 57–74.

2008. *Capital, Interrupted: Agrarian Development and the Politics of Work in India*. Minneapolis: University of Minnesota Press.

Gold, A., and Gujar, B. 2002. *In the Time of Trees and Sorrows: Nature, Power, and Memory in Rajasthan*. Durham, NC: Duke University Press.

Gooch, P. 1998. 'At the tail of the buffalo: Van Gujjar pastoralists between the forest and world arena', Ph.D. dissertation, University of Lund.

Goodman, D., and Watts, M. 1997. *Globalising Food: Agrarian Questions and Global Restructuring*. London: Routledge.

Goodwin, M. 2006. *The Hidden Life of Girls: Games of Stance, Status and Exclusion*. Oxford: Blackwell.

Gooptu, N. 2009. 'Neoliberal subjectivity, enterprise culture and new workplaces: organised retail and shopping malls in India', *Economic and Political Weekly* 44 (22), 45–54.

Gramsci, A. 1971. *Selections from the Prison Notebooks* (ed., trans. Q. Hoare and G. Nowell-Smith). London: Lawrence & Wishart.

Gratz, T. 2004. 'Friendship among young artisanal gold miners in northern Benin (west Africa)', *Afrika Spectrum* 39 (1), 95–117.

Green, J., and Hart, L. 1999. 'The impact of context on data', in Barbour, R., and Kitzinger, J. (eds.) *Developing Focus Group Resource: Politics, Theory and Practice*, 21–35. London: Sage.

Griffiths, V. 1995. *Adolescent Girls and Their Friends: A Feminist Ethnography*. Brookfield: Ashgate.

Guha, R. 1989. *The Unquiet Woods: Ecological Change and Peasant Resistance in the Himalaya*. New Delhi: Oxford University Press.

Guha, R., and Gadgil, M. 1992. *This Fissured Land: An Ecological History of India*. Berkeley: University of California Press.

Gupta, A. 1998. *Postcolonial Developments: Agriculture in the Making of Modern India*. Durham, NC: Duke University Press.

Gururani, S. 2001. 'Regimes of control, strategies of access: politics of forest use in the Uttarakhand Himalaya', in Agrawal, A., and Sivaramakrishnan, K. (eds.) *Social*

Nature: Resources, Representations and Rule in India, 170–90. New Delhi: Oxford University Press.

2002. 'Forests of pleasure and pain: gendered practices of labor and livelihood in the forests of the Kumaon Himalayas, India', *Gender, Place and Culture* 9 (3), 229–43.

Hall, G. 1904. *Adolescence: Its Psychology and Its Relations to Physiology, Anthropology, Sociology, Sex, Crime, Religion, and Education* (2 vols.). New York: D. Appleton.

Harriss, J. 2002. *Depoliticizing Development: The World Bank and Social Capital*. London: Anthem.

Hart, R. 1979. *Children's Experiences of Place*. New York: Irvington.

Harvey, D. 1989. *The Condition of Post Modernity: An Inquiry into the Origins of Cultural Change*. Oxford: Blackwell.

Hebdige, D. 1979. *Subculture: The Meaning of Style*. London: Methuen.

Heissler, K. 2011. '"We are poor people so what is the use of education?" Tensions and contradictions in girls' and boys' transitions from school to work in rural Bangladesh', *European Journal of Development Research* 23 (5), 729–44.

Herzfeld, M. 2005. *Cultural Intimacy: Social Poetics in the Nation-State*. London: Routledge.

Hey, V. 1996. *The Company She Keeps: An Ethnography of Girls' Friendships*. Buckingham: Open University Press.

Hirschkind, C. 2011. 'The road to Tahrir', Social Science Research Council, http://blogs.ssrc.org/tif/2011/02/09/the-road-to-tahrir (last accessed 11 December 2012).

Hodson, R. 2001. *Dignity at Work*. Cambridge University Press.

Hoechner, H. 2011. 'Striving for knowledge and dignity: how Qur'anic students in Kano, Nigeria, learn to live with rejection and educational disadvantage', *European Journal of Development Research* 23 (5), 712–28.

Hoffman, D. 2008. 'Rocks: a portrait of Mohammed', in Jeffrey, C., and Dyson, J. (eds.) *Telling Young Lives: Portraits of Global Youth*, 123–35. Philadelphia: Temple University Press.

Holloway, S., and Valentine, G. 2000. *Children's Geographies: Living, Learning, Playing*. London: Routledge.

Honwana, A., and de Boeck, F. (eds.) 2005. *Makers and Breakers: Children and Youth in Postcolonial Africa*. Oxford: James Currey.

Hoon, V. 1996. *Living on the Move: Bhotiyas of the Kumaon Himalaya*. New Delhi: Sage.

Huizinga, J. 1955. *Homo Ludens: A Study of the Play Element in Culture*. Boston: Beacon Press.

Ingold, T. 1992. 'Culture and the perception of the environment', in Park, D., and Croll, E. (eds.) *Bush Base: Forest Farm: Culture, Environment and Development*, 39–56. London: Routledge.

2007. *Lines: A Brief History*. London: Routledge.

Jackson, C. 1999. 'Men's work, masculinities and gender divisions of labour', *Journal of Development Studies* 36 (1), 89–108.

2000. 'Men at work', *European Journal of Development Studies* 12 (2), 1–22.

Jackson, C., and Palmer-Jones, R. 1999. 'Rethinking gendered poverty and work', *Development and Change* 30 (1), 557–83.

James, A., Jenks, C., and Prout, A. 1998. *Theorizing Childhood*. Cambridge: Polity Press.

Jayal, N. 2001. 'Democracy and social capital in central Himalaya: tale of two villages', *Economic and Political Weekly* 26 (8), 655–64.

Jeffery, P., and Jeffery, R. 1996. *Don't Marry Me to a Plowman! Women's Everyday Lives in Rural North India*. Boulder, CO: Westview Press.

Jeffery, R. and Jeffery, P. 1997. *Population, Gender and Politics: Demographic Change in Rural North India*. Cambridge University Press.

Jeffrey, C. 2002. 'Caste, class and clientelism: a political economy of everyday corruption in rural north India', *Economic Geography* 78 (1), 21–42.

2010. *Timepass: Youth, Class and the Politics of Waiting in India*. Stanford University Press.

Jeffrey, C., and Dyson, J. (eds.) 2008. *Telling Young Lives: Portraits of Global Youth*. Philadelphia: Temple University Press.

Jeffrey, C., Jeffery, P., and Jeffery, R. 2008. *Degrees without Freedom? Education, Masculinities, and Unemployment in North India*. Stanford University Press.

Jeffrey, C., and McDowell, L. 2004. 'Youth in a comparative perspective: global change, local lives', *Youth and Society* 36 (2), 131–42.

Johnson-Hanks, D. 2002. 'On the limits of life stages in ethnography: toward a theory of vital conjunctures', *American Anthropologist* 104 (3), 865–80.

Jones, G., and Chant, S. 2009. 'Globalising initiatives for gender equality and poverty reduction: exploring "failure" with reference to education and work among urban youth in The Gambia and Ghana', *Geoforum* 40 (2), 184–96.

Joyce, P. (ed.) 1987. *The Historical Meanings of Work*. Cambridge University Press.

Juris, J., and Pleyers, G. 2009. 'Alter-activism: emerging cultures of participation among young global justice activists', *Journal of Youth Studies* 12 (1), 57–70.

Kabeer, N., Nambissan, G., and Subrahmanian, R. (eds.) 2003. *Child Labour and the Right to Education in South Asia: Needs versus Rights?*. New Delhi: Sage.

Kakar, S. 1978. *The Inner World: A Psychoanalytic Study of Childhood and Society in India*. New Delhi: Oxford University Press.

Katz, C. 1989. 'Herders, gatherers and foragers: the emerging botanies of children in rural Sudan', *Children's Environmental Quarterly* 6 (4), 46–53.

1991. 'Sow what you know: the struggle for social reproduction in rural Sudan', *Annals of Association of American Geographers* 81 (3), 488–514.

2004. *Growing Up Global: Economic Restructuring and Children's Everyday Lives*. Minneapolis: University of Minnesota Press.

Keniston, K. 1971. *Youth and Dissent: The Rise of a New Opposition*. New York: Harcourt Brace Jovanovich.

Klenk, R. 2010. *Educating Activists: Development and Gender in the Making of Modern Gandhians*. London: Lexington Books.

Kothari, S. 1983. 'There's blood on those matchsticks: child labour in Sivakasi', *Economic and Political Weekly* 18 (27), 1191–202.

Kulkarni, M. 1983. 'Match-making in Sivakasi', *Economic and Political Weekly* 18 (43), 1855–6.

Kumar, N. 2000. *Lessons from Schools: The History of Education in Banaras*. New Delhi: Sage.

Kumar, S. 2004. 'Does "participation" in common pool resource management help the poor?', in Corbridge, S., Jewitt, S., and Kumar, S. (eds.) *Jharkhand: Environment, Development, Ethnicity*, 232–63. New Delhi: Oxford University Press.

Kumar, V. 2001. 'Untouchability in Uttaranchal', *Economic and Political Weekly* 36 (49), 4536–7.

Kurtz, S. 1992. *All the Mothers Are One: Hindu India and the Cultural Reshaping of Psychoanalysis*. New York: Columbia University Press.

Latour, B. 2005. *Reassembling the Social: An Introduction to Actor–Network Theory*. Oxford University Press.

Lave, J., and Wenger, E. 1991. *Situated Learning: Legitimate Peripheral Participation*. Cambridge University Press.

Lem, W. 1999. *Cultivating Dissent: Work, Identity and Praxis in Rural Languedoc*. Albany: State University of New York Press.

Lerche, J. 1999. 'Politics of the poor: agricultural labourers and political transformations in Uttar Pradesh', in Byres, T., Kapadia, K., and Lerche, J. (eds.) *Rural Labour Relations in India*, 182–243. London: Frank Cass.

Lewis, A., and Lindsay, G. (eds.) 2000. *Researching Children's Perspectives*. Buckingham: Open University Press.

Li, T. 1996. 'Images of community: discourses and strategy in property relations', *Development and Change* 27 (3), 501–28.

Linkenbach, A. 1998. 'Forests in Garhwal and the construction of space', in Jeffery, R. (ed.) *The Social Construction of Indian Forests*, 79–106. New Delhi: Manohar.

Lloyd, C. 2005. *Growing Up Global: The Changing Transitions to Adulthood in the Developing World*. Washington, DC: National Academies Press.

Lorimer, J. 2012. 'Multinatural geographies for the Anthropocene', *Progress in Human Geographies* 36 (5), 593–612.

Lukose, R. 2005. 'Consuming globalization: youth and gender in Kerala, India', *Journal of Social History* 38 (4), 915–35.

Maguire, M., and Macrae, S. 2000. *Choice, Pathways and Transitions Post-16: New Youth, New Economies in the Global City*. London: Routledge Falmer.

Maharatna, A. 1997. 'Children's work activities, surplus labour and fertility: case study of six villages in Birbhum', *Economic and Political Weekly* 32 (7), 363–9.

Mahmood, S. 2005. *Politics of Piety: The Islamic Revival and the Feminist Subject*. Princeton University Press.

Mains, D. 2007. 'Neoliberal times: progress, boredom, and shame among young men in urban Ethiopia', *American Ethnologist* 34 (3), 659–73.

Malone, K. (ed.) 2007. *Child Space: An Anthropological Exploration of Young People's Use of Space*. New Delhi: Concept.

Mamgain, R. 2003. 'Out-migration among rural households in Uttaranchal: magnitude and characteristics', *Labour and Development* 9 (2), 259–87.

Mandelbaum, D. 1970. *Society in India* (2 vols.). Berkeley: University of California Press.

Mannheim, K. 1956 [1923]. 'The problem of generations', in *Collected Works of Karl Mannheim* (vol. V), 276–320. London: Routledge.

Marriott, M. 1966. 'The feast of love', in Singer, M. (ed.) *Krishna: Myths, Rites, and Attitudes*, 200–12, 229–31. Honolulu: East–West Center Press.

Massey, D. 2005. *For Space*. London: Sage.

Mawdsley, E. 1997. 'Non-successionalist regionalism in India: the Uttarakhand separate state movement', *Environment and Planning A* 29 (12), 2217–35.

1998. 'After Chipko: from environment to region in Uttaranchal', *Journal of Peasant Studies* 25 (4), 36–54.

1999. 'A new Himalayan state in India: popular perceptions of regionalism, politics and development', *Mountain Research and Development* 19 (2), 101–12.
McCormack, D. 2008. 'Geographies for moving bodies: thinking, dancing, spaces', *Geography Compass* 2 (6), 1822–36.
McDowell, L. 2003. *Redundant Masculinities? Employment Change and White Working Class Youth*. Oxford: Blackwell.
McFarlane, R. 2012. *The Old Ways: A Journey on Foot*. London: Penguin Books.
McKibbin, R. 1990. *The Ideologies of Class: Social Relations in Britain 1880–1950*. Oxford: Clarendon Press.
McRobbie, A. 2004. 'Post-feminism and popular culture', *Feminist Media Studies* 4 (3), 255–64.
Mead, M. 1928. *Coming of Age in Samoa*. New York: William Morrow.
Mehta, M. 1995. 'Cultural diversity in the mountains: issues of integration and marginality in sustainable development', paper prepared for the 'Consultation on the mountain agenda' meeting, Lima.
1996. '"Our lives are no different from that of our buffaloes": agricultural change and gendered spaces in a central Himalayan valley', in Rocheleau, D., Thomas-Slayter, B., and Wangari, E. (eds.) *Feminist Political Ecology: Global Issues and Local Experiences*, 180–210. London: Routledge.
Ministry of Home Affairs 1991. *Census of India*. New Delhi: Ministry of Home Affairs.
2001. *Census of India*. New Delhi: Ministry of Home Affairs.
Mishra, L. 2000. *Child Labour in India*. New Delhi: Oxford University Press.
Moller, J. 2003. 'Responses to modernity: female education, gender relations and regional identity in the hills of Uttar Pradesh', in Jeffery, R., and Lerche, J. (eds.) *Social and Political Change in Uttar Pradesh: European Perspectives*, 103–28. New Delhi: Manohar.
Montaigne, M. de 1972 [1603]. *Essays of Michel de Montaigne*. Garden City, NY: Doubleday.
Morarji, K. 2010. 'Where does the rural educated person fit? Development and social reproduction in contemporary India', in McMichael, P. (ed.) *Contesting Development: Critical Struggles for Social Change*, 50–64. London: Routledge.
Morrow, V. 1994. 'Responsible children? Aspects of children's work and employment outside school in contemporary UK', in Mayall, B. (ed.) *Children's Childhoods: Observed and Experienced*, 128–43. London: Falmer Press.
Mukhopadhyay, B. 2004. 'Between elite hysteria and subaltern carnivalesque: the politics of street-food in the city of Calcutta', *South Asia Research* 24 (1), 37–50.
Nambissan, G. 2003. 'Social exclusion, children's work and education: a view from the margins', in Kabeer, N., Nambissan, G., and Subrahmanian, R. (eds.) *Child Labour and the Right to Education in South Asia: Needs versus Rights?*, 109–42. New Delhi: Sage.
Nautiyal, M. 2000. 'Medicinal plants: a resource for Uttaranchal', in Sati, M., and Sati, S. (eds.) *Uttarakhand Statehood: Dimensions of Development*, 302–13. New Delhi: Indus Publishing.
Nautiyal, S., Rao, K., Maikhuri, R., Rakesh, K., and Saxena, K. 2003. 'Transhumant pastoralism in the Nanda Devi Biosphere Reserve, India', *Mountain Research and Development* 23 (3), 255–62.
Nieuwenhuys, O. 1994. *Children's Lifeworlds: Gender, Welfare and Labour in the Developing World*. London: Routledge.

1996. 'The paradox of child labor and anthropology', *Annual Review of Anthropology* 25, 237–51.

2007. 'Embedding the global womb: global child labour and the new policy agenda', *Children's Geographies* 5 (1/2), 149–63.

Nisbett, N. 2007. 'Friendship, consumption, morality: practising identity, negotiating hierarchy in middle-class Bangalore', *Journal of the Royal Anthropological Institute* 13 (4), 935–50.

2009. *Growing Up in the Knowledge Society: Living the IT Dream in Bangalore*. New Delhi: Routledge.

Oldman, D. 1994. 'Childhood as a mode of production', in Mayall, B. (ed.) *Children's Childhoods Observed and Experienced*, 153–66. London: Falmer Press.

Orkin, K. 2012. 'Are work and schooling complementary or competitive for children in rural Ethiopia? A mixed-methods study', Working Paper 77, Young Lives, University of Oxford.

Ortner, S. 1995. 'Resistance and the problem of ethnographic refusal', *Comparative Studies in Society and History* 37 (1), 173–93.

2004. *Anthropology and Social Theory: Culture, Power, and the Acting Subject*. Durham, NC: Duke University Press.

Osella, C., and Osella, F. 1998. 'Friendship and flirting: micro-politics in Kerala, south India', *Journal of the Royal Anthropological Institute* 4 (2), 189–206.

2006. *Men and Masculinities in South India*. New York: Anthem Press.

Pahl, R. 1998. 'Friendship: the glue of contemporary society?', in Franklin, J. (ed.) *The Politics of Risk Society*, 99–120. Cambridge: Polity Press.

Paine, R. 1969. 'In search of friendship', *Man* (new series) 4 (4), 505–24.

Palni, L., Maikhuri, R., and Rao, K. 2001. 'Conservation in the Himalayas agroecosystems: issues and priorities', in Pandey, P., Pande, D., Bisht, P., and Pande, R. (eds.) *Economy of Uttaranchal: Profile and Dynamics of Change*, 135–76. New Delhi: Anamika.

Pande, D., and Pande, S. 2001. 'Importance of non-timber forest products', in Pandey, P., Pande, D., Bisht, P., and Pande, R. (eds.) *Economy of Uttaranchal: Profile and Dynamics of Change*, 219–31. New Delhi: Anamika.

Pande, G., and Pandey, P. 2001. 'Economy of Uttaranchal state: prospects and the case of tourism as a key sector', in Pandey, P., Pande, D., Bisht, P., and Pande, R. (eds.) *Economy of Uttaranchal: Profile and Dynamics of Change*, 27–40. New Delhi: Anamika.

Pandey, D., and Rawat, D. 2000. 'Aspects and prospects of horticulture in Uttarakhand', in Sati, M., and Sati, S. (eds.) *Uttarakhand Statehood: Dimensions of Development*, 181–205. New Delhi: Indus Publishing.

Pandian, A. 2009. *Crooked Stalks: Cultivating Virtue in South India*. Durham, NC: Duke University Press.

Parry, J. 1999. 'Lords of labour: working and shirking in Bhilai', *Contributions to Indian Sociology* 33 (1), 107–40.

Parry, J., Breman, J., and Kapadia, K. 1999. *The Worlds of Indian Industrial Labour*. New Delhi: Sage.

Pathak, S. 1997. 'State, society and natural resources in Himalaya: dynamics of change in colonial and post-colonial Uttarakhand', *Economic and Political Weekly* 32 (17), 908–12.

Pauw, E. 1896. *Report on the Tenth Settlement of the Garhwal District*. Allahabad: Government Press.

Pearce, F. 1991. 'Building a disaster: the monumental folly of India's Tehri Dam', *Ecologist* 21 (3), 123–8.

Pfaff, J. 2009. 'Youth culture as a context of political learning: how young people politicize amongst each other', *Young* 72 (2), 167–89.

Philo, C., and Smith, F. 2003. 'Guest editorial: political geographies of children and young people', *Space and Polity* 7 (2), 99–115.

Piaget, J. 1955. *The Construction of Reality in the Child* (trans. M. Cook). London: Routledge & Kegan Paul.

Piaget, J., and Inhelder, B. 1958. *The Growth of Logical Thinking from Childhood to Adolescence*. New York: Basic Books.

1969. *The Psychology of the Child*. New York: Basic Books.

Pile, S. 1997. 'Introduction: opposition, political identities and spaces of resistance', in Pile, S., and Keith, M. (eds.) *Geographies of Resistance*, 1–32. London: Routledge.

Pinto, S. 2008. *Where There Is No Midwife: Birth and Loss in Rural India*. New York: Berghahn Books.

Poffenberger, M., and McGean, B. (eds.) 1996. *Village Voices, Forest Choices: Joint Forest Management in India*. New Delhi: Oxford University Press.

Punch, S. 2000. 'Children's strategies for creating playspaces: negotiating independence in rural Bolivia', in Holloway, S., and Valentine, G. (eds.) *Children's Geographies: Playing, Living, Learning*, 48–62. London: Routledge.

2001. 'Negotiating autonomy: childhood in rural Bolivia', in Alanen, L., and Mayall, B. (eds.) *Conceptualising Adult–Child Relations*, 23–36. London: Routledge Falmer.

Putnam, R. 1993. *Making Democracy Work: Civic Traditions in Modern Italy*. Princeton University Press.

Raheja, G. 1988. *The Poison in the Gift: Ritual, Prestation, and the Dominant Caste in a North Indian Village*. Chicago University Press.

Ramamurthy, P. 2010. 'Why are men doing floral sex work? Gender, cultural reproduction, and the feminization of agriculture', *Signs: Journal of Women in Culture and Society* 35 (2), 397–424.

Rana, R. 1996. 'Garhwali women: limits of change', *Economic and Political Weekly* 31 (19), 1125–6.

Rangan, H. 1997. 'From Chipko to Uttaranchal: development, environment, and social protest in the Garhwal Himalayas, India', in Peet, R., and Watts, M. (eds.) *Liberation Ecologies: Environment, Development and Social Movements*, 205–27. London: Routledge.

2001. *Of Myths and Movements: Rewriting Chipko into Himalayan History*. New Delhi: Oxford University Press.

Razavi, S. 1992. 'Fieldwork in a familiar setting: the role of politics at the national, community and household levels', in Devereux, S., and Hoddinott, J. (eds.) *Fieldwork in Developing Countries*, 132–48. London: Harvester Wheatsheaf.

Reed-Danahay, D. 1999. 'Friendship, kinship and the life course in rural Auvergne', in Bell, S., and Coleman, S. (eds.) *The Anthropology of Friendship*, 137–54. Oxford: Berg.

Reynolds, P. 1991. *Dance Civet Cat: Child Labour in the Zambezi Valley*. London: Zed Books.
Riley, M. 2009. 'The next link in the chain: children, agricultural practices and the family farm', *Children's Geographies* 7 (3), 245–60.
Robinson, J. 1994. 'White women research/representing "others": from antiapartheid to postcolonialism?', in Blunt, A., and Rose, G. (eds.) *Writing Women and Space: Colonial and Postcolonial Geographies*, 197–226. New York: Guilford Press.
Robson, E. 2004. 'Hidden child workers: young carers in Zimbabwe', *Antipode* 36 (2), 227–48.
Rogers, M. 2008. 'Modernity, "authenticity", and ambivalence: subaltern masculinities on a south Indian college campus', *Journal of the Royal Anthropological Institute* 14 (1), 79–95.
Roitman, J. 2004. *Fiscal Disobedience: An Anthropology of Economic Regulation in Central Africa*. Princeton University Press.
Rose, N. 1998. *Inventing Our Selves: Psychology, Power and Personhood*. Cambridge University Press.
Roulet, M. 1996. 'Dowry and prestige in north India', *Contributions to Indian Sociology* 30 (1), 98–107.
Rudolph, L., and Rudolph, S. 1967. *The Modernity of Tradition: Political Development in India*. Chicago University Press.
Rudolph, S., and Rudolph, L. 1976. 'Rajput adulthood: reflections on the Amar Singh diary', *Daedalus* 105 (6), 145–67.
Saberwal, V. 1999. *Pastoral Politics: Shepherds, Bureaucrats, and Conservation in the Western Himalaya*. New Delhi: Oxford University Press.
Sangtin writers and Nagar, R. 2006. *Playing with Fire: Feminist Thought and Activism through Seven Lives in India*. Minnesota University Press.
Santos, G. 2008. 'On same-year siblings in rural south China', *Journal of the Royal Anthropological Institute* 14 (3), 535–53.
Santos-Granero, F. 2007. 'Of fear and friendship: Amazonian sociality beyond kinship and affinity', *Journal of the Royal Anthropological Institute* 13 (1), 1–18.
Sarangapani, P. 2003. *Constructing School Knowledge: An Ethnography of Learning in an Indian Village*. New Delhi: Sage.
Sarkar, R. 1998. 'Understanding sustainability: study of a hill settlement', *Economic and Political Weekly* 33 (44), 2800–6.
Savage, M. 2003. 'A new class paradigm?', *British Journal of Sociology of Education* 24 (4), 535–41.
Sax, W. 1993. *Mountain Goddess: Gender and Politics in a Himalayan Pilgrimage*. New York: Oxford University Press.
2002. *Dancing the Self: Personhood and Performance in the Pandav Lila of Garhwal*. New York: Oxford University Press.
Schildkrout, E. 1980. 'Children's work reconsidered', *International Social Sciences Journal* 32 (3), 479–90.
Scott, J. 1985. *Weapons of the Weak: Everyday Forms of Peasant Resistance*. New Haven, CT: Yale University Press.
Searle-Chatterjee, M. 1979. 'The polluted identity of work: a study of Benares sweepers', in Wallman, S. (ed.) *Social Anthropology of Work*, 269–85. London: Academic Press.

Sen, I. 1998. 'Class and gender in work time allocation', *Economic and Political Weekly* 23 (33), 1702–6.
Shahine, S. 2011. 'Youth and the revolution in Egypt', *Anthropology Today* 27 (2), 1–3.
Sharma, V. 2001. 'Role of medicinal herbs and wildlife trade in mountain environments', in Pandey, P., Pande, D., Bisht, P., and Pande, R. (eds.) *Economy of Uttaranchal: Profile and Dynamics of Change*, 205–18. New Delhi: Anamika.
Sharp, J., Routledge, P., Philo, C., and Paddison, R. (eds.) 2000. *Entanglements of Power: Geographies of Domination/Resistance*. London: Routledge.
Shiva, V. 1989. *Staying Alive: Women, Ecology and Development*. London: Zed Books.
Shiva, V., and Bandyopadhyay, J. 1986. *Chipko: India's Civilisational Response to the Forest Crisis*. New Delhi: Intach.
Sivaramakrishnan, K., and Agrawal, A. (eds.) 2003. *Regional Modernities: The Cultural Politics of Development in India*. New Delhi: Oxford University Press.
Solberg, A. 1997. 'Negotiating childhood: changing constructions of age for Norwegian children', in James, A., and Prout, A. (eds.) *Constructing and Reconstructing Childhood* (2nd edn), 123–40. London: Falmer Press.
Somanathan, E. 1991. 'Deforestation, property rights and incentives in central Himalaya', *Wasteland News* August–October, 14–27.
Sugden, F., and Punch, S. 2013. 'Work, education and out-migration among children and youth in upland Asia: changing patterns of labour and ecological knowledge in an era of globalization', *Local Environment* 18 (13), 255–70.
Sundar, N., Jeffery, R., and Thin, N. 2001. *Branching Out: Joint Forest Management in India*. New Delhi: Oxford University Press.
Swaninathan, M. 1998. 'Economic growth and the persistence of child labor: evidence from an Indian city', *World Development* 26 (8), 1513–28.
Swanson, K. 2009. *Begging as a Path to Progress: Indigenous Women and Children and the Struggle for Ecuador's Urban Spaces*. Atlanta: University of Georgia Press.
Tewari, R., and Mujoo, R. 2001. *Uttaranchal: Infrastructure and Economic Development*. New Delhi: APH Publishing.
Thieme, T. 2010. 'Youth, waste and work in Mathare: whose business and whose politics?', *Environment and Urbanization* 22 (1), 1–20.
Thomas, M. 2009. 'The identity politics of school life: territoriality and the racial subjectivity of teen girls in Los Angeles', *Children's Geographies* 7 (1), 7–19.
Trawick, M. 1990. *Notes on Love in a Tamil Family*. Berkeley: University of California Press.
2007. 'Freedom to move: a bike trip with Menan', in Malone, K. (ed.) *Child Space: An Anthropological Exploration of Young People's Use of Space*, 21–40. Delhi: Concept.
Tsing, A. 1993. *In the Realm of the Diamond Queen*. Princeton University Press.
Uberoi, P. 1994. *Family, Kinship and Marriage in India*. New Delhi: Oxford University Press.
Valentine, G., and Holloway, S. 2002. 'Cyberkids? Exploring children's identities and social networks in on-line and off-line worlds', *Annals of the Association of American Geographers* 92 (2), 302–19.
Van Blerk, L. 2006. 'Diversity and difference in the everyday lives of Ugandan street children', *Social Dynamics* 32 (1), 47–74.

Verkaaik, O. 2004. *Migrants and Militants: Fun and Urban Violence in Pakistan*. Princeton University Press.

Vigh, H., 2006. *Navigating Terrains of War: Youth and Soldiering in Guinea-Bissau*. New York: Berghahn Books.

Wadley, S. 1994. *Struggling with Destiny in Karimpur, 1925–1984*. Berkeley: University of California Press.

Wallman, S. (ed.) 1979. *Social Anthropology of Work*. London: Academic Press.

Walton, H. 1910. *British Garhwal: A Gazetteer*, vol. XXXVI, *District Gazetteers of the United Provinces of Agra and Oudh*. Allahabad: Government Press.

Walvin, J. 1982. *A Child's World: A Social History of English Childhood 1800–1914*. Harmondsworth: Penguin Books.

Weiner, M. 1991. *The Child and the State in India*. New Delhi: Oxford University Press.

Weiss, B. 2009. *Sweet Dreams and Hip Hop Barbershops: Global Fantasy in Urban Tanzania*. Bloomington: Indiana University Press.

Whatmore, S. 2009. 'Environment', in Gregory, D., Johnston, R., Pratt, G., Watts, M., and Whatmore, S. (eds.) *The Dictionary of Human Geography* (5th edn), 202–3. Oxford: Wiley-Blackwell.

Willis, P. 1977. *Learning to Labor: How Working Class Kids Get Working Class Jobs*. New York: Columbia University Press.

1982. 'Cultural production and theories of reproduction', in Barton, L., and Walker, S. (eds.) *Race, Class and Education*, 107–39. London: Croom Helm.

Winsvold, A. 2004. 'When children unite: child workers' organisation in India', Ph.D. dissertation, University of Lund.

Woodhead, M. 1998. *Children's Perspectives on Their Working Lives: A Participatory Study in Bangladesh, Ethiopia, the Philippines, Guatemala, El Salvador and Nicaragua*. Sweden: Radda Barnen.

World Bank 2007. *World Development Report: The Next Generation*. Washington, DC: World Bank.

Wyers, J. 1986. 'Child labour in Brazilian agriculture', *Critique of Anthropology* 6 (2), 63–80.

Yon, D. 2000. *Elusive Culture: Schooling, Race and Identity in Global Times*. Albany: State University of New York Press.

Index